IMPERIALISM
MEDIA
AND
THE GOOD NEIGHBOR

IMPERIALISM, MEDIA, AND THE GOOD NEIGHBOR:

New Deal Foreign Policy and United States Shortwave Broadcasting to Latin America

FRED FEJES

Florida Atlantic University

ABLEX PUBLISHING CORPORATION
NORWOOD, NEW JERSEY

Library of Congress Cataloging-in-Publication Data

Fejes, Fred.
   Imperialism, media, and the good neighbor.

   (Communication and information science)
   "July 1984"
   Bibliography: p:
   Includes index.
   1. Latin America—Relations—United States.
2. United States—Relations—Latin America.
3. United States—Foreign relations—1933–1945.
4. Radio, Short wave—Latin America. 5. Radio, Short wave—United States. I. Title. II. Series
F1418.F38   1986   327′7308   86-10882
ISBN 0-89391-321-9

ABLEX Publishing Corporation
355 Chestnut Street
Norwood, New Jersey 07648

CONTENTS

v

PREFACE

Throughout United States history, Latin America has regularly alternated between occupying a position of prominence in both our foreign policy and in the public mind and being ignored or casually regarded as a colorful but relatively unimportant region of the world that did not merit serious attention. Since the turn of this century, there have been roughly four times in which the affairs of Latin America emerged to nearly dominate United States thinking about its position and role in the world. In the first decade of this century, with the victory over Spain, subsequent expansion into Latin America, and the building of the Panama Canal, the United States dramatically asserted its leadership in the Western Hemisphere. In the late 1930s and during World War II, both United States policymakers and the American public became acutely aware of the need of the support and cooperation of the other American republics in the face of the Axis threat. In the early 1960s, with the establishment of a socialist state in Cuba, Latin America became a major problem area for the United States. And currently, with the creation of the Sandinista state in Nicaragua and the war in El Salvador, Latin America again dominates the news.

It is left to scholars and students of Latin America to stand back and try to make some sense of the overall pattern of United States–Latin American relations as they emerged over the decades. United States involvement in Latin America has been analyzed in terms of its political, military, economic, and social dimensions. Only now are we beginning to appreciate the significance of communications and culture as a dimension of United States–Latin American relations worthy of study in its own right. This book focuses on this dimension as it analyzes the development of United States–Latin American communication media ties during the era of the Franklin Roosevelt administration. It examines how the building of communication and cultural ties interacted with the political, economic, military, and social dimensions of United States foreign policy in the region.

The development of media relations with Latin America was closely tied to the goals and interests of both the United States government and private companies. Yet, the use of communications media, such as shortwave, represented more than just another method by which United States interests could achieve their goals in the region. Just as the development of radio, and later television broadcasting, transformed the character and quality of domestic politics, so also did the creation of international broadcasting alter the character of international politics. International politics was no longer a matter of state to state or government to government relations. The public opinion of nations was now an important element in international politics.

In analyzing the development and role of United States shortwave broadcasting in Latin America, I do not attempt to make a radically new interpretation of either American history or United States–Latin American relations. Generally, American historical studies of mass communications tend not to be very conscious of any underlying historical framework or interpretation. To the extent that they are informed by any view of the American past, it is the progressive-liberal view best represented in the works of Turner, the early Beard, Becker, the Schlesingers, and Commager and popularized in countless high school and college textbooks. This book, however, draws upon a different, more recent current of historical research and interpretation, a current that has often been labeled "revisionist history." The major thrust of revisionist historical scholarship has been to unravel and understand the complex dynamics between economic interests and public policy and how these are interrelated and revealed, not only in domestic, but also in international political and economic activity. The most general statement of the basic analytical context of this work can be found in the works of William Appleman Williams, particularly in *The Tragedy of American Diplomacy*. With regard to United States–Latin American relationships, this book draws heavily upon the research and analysis of Lloyd C. Gardner, a close colleague of Williams, and his work, *Economic Aspects of New Deal Diplomacy*. Equally helpful in formulating some of the elements of this analysis has been David Green's *The Containment of Latin America*. In dealing with the domestic aspects of United States politics and economics during the period covered, two essays by Barton J. Bernstein, "The New Deal: The Conservative Achievements of Liberal Reform" and "America in War and Peace: The Test of Liberalism," have been extremely useful in an understanding of the New Deal.

In the various contemporary discussions and accounts of both the short-wave activity of the commercial networks and that of the United States Government, terms such as "propaganda," "cultural warfare," "information campaign," "information activity," and "cultural campaign" were used to describe the nature and purpose of the shortwave broadcasts to

Latin America. Such a diversity of terms reflected the lack of consensus at that time in defining the nature of shortwave broadcasting to the region. As Latin American nations were allied of the United States, government officials were hesitant to describe their activities as propaganda. Yet, the overall goal was to mobilize public opinion in Latin America on behalf of United States war aims. An examination of the terminology used during this period to describe the activities of the United States government in the information field would make a fascinating study in itself. However, an effort has been made to remain faithful to the confusion and ambiguity surrounding the efforts of the United States government. Thus, terms like "propaganda," "information activities," and so on are used interchangeably.

Another troublesome term is "policy." Today, largely as a result of efforts at technocratic management meant to depoliticize large areas of public life and decisionmaking, the term "policy" and its derivatives, e.g., policy "making" and policy "formation," have connotations of rationality, science, and impartial and nonideological analyses. To restate the old joke, "I'm a policy-maker, you're a politician, and he's an ideologue." However, in this analysis, the word policy is not meant to have such connotations. Policy here is meant simply to describe the set of principles and goals used to guide action in a specific area. The making and carrying out of policy is an intensely political process, heavily imbued with elements of irrationality and ideology.

Finally, the notion of imperialism looms large in this work. Although there are a number of definitions of the word, the notion of imperialism that underlies this analysis is based on a Marxist perspective which views imperialism as a complex integrated system of power relations founded in a system of production. Because of the dynamics of unequal exchange built into this system, certain nations and social classes benefit at the expense of others. However, while a centrality is ascribed to economic factors, one must also understand and examine the power and significance of the cultural, social and political factors and how they interact with the economic base. In trying to articulate and examine a notion of media imperialism, I am not arguing that communication forms an independent system of variables, or that media imperialism is a new form of imperialism, distinct and autonomous from economic and political forces. Rather, I am trying to define and accentuate the role that communication occupies in the overall dynamics of imperialism. In a sense, this book is an attempt to redefine and broaden the general Marxist concept of imperialism in order to bring into sharper focus the position and importance of communication and the part it plays in the dynamics of imperialism.

A number of people and institutions were very helpful to me during the research and writing of this book. The Institute of Communications Research at the University of Illinois and Wayne State University provided funding to support the research. The staffs of the United States National Archives, the David Sarnoff Memorial Library, the CBS News Division, and the State Historical Society of Wisconsin all provided friendly, but crucial assistance. In addition, Eleanor Blum, Nancy Allen, and Carl Deal of the University of Illinois Library made special efforts to get needed material and documents for me. Thomas Guback and Paul Drake, through their teaching and scholarship, stimulated my interest in this topic and provided me with numerous helpful comments and criticisms. In addition to these individuals, a number of others provided helpful comments and professional and personal support. Among these, I particularly wish to thank Marvene Blackmore, James Carey, Jim Chestnut, Ben Helmke, Mark Katz, Eileen Meehan, Vincent Mosco, Tim Napier, Pablo Poveda, Jennifer Slack, Rafael Roncagliolo, Mary Laurel Reynolds, Mel Voigt, and Anna Zornosa. Whether by professional assistance, personal friendship, or both, these people made this experience a rewarding one.

CHAPTER 1

INTRODUCTION

Within the last 10 years there has been a dramatic change in what is considered important in the study of international communications, as well as in our understanding of the role of modern communications in the development of the Third World.

During the 1960s, communications researchers focused on the ways in which they thought media could assist the social and economic development of the nations of Africa, Asia, and Latin America. Beginning in the 1970s, though, there emerged a radically different perspective and evaluation of the role of modern communications in development. Frequently, the term "media imperialism" is used to describe the concerns of this new approach. The overall focus of this new orientation is the study of the processes by which modern communications media have operated to create, maintain, and expand systems of dominance and dependence on a world scale.

The media imperialism approach attempts to deal with those questions and areas of concern that earlier communication models and scholarship generally ignored. Previous models focused on the national level and on social psychological factors in order to determine how modern communications media could help accelerate the process of development and modernization. In contrast, the media imperialism approach is based on "an emphasis on global structure, whereby it is precisely the international socio-political system that determines the course of development within the sphere of each nation."[1] Whereas earlier models viewed communications media as a "tool" for development, the media imperialism approach views the media, situated as they are in a transnational context, as potential obstacles to meaningful and well-balanced socio-economic progress.

The major thrust and greatest accomplishment of the work undertaken within this approach so far has been an empirical description of the manner in which communications media operate on a global level. As reflected

in the works of Herbert Schiller, Armand Mattelart, and others, the research in this area tends to focus on the operation of transnational agents,
either transnational corporations or transnational media industries, and
their role in international communications. Such works attempt to describe in detail the manner in which such transnational agents dominate
the international structure and flow of communications. Often, an important element in such studies is an examination of how the policies and
practices of the core country government, particularly that of the United
States, assist these transnational agents in achieving global dominance in
communication.

Overall, as a scholarly position and paradigm, the media imperialism
approach must be judged a success, in that it has fundamentally changed
the orientation and research agenda in the field of international communications and communications and development. Of course, the success of
this approach must be seen in a larger context. Its growth and prominence
is one reflection of the general critical assessment and rejection by many
Third World countries of western models of modernization, of which
earlier communications models were a part. Along with calls for a "New
International Economic Order," there have been calls for a "New International Information Order." Much of the current research within this
approach has direct and important relevance for communication policy
formation in Third World countries.

While acknowledging its success and the important issues it has raised
about international communications and the role of communications in
social and economic development, both critics and adherents of the media
imperialism approach have noted that the research undertaken within
this approach has failed to deal adequately with a number of important
issues and areas of concern.[2] For example, while at the empirical level
there has been much progress dealing with the concerns of media imperialism, such progress has not been matched at the theoretical level. In one
sense, the research on media imperialism can be situated within the broad
tradition of a Marxist critique of capitalism. In the global growth of modern
communications media, researchers see a reflection of the broader imperialist expansion of western capitalism. In a more specific sense, one
can situate the research on media imperialism in the context of the dependency approach to the problems of development that have emerged since
the late 1960s. Yet, such affinities are implicit rather than explicit. Very
little effort has been made to articulate and develop the media imperialism approach as a comprehensive theoretical construct by which future
research can be guided.

A second major deficiency of the media imperialism approach has been
a lack of attention to the *intranational* factors and dynamics as they form
a part of the communication practices and policies of both the core and

periphery countries. The major focus of the approach has been on the role of transnational agents and interests in shaping communications between developed and Third World countries. While such a focus is, of course, a necessary corrective to earlier models of communications and development, and does perform the very necessary task of establishing the overwhelming role of transnational interests in world communications, it nonetheless tends to ignore the forces and factors operating on national and local levels. The complex relations and dynamics among institutions, social classes, and groups are deemphasized in favor of highlighting the actions of the transnational agents.

In addition to the lack of theoretical development and examination of intranational factors and forces, the media imperialism approach, as embodied in the various empirical studies, lacks a sensitivity to the historical dimension. Tied as it is to the pressing concerns over current problems, the approach tends to define the issues of media imperialism primarily in the context of the United States post-World War II ascendancy to world power. As such, it has little to offer in describing the role of communications media in the relations of dominance and dependence prior to the war. This is ironic, since the media imperialism approach, in one sense, really does not represent any radical new breakthrough in the study of communications. It is more a revival and reformulation of an older concern, perhaps best represented in the works of the Canadian economic historian, Harold Innis, of the relations that have existed throughout human history between the development of communications media and the extension of domination by particular societies.

This last point needs to be emphasized. It is important to place media imperialism in a larger historical perspective, not only to give the approach more breadth and power, but also to reveal the extremely complex relationships that have existed over time between the development and expansion of communication media and the creation of new structures of dominance and dependence. Only with a knowledge of media imperialism as an historical phenomenon operating in the larger context of the relations of power can one begin to develop a comprehensive theoretical understanding of its nature and characteristics. Only with an understanding of the historical nature of media imperialism can one hope to formulate effective and meaningful contemporary strategies to overcome it.

This present work is written as a contribution to the development of an understanding of media imperialism as an historical phenomenon. It is devoted to an examination of United States shortwave broadcasting to Latin America in the context of the foreign policy of the administration of Franklin D. Roosevelt. There are a number of reasons why this topic and period are of special relevance to an understanding of media imperialism. As noted above, much of the empirical work within the approach tends to focus on an examination of media imperialism as a part of the post-World War II global expansion of United States military, economic, and political power. Yet, if one dates United States ascendancy to world power as 1945, one must remember that the United States had a great deal of experience in influencing and controlling the destinies of other nations prior to World War II. In the first third of this century, Latin America was the major arena for United States economic and political expansion. By 1920 the United States had achieved overwhelming economic and political dominance in that region. Many of the techniques, practices, and policies that the United States employed after World War II in expanding its dominion over the globe were first developed through trial and error in Latin America. As one observer noted soon after World War II, in commenting upon the United States foreign policy in Latin America, "Latin America is a laboratory in which much of the application of foreign policy can get its first workout."[3]

An important element in the establishment of United States power in the hemisphere was the control of communications, first point-to-point, and later the mass media. The United States demanded that both European and Latin American nations adhere to an "open-door" policy in cable communications in the hemisphere. With the development of radio-telegraphy, the United States demanded that all nations recognize this country's preeminence in hemispheric radio communications. In time the various mass media—first film, then newspapers and magazines, and lastly radio broadcasting—were integrated into the media structure of the United States. By 1945, United States hegemony in hemispheric communications was complete.

One could well focus on the experience of the United States in any one of the Latin American media in order to reveal the larger patterns of the development of a media dependency. However, a study of United States shortwave broadcasting to Latin America, far from being a prosaic affair, illustrates particularly well the complex interrelationships between economic interests, public policy, and domestic and international politics, all of which comprise the phenomenon of media imperialism. The United States economic, political, and communications expansion into Latin America was an integral part of major social and political transformations in the United States. Through a study of shortwave broadcasting to Latin America during the Roosevelt administration, one can reveal, in part, the major restructuring of relationships that were occuring between major domestic institutions in the United States. In many senses, a study of shortwave broadcasting requires a critical understanding of the major dynamics that underlie United States actions both at the domestic and international levels.

American international shortwave broadcasting was developed in the 1920s and was controlled by those same interests and groups that controlled the development of American domestic broadcasting. Chief among the companies involved were the National Broadcasting Company (NBC) and the Columbia Broadcasting System (CBS). While initially there was a great deal of enthusiasm about the possibilities of this new technology, by the mid 1930s the private companies realized that the commercial broadcasting application of this technology was very limited. They reduced their shortwave activities significantly; ironically, this was done at a time when foreign governments were realizing the political uses of shortwave broadcasting and were thus expanding their international shortwave activities. In the late 1930s the United States government also began to realize the capability of shortwave to help achieve foreign trade and policy goals, particularly in Latin America. Yet, given the fact that American shortwave broadcasting was in private hands, the government had to act slowly and reach a modus vivendi with the private broadcasters. Very suspicious of the New Deal administration, private broadcasters feared that any direct government involvement in shortwave would be but a first step toward the direct control of domestic broadcasting. So as to remove any cause for direct government involvement in shortwave, the broadcasters upgraded and expanded their shortwave services, particularly to Latin America. Moreover, in order to assist private broadcasters in their efforts, in 1939 the United States government allowed the sale of commercial time of shortwave broadcasts. Yet, whatever commercial possibilities existed were quickly disrupted by the beginning of the war in Europe. Under wartime conditions, the government began to exert more and more control over private broadcasters' activities. The private broadcasters, realizing that their fears of government control of domestic broadcasting were unfounded, cooperated with the government. Finally, in 1942, the government leased all the shortwave facilities and took control of all programming. The World War II experience laid the foundation for the post-war development of the Voice of America.

This basic outline of events does not do justice to the complexity of the historical process or explain how the development of government interest and activity in shortwave reflected its shifting foreign policy strategy and the restructuring of relations that occurred between business and government during World War II. Government interest in shortwave arose as part of the Roosevelt Administration's larger effort to develop a new approach to inter-American affairs, which went under the name of the Good Neighbor Policy. As an integral part of its domestic program to deal with the economic crisis of the 1930s, the administration sought to open the hemisphere further to United States exports, while concomitantly expanding and consolidating its influence throughout the southern continent. The Roosevelt Administration rejected a reliance on force and unilateral intervention as counter-productive. It sought instead to organize a system of inter-American cooperation and solidarity, based on the protection and expansion of United States hemispheric interests and dominance. Essential elements in this system were liberal trade policies and an emphasis on inter-American unity in opposition to European interests and intervention. While hailed at the time as a radical reversal of United States policy in the region, the new approach embodied in the Good Neighbor Policy did not represent a liquidation of past imperialist goals, but rather a creative transformation of the methods of control and dominance.

Essential to the success of the Good Neighbor Policy was the development of a consensus on hemispheric affairs among the governments of American nations which would give centrality to United States interests and goals. Thus, the cultural element in foreign policy assumed new importance, and attempts were made to complement commercial, political, and military ties with cultural ones. Initially, such efforts in the late 1930s were limited to educational exchanges. However, the war in Europe and the threat it posed to United States hemispheric interests required that such cultural efforts be greatly expanded. The United States government turned to shortwave and other mass media in order to mobilize broad support among the Latin American public for United States goals and aims. While cultural diplomacy was initiated on the high plane of intellectual cooperation among educators, the political situation in the early 1940s soon transformed it into an enormous public relations campaign.

If war-time cooperation is used as the measure of success, then the Good Neighbor Policy in its economic, political, and cultural manifestations must be regarded as a vast success. By the end of the war, all Latin American nations had declared war on the Axis powers, in contrast to World War I, when seven of the twenty Latin American republics—including Argentina, Mexico, and Chile—remained neutral. Latin American nations supplied the Allies with essential war materials and cooperated with the United States in its efforts to root out any Axis interests or presence in the hemisphere. As one historian of inter-American relations noted, "During World War II, the New World attained the high points of solidarity which had been envisioned for it by Henry Clay a century and a quarter earlier. . . . [Such solidarity] now came to include not only expanded trade relations, but also financial, military, political, and particularly moral cooperation."[4]

A less optimistic way of looking at Inter-American solidarity during World War II is to note that one of the explicit aims of United States activity in Latin America during the war was to decrease the dependency of Latin America on European trade, politics, and culture as much as possible, and to increase the region's ties with the United States. As a result of the war, the economies of the Latin American nations became highly integrated into the economy of the United States, their foreign policy became an adjunct to United States policy, and their media began to be explicitly patterned after those of the United States.

Additionally, the United States sought to blunt the demands of Latin American nationalism in their economic, political, and cultural manifestations. The United States demanded that Latin American nations eschew a program of economic development that would lead to greater industrial growth and thus restrict the importation of United States products. The United States was quick to identify strong, emerging nationalist movements in Bolivia and Argentina as pro-Axis, and sought to isolate them politically. The influence the United States was able to exercise on the Latin American media through its control of advertising revenue and newsprint was aimed at supporting those media friendly to United States aims and silencing those that were either pro-Axis, strongly nationalist, or simply independent. While, of course, the defeat of fascism was an urgent necessity during World War II, the United States seized this crisis as an opportunity to integrate the Latin American nations even more into a system of client states.

After the war, the focus of United States interest in foreign matters became fixated on the post-war problems of Europe and the issues of global order and dominance. The United States now insisted that the inter-American system it had cultivated so carefully give priority to the larger world order it was trying to create. Throughout the war, Latin American nations cooperated closely with the United States in the hope that, after the war, the United States would give special assistance and attention to Latin American efforts at social and economic development. Overall, such hopes were disappointed. The United States advised Latin American nations to rely on private foreign capital for their development needs, while the government was giving billions for the post-war reconstruction of Europe. While Latin America was not exactly relegated to the backwaters of United States foreign and economic policy, post-war United States–Latin American relations hardly lived up to the picture of inter-American assistance and cooperation painted by the United States government during the war.

To some, this development reflected the abandonment of the Good Neighbor Policy by the United States. In a strictly literal sense, this is true. However, in a more profound sense, this development reflected the outstanding success of the Good Neighbor Policy. Politically, economically, and militarily, United States interests in Latin America were secure. The United States did not so much abandon the Good Neighbor Policy as it made it a part of a global policy to deal with the post-war world. Its goals and methods—free trade and a reliance on political rather than military means—were reformulated as the aims and methods of its general foreign policy. The experience and lessons it had learned in establishing its dominance in Latin America were now being applied on a world scale.

As a laboratory for economic policy and political diplomacy, Latin America served as a testing ground for United States policies and practices in the area of communications and media. Just as the modern United States policy of free trade received its first manifestation in Latin America in the form of reciprocal trade treaties and Export-Import Bank loans, so also United States policies and practices of control over international communications and cultural diplomacy received their first workout. By 1945, the United States had developed communications practices and policies in Latin America designed to complement and enhance its economic, military, and political control of the region. In those areas where private media interests were successful in penetrating Latin American nations, such as the film and advertising industries, the United States government lent assistance and encouragement. In the areas where private interests were not successful, such as in shortwave broadcasting, the government itself stepped in and undertook media activities. Thus the United States faced the post-war era of world expansion with a partnership between government and media interests that had been worked out on the basis of the Latin American experience.

Yet, it is a mistake to think that the consummation of this partnership occurred smoothly and without any problems. An important part of an understanding of media imperialism as an historical dynamic is a comprehension of the factors, forces, and relationships at the national level which produce it and determine its specific characteristics. In discussions of media imperialism, there is often the assumption that the relations between government and business are unproblematic and that they share the same interests and goals. However, such relations are very complex. An important part of the development of United States broadcasting to Latin America was the conflict between United States private broadcasters and the government.

There are a number of different dimensions to this conflict. On one level, it reflected the antagonistic relations between the broadcasting industry and the government. While broadcasters welcomed government regulation by Republican administrations in the 1920s, they feared possible government takeover under the New Deal. Thus, they opposed any direct government involvement in shortwave, seeing such involvement as the first step toward a larger government role in domestic broadcasting.

Nonetheless, the broadcasters recognized that the United States' growing commercial and political dominance in the hemisphere, and the threat to that dominance raised by the growing crisis in Europe, required that they be more cognizant of the political impact their international broadcasting activities could have on the conduct of United States hemispheric policy. Rather than merely oppose greater government involvement in shortwave, the broadcasters tried to remove any justification the government might have had for direct activity in the field. In the late 1930s, they expanded and reshaped their own shortwave efforts in order to meet the government's political needs in hemispheric affairs.

This informal arrangement became less satisfactory to the government as the world crisis deepened. While respecting, and in some cases manipulating, the broadcasters' fears about government intervention, the government began to play a larger role in shortwave activities. In the 2 year period prior to Pearl Harbor, it encouraged and assisted broadcasters in their efforts and offered more guidance and direction as to the political role shortwave should play. Moreover, the government sought to disabuse the broadcasters of their fears of government intervention in the field of domestic broadcasting, and assured them of the government's support of the commercial structure of private broadcasting. The government was successful, and, by 1942, many of the fears that shaped relations between the government and the broadcasting industry during the 1930s were quieted.

No longer fearing government involvement in shortwave as a prelude to greater domestic control, shortwave broadcasters were able to reassess their activities in the field. It was evident that the political importance of international broadcasting in the conduct of United States foreign affairs far outweighed any commercial possibilities shortwave might have had. Thus, broadcasters were willing to allow greater government control and direction of their activities. This was formalized in 1942, when the government leased time on all private shortwave transmitters and assumed control over all programming activities, manifesting the politicization of shortwave broadcasting. In the context of this arrangement and agreement between the broadcasters and government on the nature and use of shortwave broadcasting, the post-war development of the Voice of America took place.

Yet, a focus on the particulars of government-broadcasters relations should not obscure the larger development taking place. Both the conflict between the broadcasters and the government, and the nature of its eventual resolution, took place in the context of more basic changes in the relations between government and business.

The government, faced with the economic crisis of the 1930s, had to take on a larger role in the management of society, not to change it, but in order to insure the survival of the system of capitalist relations of power. On the domestic level, the government attempted to rationalize the system of capitalist production by introducing elements of national planning. In order to minimize the social destructiveness of capitalism, it sponsored various social welfare measures and reforms. On the international level, it sought to intervene in international economic affairs, and attempted to evolve some type of international economic planning. With the New Deal, the shape of the modern liberal corporate state began to emerge. Rather than being the "errand boy" for specific dominant economic interests, the state began to assume a more semi-autonomous character in order to deal with the increasingly complex problems of capitalist development.

An enlarged role for the government in the management of the economy required a restructuring of relations between business and government. This process of adjustment occurred slowly and not without conflict. A number of progressive business and economic interests supported the New Deal reforms, seeing them as necessary to the survival of the system. However, many businessmen saw government intervention into the economy as a threat to free enterprise and to the opportunity to make a profit. Much of the broadcasting industry, already subject to government regulation, felt particularly threatened by an activist administration.

However, as the possibility of war grew, production for war needs assumed priority over New Deal reform. The true nature of the administration's character and agenda began to become clear. It sought to develop an active collaboration between private industry and the state. It went to great lengths to assure businessmen of its good faith and intentions. Private industrialists, particularly those from larger corporations, gladly greeted business' war-time role, particularly with its cost-plus contracts, promises of lax anti-trust enforcement, and labor peace. While many liberal New Dealers saw the war as wrecking the broad social program of reform initiated in the 1930s, a more correct assessment would be that, during World War II, many of the more basic aims and goals of the New Deal were realized. A radical restructuring of power in society was avoided, the capitalist economy was saved and revitalized, and the liberal corporate state, based on an alliance between business, the military, and the government, with labor as a very junior partner, was shaped into its modern form.

In this sense, then, the debate, conflict, and resolution of the issue of government involvement in shortwave was but a small part of the larger process of changing relations between the state and the dominant economic sectors in society. In the face of the government's enlarged role in the political and economic management of, not only the domestic, but also the international capitalist order, traditional relations between government and business, including broadcasting, had to be reevaluated and restructured.

Before one can approach an insightful understanding of United States–Latin American media relations as they have evolved over the years, one must first understand some of the basic dynamics that underlie United States–Latin American relations in general. Chapter 2 is devoted to examining the development of United States–Latin American political, economic, and military ties during the first third of this century. While much of this material will be familiar to those with an understanding of the history of United States–Latin American relations, it is necessary to lay a groundwork in order to understand subsequent events.

Chapter 3 examines the development of the technology and practice of shortwave broadcasting in the 1920s and the early 1930s by private broadcasters. Of special importance are the factors that contributed at first to the broadcasters' interest and enthusiasm and later to their near-abandonment of shortwave.

Chapter 4 looks at the growing interest of the United States government in using shortwave as an adjunct to its foreign policy and trade in Latin America in the late 1930s. This interest led to the conflict between private shortwave broadcasters and the government over the control and direction of international broadcasting. A resolution of sorts was achieved in 1939 with the commercialization of shortwave.

Chapter 5 examines the period between the commercialization of shortwave in 1939 and total government takeover in 1942. During this 3-year period, a major restructuring of relations between the broadcasting industry and the government took place, in which conflict was replaced with cooperation. On the basis of this cooperation, the United States government and media interests were able to penetrate and profoundly affect the development of Latin American media systems.

Chapter 6 looks briefly at post-war developments and at the outcomes of the war-time cooperation between the broadcasting interests and the government. Chief among them was the institutionalization of government involvement in international broadcasting that occurred with the creation of the Voice of America.

Notes

[1] See Kaarle Nordenstreng and Herbert Schiller, "Communications and National Development: Changing Perspectives—Introduction," in *National Sovereignty and International Communications*, eds. Kaarle Nordenstreng and Herbert Schiller (Norwood, New Jersey: Ablex, 1979), p. 7; see also Rita Cruise O'Brien, "Mass Communications: Social Mechanisms of Incorporation and Dependence," in *Transnational Capitalism and National Development*, ed. J.J. Villamil (Atlantic Highlands, New Jersey: Humanities Press, 1979), pp. 129–143.

[2] See Vincent Mosco and Andrew Herman, "Radical Social Theory and the Communications Revolution," in *Communications and Social Structure—Critical Studies in Mass Media Research*, eds. Emile G. McAnany, Jorge Schnitman, and Noreene Janus (New York: Praeger, 1981), pp. 58–84; Chin Chau Lee, *"Media Imperialism" Reconsidered: The Homogenizing of Television Culture* (Beverly Hills, California: Sage, 1980); and Fred Fejes, "Media Imperialism: An Assessment," *Media, Culture and Society* 3: 3 (1981) pp. 281–289. The following discussion draws heavily upon the last article.

[3] Allen Haden, "In Defense of Rockefeller," *The Inter-American* November 1945, p. 48.

[4] Donald M. Dozer, *Are We Good Neighbors?* (Gainesville, Florida: University of Florida Press, 1959), p. 147.

CHAPTER 2

THE CONTEXT: UNITED STATES–LATIN AMERICAN RELATIONS FROM THE "BIG STICK" TO "THE GOOD NEIGHBOR"

One major goal of this work is to analyze North American shortwave radio broadcasting to Latin America in the 1930s and 1940s as part of United States–Latin American relations in general. It is necessary, therefore, first to discuss the ties between the United States and Latin America, and how they evolved over time. As will be shown, the United States pursued a policy of aggressive political and economic expansion into Latin America during the first third of this century. Along with forceful military and political intervention in the affairs of Latin American countries and growing American investment in the region and increased trade, an important aspect of this overall expansion was the control the United States sought over inter-American communications.

By the end of the 1920s, the United States was the unchallenged dominant power in the Western Hemisphere. The depression and its consequences, however, threatened such hemispheric hegemony. Such threats, if they were to be met successfully, required a rethinking of goals, priorities, and practices. Franklin D. Roosevelt's early policies in both domestic and hemispheric affairs were evidence of bold attempts to devise new courses of action to deal with the radically changed conditions. As new strategies of hemispheric control were sought, shortwave radio broadcasting began to emerge as an important element in United States–Latin American relations.

United States Expansion into Latin America Prior to 1929

During the 19th century, the energies and attention of the United States were devoted first to establishing and consolidating its rule over the North

American continent and then to internal expansion and industrial development. As a result, this country maintained little consistent active interest
and involvement in the affairs of Latin America during the 1800s. The
United States government, through its proclamation of the Monroe Doctrine in 1823, defined for itself the role of protector of the American nations against the threat of European incursions in this hemisphere. In
practice, however, the doctrine's efficacy was based on the willingness
and ability of the United States to enforce it. The United States government was either silent or only lamely protested against British expansion
in the Caribbean in the 1830s and 1840s, French and British intervention
in the La Plata region of South America, reannexation by Spain of Santo
Domingo in 1861 and French occupation of Mexico in the 1860s. Among
Latin American nations, notions of Pan-American solidarity in one form
or another were enunciated as early as 1815, and a number of regional
conferences were held between 1826 and 1865 in an attempt to establish
some system of inter-American cooperation and military security. Such
efforts, however, were initiated by Latin American nations and generally
were marked by a lack of interest by the United States.

However, starting in the 1880s, United States industries began to feel
the need for foreign markets for their surplus production. The accumula-
tion of domestic capital was stimulating the search for new opportunities
for investment overseas. Thus, the United States began to take a more active interest in its Southern neighbors. One early expression of such interest was the calling of a number of hemispheric conferences of American
governments, popularly known as "Pan American conferences." The first
conference, organized by the United States, was held in Washington, D.C.
in 1889. Subsequent conferences led to the creation of the Pan American
Union, the predecessor of today's Organization of American States. Much
of the business of these conferences was devoted to commercial matters,
such as the development of uniform weight and measure standards and
merchandise nomenclature, copyright and patent protection, and the
standardization of trade regulations and practices. Such conferences also
had the potential of providing Latin American nations an opportunity to
press their interests in concert against their Northern neighbor. At the first
conference in 1889, Latin American countries, weary of past European
intervention and fearful of the possibility of future United States intervention in the region, pushed for the adoption of a resolution that drastically
restricted the right of a nation to intervene in the internal affairs of other
countries. Of all the countries present, the United States was the only government to oppose adoption of the resolution. Subsequently, the United
States made great efforts to control future conferences and to remove from
the agenda any discussion of significant political issues between the United
States and Latin America. When the Pan American Union was formed in

1910, the United States Secretary of State was designated as permanent chairman and the organization was housed in a building in Washington, D.C. adjacent to the State Department and the White House. Understandably, most of the Latin American nations were not enthusiastic about the Pan American Union, but, lacking a viable alternative for collective hemispheric action, they participated. The development of the Pan American movement and the creation of the Pan American Union reflected the United States' drive to extend its commercial hegemony over the hemisphere.[1] Such efforts were matched by more aggressive attempts to extend its political and military power.

The Monroe Doctrine, backed by the United States' increasing industrial and potential military power, was given new life in the 1890s. The United States sought to establish its priority rights over the region in opposition to the presence and claims of European nations, especially in the Caribbean and Central America. Forcefully invoking the Doctrine in a boundary dispute between Great Britain's colony of Guiana and Venezuela in 1895, the Cleveland Administration compelled the two nations to bring the matter to arbitration. While the settlement was largely in favor of British claims, the important outcome for the United States was the recognition by Great Britain of the dominant position that the United States occupied in the affairs of the hemisphere.

The 1898 war with Spain marked the beginning of a 30-year period of immense growth in the political and economic power of the United States, first in the Caribbean and later into South America. Gaining control over Spain's former colonies of Cuba and Puerto Rico and later, through its involvement in the 1903 Panama revolt, of territory in Panama on which to build a transisthmus canal, American preeminence in the Caribbean was quickly established. An indirect challenge to United States power occurred in 1902 when Great Britain, Germany, and Italy, exercising rights traditionally recognized under international law, blockaded Venezuelan ports in order to force that nation to pay its creditors. This challenge, however, was used as an occasion for the further extension of United States involvement. Recognizing that the financial and political instability common to many Latin American countries often endangered foreign lives and property, and thus provided an excuse for European intervention as occurred in Venezuela, President Theodore Roosevelt took action to preempt such future European involvement.

In order to remove any justification for European involvement in this hemisphere, Roosevelt in his 1904 Message to Congress asserted that the United States had the unilateral right to intervene militarily in the internal affairs of other American countries. The so-called "Big Stick" policy transformed the Monroe Doctrine from a passive warning aimed at European nations into an active instrument justifying unilateral intervention into the affairs of other American nations. In the first third of this century, citing reasons of political unrest, financial instability, or violation of United States rights, the United States undertook major military interventions in the Dominican Republic, Nicaragua, Honduras, Haiti, and Mexico, in addition to maintaining troops in Panama, Cuba, and exercising political suzerainty over Puerto Rico. By the time of the entry of the United States into World War I, the Caribbean had been turned into "an American lake."

With the encouragement and protection of the United States government, businessmen and investors turned South. In 1897 total United States investment in Latin America was approximately $304 million, with most of it placed in Mexican railroads and mines and Cuban sugar plantations. By 1908 total United States investment had tripled to $1,063 million, and by 1914 it totaled $1,641 million, accounting for roughly half of all United States foreign investment. United States trade showed similar increases, growing from $240 million in 1898 to $801 million in 1913. United States Latin American trade, as a share of total United States foreign trade, grew from 13 percent to 19 percent during the same period.

Prior to World War I, the greater portion of United States trade and investment in the region was in Central American and Caribbean countries. On the South American continent, Great Britain and Germany tended to be the major investors and foreign trading partners. World War I, however, provided the United States with the opportunity for uncontested economic penetration of Latin America. With European production devoted to the war effort, the United States took over Europe's role as the major supplier of goods for the South American republics. By the end of the war, the United States was Latin America's largest supplier of goods and investment. The trend continued after the war, and by 1929 the United States trade with Latin America totaled $2,080. The United States supplied Latin America with 38.7 percent of its imports and received 34.5 percent of its exports. In contrast the combined imports of Britain, France, and Germany totaled 34.5 percent, and together they received 32.8 percent of all Latin American exports. By 1929 United States investment in the region has increased to $5,370 million.[2] By the end of the 1920s, the United States had succeeded in penetrating and dominating the commerce and finance of the region.

Yet, the United States' economic expansion created political problems. The brash interventionist style of diplomacy that characterized the "Big Stick" policy of the United States in the Caribbean and Central America could not serve as a basis for United States policy with South America. Indeed, the effectiveness of direct military intervention was beginning to be doubted. Given the growing isolationist sentiment in the United States due to the disillusionment with the United States' participation in the war, it was questionable whether public opinion would allow or support an aggressive style of diplomacy. Thus the United States' new position of dominance in the Hemisphere required new forms of political techniques and policies by which it could protect and expand its interests. In the words of one historian of United States–Latin American relations, the basic problem facing United States policy makers in the post-war years was how "to formulate principles of policy flexible enough to protect America's hegemony in the hemisphere and the special situations in the Caribbean without producing the kind of involvement which had caused the United States to reduce several nations to protectorate status."[3] In confronting this problem, Charles Evans Hughes, Secretary of State under Harding and Coolidge, attempted to formulate a Latin American policy that both insured the promotion and protection of the broad strategic interests of the United States in the region, such as access to petroleum, an open door for North American trade and investment, the limitation of indebtedness by Latin American governments to European financiers, and the control over hemispheric communication; and, at the same time, backed away from an active involvement in Latin American politics and an active defence of specific North American business interests in the region. Much of the active promotion of United States trade and investment and active championing of individual business interest in Latin America was undertaken instead by the Commerce Department under Herbert Hoover. In general, the State Department was circumspect in using its power and influence to further individual United States interests and tried to remain aloof in disputes between United States nationals and Latin American governments.

By the end of the 1920s, with its economic preeminence established by the war and its political preeminence recognized by the major European powers, the dominant position of the United States in the affairs of the Western Hemisphere was unchallenged. Along with a continuation of the steady, quiet, and almost routine expansion of United States investment and trade in the region, the aggressive interventionist policies of past administrations gave way in the 1920s to a search for more refined and indirect means of control. While many Latin American governments objected to the presumed right of the United States to intervene in their internal affairs, such objections did not constitute any immediate threat to United States hegemony. Protest as they might, most of the ruling elites in Latin America welcomed North American investment and trade. As the economies and political regimes of the region were based on the export of raw materials and agricultural goods, the strong world demand for Latin American goods during much of this decade led to prosperity and the continued political rule by export oriented elites. Thus, there was, as yet, very little incentive to radically alter the existing state of hemispheric affairs.

United States Expansion in Latin American Communications

Complementing United States economic penetration of Latin America was the expansion by American communication interests in the region and the general increase in the control by United States companies over Latin American communications media. A major area of such penetration was cable and radio communication.

The United States owned Central and South American Telegraph Company, renamed All American Cables in 1920, laid a cable line in the 1880s and 1890s down the western coast of the southern continent. The company received monopoly cable concessions from the governments of Mexico, Guatemala, Nicaragua, Columbia, Ecuador, and Peru. Eventually the cable company succeeded in connecting the United States with Chile and, by overland route, Argentina. However, all cable communication on the eastern coast of the southern continent was dominated by British interests. The situation was particularly critical, as the British-owned Western Telegraph Company had monopoly concessions on underwater cable communications in Argentina, Brazil, and Uruguay. By World War I, it was evident that such British control could seriously hamper United States expansion in the region. Given the prospect of post-war hemispheric rivalry between Britain and the United States, United States business and military interests did not feel secure in transmitting information on commercial and military matters, often of a confidential nature, over British controlled facilities. Attempts by All American Cable to expand were met by opposition by Western Telegraph.

The United States government dealt with the situation after the war by establishing an "open door" policy in cable communications. The State Department actively opposed the continuation of any monopoly concession grant by any Latin American government in cable communication. It brought pressure on the British government and the various Latin American governments to drop exclusive cable concessions. More importantly, it withheld from Western Telegraph and its United States ally, Western Union, landing rights in the United States for its Latin American cables. Eventually, the State Department was able to force Western Telegraph to waive its monopoly rights in Latin American countries. United States cable companies also relinquished their monopoly concessions in Latin America. The continent was thus opened to expansion by United States cable companies, an opportunity which a number of them quickly took advantage by laying new cable lines and buying up smaller existing cable companies. By 1924 it was possible to send a message to any country in the hemisphere over United States-owned facilities.[4]

In the area of radio communications, it was regarded as equally important that the United States establish a dominant position in Latin America, particularly since this was a developing new technology in which no company or country had, as yet, established a dominant position in Latin America. In October 1915, Secretary of State Robert Lansing, in a circular to all United States embassies in Latin America, noted that the State Department, given the war in Europe, was very concerned that the ownership and control of radio communication in the Americas should not "pass beyond this hemisphere and into European or Asiatic hands." The circular instructed the embassies to communicate to the various Latin American governments that "the Department would accordingly be inclined to look with favor, and believes that other American governments share this view, upon any mutually acceptable agreement whereby the control of this vitally important method of communications between the American continent might rest wholly in sympathetic and disinterested hands, thus realizing another conception of a broad and beneficial Pan Americanism." Lansing proposed that an informal exchange of views on this matter take place among the representatives of the American governments attending an upcoming Pan American Scientific Congress to be held in Washington that December.

On January 7, 1916, delegates of all the Latin American governments represented at the scientific congress met at the State Department to discuss the issue of the control of hemispheric radio communications. It quickly became evident that the United States had something more in mind than a general discussion of the issue of radio control in the Americas. The United States representatives outlined a broad plan for the organization and construction of a Pan American system of radio communications which would link all the nations of the hemisphere. This system would be based on government ownership and control of all radio communication facilities and would conduct all military, governmental, and commercial radio communications within the hemisphere and with other parts of the globe, thus allowing American nations to bypass British control of world cable communications. Within this system the United States would take leadership, as government controlled stations would "be rendered available for the use of all American governments in case of exigencies demanding united action by them or by the United States." While all Latin American delegates agreed informally on the need to keep control of radio in the Americas in hemispheric hands, they could not officially commit their governments in any manner to any plan or agreement, other than to study the proposals put forward on the matter.

The United States plan was given more definite form in a memorandum circulated by the State Department to United States embassies in Latin America in March 1916. This memorandum, to be formally presented to the various Latin American governments, contained the proposals made by the United States for a hemispheric radio relay network which would be centered in the Canal Zone, with major relay stations in Washington, D.C., Cuba, Guatemala, Paraguay, and Argentina. Latin American governments were asked to study this proposal as the basis for a planned Pan American conference which would establish a hemispheric radio network. While the immediate purpose of this plan was to establish a system of radio communication for the military defense of the hemispheric, the consequence of such a proposal was that it would organize hemispheric radio communication on the basis of United States interests and control. The Latin American governments were understandably not excited about the proposal and the planned conference never took place.[5]

While its growing involvement in the European war shifted the United States governments attention away from Latin America, the concern over North American control over hemispheric radio communications was never really abandoned, and such a goal was again actively pursued after the war. An internal State Department memorandum, dated June 16, 1919, noting the post-war prospect of the growth of British and German interests in Latin American radio communications, stated, "It is vital that the American interest dominate wireless communication in this hemisphere, vital from a military, naval and communications point of view." As the issue of the ownership of radio communication had, by this time, more or less been settled against the formation of a government monopoly, the memorandum noted that "The only practical method we know by experience to have proven its worth is the selection of some powerful American interest and persuading it to go down into that field and the rendering to it of every possible government support whether it be diplomatic or financial." The memorandum suggested that Latin America be divided between two American radio companies: The Tropical Radio Company, the radio subsidiary of United Fruit, taking Central America, the Caribbean, and Mexico; and the Pan American Wireless Company, taking South America. It further suggested that these companies' expansion in radio communications be financed, in part, through government funds, as they would be fulfilling a governmental aim "in obtaining for the United States a dominance of radio communication in the western world."[6]

While the State Department was concerned about Latin American radio communications, more definite plans were taking shape in the Department of the Navy. Admiral W.H.G. Bullard, chief of the Naval Communications Service, was deeply involved in assisting the General Electric Company in its planned formation of the Radio Corporation of America (RCA) and that company's subsequent purchase of the American holdings of the Marconi Company, a purchase designed to protect the United States against British control of radio communications. In the original agreement between the Marconi Company and General Electric, in which the British company agreed to sell its American assets, it was recognized by both parties that the soon-to-be-formed RCA and the Marconi Company would work together in the development of Latin American radio communications. Both companies would form and jointly own a new company called the South American Radio Corporation, which would build stations and conduct radio traffic in Latin America. However, in line with its informal compact with the United States government that all American radio communications would be controlled by American citizens, RCA was to dominate the new company both by having sole control of the management and by having five seats on the company's seven-member board. RCA, deeply involved in organzing its radio service in the United States, was not ready to act in South America, and plans for the construction of the first radio station there, to be built in Argentina, were left to the Marconi Company. However, the British government objected to such a large measure of North American control over the new South American Radio Corporation, and the Marconi Company asked for increased representation on the Board of Directors before proceeding with its plans for a station in Argentina.

The picture was further complicated by the fact that the German radio company, Gesellschaft Für Drahtlose Telegraphie (Telefunken) had organized an Argentine company for the purpose of constructing a radio station in Buenos Aires for communication with Europe. The French radio company, Compagnie Générale de Télégraphie (CGT) was also expressing interest in constructing Latin American stations. RCA's and Marconi's delay, and the German and French plans, worried the American government. While an "open door" policy worked to American advantage in the already established field of cable communication, in the as yet undeveloped field of international radio communication it could be disastrous. Given the expense of constructing a radio station and the probability of a low volume of commercial radio business in Latin America, competition would make any Latin American radio station unprofitable. More importantly, at a time when the potential of shortwave radio communication was as yet undiscovered and international radio communication was based on high-power, long-wave communication, there was only very limited spectrum space available for the new South American stations. To avoid probable interference, most likely Latin American governments would give priority rights over frequencies to the first station built. In a letter to the RCA Board of Directors in July 1920, Admiral Bullard expressed his concern over the situation and appealed for measures which would exclude Europeans from gaining control over communications in the Western Hemisphere. RCA, unable to act in South America, could only try to meet the British objections and get the Marconi Company started on a South American station. In September, the RCA Board of Directors agreed to increase Marconi's representation on the Board of the South American Radio Corporation to four Marconi representatives and five RCA representatives. This, however, was still unacceptable to the British.

In November 1920, RCA and Marconi officials met and decided that the best way to deal with the South American matter, given the progress of the German company in constructing its radio station in Argentina, was to recognize German and French claims in Latin American radio communication and form a consortium of the American, British, German, and French radio interests for the purpose of developing Latin American radio. The German and French interests were receptive to the idea, and the four companies met in Paris in August 1921 to work out the details of the new organization. Before proceeding to the South American matter, the companies agreed to refrain from competing with each other within their own national boundaries or in territories controlled by their respective governments. Thus, the world was partially carved up among the four radio companies, with the Marconi Company receiving Great Britain and its colonies; the CGT, France and its colonies and dependencies; RCA, the United States and its dependencies; and Telefunken restricted to operating primarily within Germany. South America was to be developed by all four of the companies through the consortium. However, as with the prior arrangement between RCA and Marconi, the major point of contention was the degree of control RCA was to exercise in the consortium. The RCA delegation, led by RCA's president, Owen D. Young, argued that given the political and military importance of radio communication and the dominant position of the United States in Latin America, American interests should have priority in the South American radio situation. He proposed the board of directors of the consortium consist of two representatives from each company, plus an American chairman chosen by RCA but not directly associated with RCA. Not only would the chairman be able to break ties, but he also would be able to veto any decision made by the board. The Marconi delegation, the principal opponent of this plan, countered with a proposal for a board of directors consisting of two representatives from each company. One of the RCA representatives would be chairman and would have two votes in case of a tie. After 2 months of heavy argument, and only after RCA threatened to break off negotiations and form a separate South American radio company with the German interests, the Marconi delegation gave in and accepted the American proposal. The new consortium, known as the AEFG Trust, was to control all the radio facilities owned and built by the four companies in South America. Plans were made for the completion of the Argentine station and for the construction of new stations in Brazil, Chile, and Columbia. United States control thus was assured over Latin American point-to-point radio communications. Owen D. Young proudly hailed the creation of the AEFG

Trust as the extension of the Monroe Doctrine into hemispheric radio communications.[7]

Paralleling the creation of the AEFG Trust was the emergence of another North American company in the field of Latin American electronic communication. In 1920, the North American concern, the International Telephone and Telegraph Company (ITT), was organized with initial assets consisting of telephone companies in Puerto Rico and Cuba. During the next decade, the company pursued an aggressive expansion policy in Latin America. By 1930, ITT had acquired the principal telephone systems in Mexico, Chile, Uruguay, Argentina, and the state of Rio Grande do Sul in Brazil. Although ITT's major business was the operation of telephone systems, it also quickly expanded into other areas of electronic communications in Latin America. In 1927, it acquired controlling interest in All American Cables, the principal North American cable company in Latin America and the only cable company with facilities in every Latin American country except Paraguay. The next year, gaining control of the Mackay Radio and Telegraph Company and utilizing the newly discovered potential of shortwave radio communication, ITT proceeded to organize radio communication companies in Argentina, Brazil, and Chile. This was part of a larger ITT effort to establish and operate an international radio communication system to compete with RCA. In Latin America, the Mackay company became the chief competitor or the AEFG Trust. Taking into account the Latin American investments of ITT and the AEFG Trust, together with investments by smaller North American radio companies such as United Fruit's Tropical Telegraph Company, by the end of the decade United States interests organized and controlled the major elements in the entire system of Latin American electronic point-to-point communications. The only major exceptions were national telegraph systems that were generally state owned.[8]

Although electronic point-to-point communication was the major area of penetration by United States interests in Latin American communications, the overall growing dominance by the United States in the hemisphere was also reflected in the Latin American mass media. In the dissemination of news to Latin America, the end of World War I saw the North American news agencies, United Press and Associated Press, successfully challenge European control over the distribution of foreign news to Latin American newspapers. Until the beginning of the war, the three major European news agencies, Reuters (Great Britain), Havas (France), and Wolff (Germany), along with the Associated Press, agreed upon a system of news exchange among themselves which divided the world into exclusive spheres of activity which tended to follow the divisions of global political power and influence. The news-gathering and dissemination activities of Associated Press were limited by this agreement to the United States and parts of the Caribbean and Central America, with Havas having exclusive press rights in the rest of the Caribbean and Central America and on the entire southern continent.

However, after the outbreak of the war, a number of Latin American newspapers objected to Havas' refusal to disseminate German war communiques and to the press agency's strong bias in favor of the French war effort. A number of papers requested international news from Associated Press, which it could not provide due to its agreement with the other news agencies. The Latin American papers turned to Associated Press' main competitor, United Press, which, not bound by the Agreement with the European agencies, provided them with news. Moreover, as part of its war-time propaganda campaign, the Wilson Administration actively encouraged and supported the efforts of United Press to expand its activities into Southern America. Associated Press, sensing the danger of news dissemination in South America being taken over by its domestic rival, negotiated a change in the agreement with Havas in 1918. With French interests in Latin America experiencing a decline because of the war, the French agency could do little but recognize the right of Associated Press to organize a news distribution system in South America.

The next year Associated Press signed contracts for the distribution of news with 24 Latin American newspapers, including *La Nación* and *La Prensa* of Lima. Associated Press' policy of supplying news to rival newspapers, however, proved incompatible with the fierce newspaper competition in Latin America, and a number of Associated Press' new clients subsequently dropped the news agency in favor of United Press. Not only did Associated Press and United Press provide Latin American newspapers with the bulk of their foreign news, but they also, in time, came to operate major domestic news agencies in a number of Latin American countries, such as Argentina, due to the unwillingness of many of the Latin American newspapers to cooperate with one another to the extent of forming national newsgathering pools.

The growing ties between the United States and Latin American press were reflected in the First Pan American Congress of Journalists held in Washington in 1926. This Congress, whose organizing committee was headed by the president of the American Newspaper Publishers Association, was attended by over one hundred Latin American publishers, editors, and reporters representing the most powerful and influential newspapers in the Southern Hemisphere. It had the status of a semi-diplomatic affair, with the Latin American newspapermen being given diplomatic privileges of going through United States customs. Messages of welcome were voted by both houses of Congress, and the meeting was addressed by both President Coolidge and Secretary of State Frank B. Kellogg. After a week-long meeting in Washington, the group was conducted on a 3-week tour of the

Eastern and Central United States, during which they were feted by local newspapers, chambers of commerce, and other groups and individuals.[9]

Another area of the Latin American mass media which North American interests penetrated and controlled was the film market. Prior to World War I, much of the Latin American film market was supplied by French products, particularly films from the French film company, Pathé, which maintained distribution offices in Buenos Aires, Rio de Janeiro, Havana, and Mexico City. However, the war forced European producers to discontinue making and marketing films, thus leaving the Latin American market completely open to products from the United States. In 1914, Universal Pictures Corporation sent a film scout to investigate the Latin American market and, by the end of the war, Hollywood film producers successfully captured Latin American screens. Although Hollywood's domination of Latin American film reflected its domination of the world film market in general at that time, in Latin America it was particularly overwhelming. One source estimated that in 1922 North American films took up 95 percent of the Latin American film market, as compared to controlling 90 percent of Australia's and 85 percent of Continental Europe's. Little local production was attempted, and it was rarely commercially successful or popular because American films had already defined the style of film making popular with Latin American audiences. Latin American producers and film companies could rarely hope to compete with the technical excellence and pervasiveness of the North American product.[10]

With the United States looking to Latin America as a market for its goods, there was growing attention given to the various Latin American mass media and their potential as advertising media. The Bureau of Foreign and Domestic Commerce of the Department of Commerce was particularly active in exploring the use of advertising as an aid to promote United States exports. As early as 1917, when the war in Europe had cut off European goods to Latin America, the Bureau had initiated an investigation of advertising practices and media in the various Latin American countries. The results of this investigation, published in a series of pamphlets in 1919 and 1920,[11] offered the North American exporter a comprehensive and detailed analysis of the state of advertising in the various Latin American countries, and a discussion of the advantages and disadvantages of a broad and diverse range of Latin American advertising media, including not only newspapers and magazines, but also billboards, trolley car posters, and calendars. In general, the investigations revealed that throughout Latin America, with the possible exception of Buenos Aires, the practice of advertising as a form of sales promotion was very undeveloped. Most newspaper advertising consisted of close copy ads for patent medicine, cigarettes, and sundry personal items. Audited circulation of newspapers and magazines was unknown, as were rate cards and discounts. Advertising agents, where they existed, were generally nothing more than space brokers.

Yet this state of affairs had promise, as the entire field of Latin American advertising was open to development along the lines of practices and ideas in the United States. As the pamphlet on advertising in Argentina noted about the Argentine public:

> While Europe influences them from almost every other angle, its advertising has scarcely ever touched them. The whole field of modern advertising is peculiarly an American development of selling. Nowhere in this field are there better evidences of American originality than in copy and illustration, and nowhere is Argentine advertising more poorly developed. The Argentine gives no particular indication of taking to advertising as a business and of becoming his own copy writer. The European nations have not developed either the science or the art of advertising as has the United States, and it lies largely with the advertising men of this country to take the opportunity that the media, the intelligence, and the purchasing power of the Argentina offer and turn it to good account for the American export trade.[12]

Continually stressed in all of the Bureau's pamphlets on advertising in Latin America was the recommendation that United States advertising agencies set up branches in the principal cities of Latin America.

During the 1920s, United States advertising agencies handling the accounts of large exports such as Ford and General Motors set up branch offices in a number of Latin American cities in order to handle the advertising of their clients. Such arrangements, however, were exceptional. Generally, most North American companies doing business in Latin America worked through local sales representatives or distributors in placing their advertisements in local Latin American media. Usually, the advertising division of a company in the United States would prepare advertisements for a particular Latin American market, often just translating domestic advertisements into Spanish or Portuguese. They would then send them to their sales representative or distributor in Latin America, who would place the advertisements in the local media. Much of the early advertising by North American exporters was of the "hit or miss" variety, with very little attempt to develop a consistent advertising campaign based on the utilization of local themes or tastes, and with very little thought given to proper media selection or appropriate audience. Some of the larger newspapers, however, such as *La Nación* of Buenos Aires, established offices in New York in the early 1920s in order to advise companies on their advertisements and to handle placement of advertising directly.

Despite the numerous inadequacies and mistakes, North American exporters began to rely on advertising as a means of sales promotion. With the growing popularity of radio in Latin America in the late 1920s, the Bureau

of Foreign and Domestic Commerce conducted a survey
amination of Latin American radio as a possible adverti
concluded that it had great potential for United State:

By the 1930s, American advertising had become a n
port of Latin American media. Despite the great decli...
Latin American trade due to the Depression, a survey undertaken
United States consulate officials in Brazil in the mid-1930s revealed that
approximately 64 percent of all advertising space over a 30-day period, in
21 of the country's most prominent daily newspapers and 10 of the leading
weekly magazines, was devoted to products imported from the United
States. Moreover, it is evident that North American exporters heeded well
the Bureau's advice about radio advertising. It was estimated that, in
1935, United States sponsors provided one-third of Argentina's total commercial radio revenue.[14] There was thus a growing mutual dependency in
which United States exporters depended on Latin American print and
broadcasting media to advertising and sell their products. Latin American
publishers and broadcasters in turn depended on American advertising
dollars. It was a relationship that would have serious consequences for the
Latin American media during World War II.

The Depression and the Initial Formulation of the Good Neighbor Policy

Although the United States expansion and consolidation of its economic
and political hegemony over Latin America in the 1920s occurred in the
context of regional prosperity and relative political stability and amica-
bility in diplomatic affairs, American power was built on very insecure
foundations. In the area of trade and investment, the United States government and private businesses during the 1920s pursued policies which
crudely exploited Latin American resources. At the same time United
States companies, under the active encouragement of the Department of
Commerce, were energetically developing export markets for American
goods, the Republican administrations of the 1920s were actively seeking
to close United States markets to any goods or products which might compete with domestic producers. Tariff legislation in 1921 and 1922 raised
tariffs to their highest level in 11 years. The impact of such restrictions was
not heavily felt at first, as during the 1920s world demand for Latin American goods remained strong and Latin America enjoyed a positive trade
balance with the United States. Yet, to Latin American countries whose
economies depended on the export of one or two primary products, the
lack of free access to the United States market was a potentially serious
issue. During this decade, United States trade policies were governed by
narrow concepts of national self-interest.

United States investment activity in the region was likewise based on quick short-term gain and narrow self-interest. Latin American investments were extremely attractive to North American investors during the 1920s, as reflected by a more than doubling of United States investment in the region between 1919 and 1929. In South America, the area of greatest new United States investment, the increase was almost 300 percent. Much of this new investment was in government and private bonds, which were offered on United States bond markets with high rates of return. Yet, in spite of this large growth of investment, a process of decapitalization was actually occurring, due to the high rates of investment returns and profits. According to one estimate, during the second half of the 1920s, new investments by the United States in Latin America totaled approximately $200 million.[15] However, investment return flowing out of Latin America in the form of interest payments and profit to United States investors totaled $300 million. Moreover, as much of the new United States capital was in nonproductive investments, such as government bonds, or in export-oriented production, such as mining, they did little to stimulate the growth and development of a local national economy. Both the products and profits of foreign investments normally left the region and contributed little to overall beneficial and balanced economic development.

In the area of politics, United States policy was confused due to this country's unwillingness to renounce its self-proclaimed right of military and political intervention, while at the same time recognizing that such intervention was generally costly and ineffective. While pre-war administrations could ostensibly justify intervention on the basis of the threat of European military and political incursions in the hemisphere, after the war, with the worldwide decline of European power, such threats became less compelling and the justification of the right of intervention less convincing. By 1928, even such a figure as Thomas P. Lamont, a senior partner in the J.P. Morgan Company, the banking house responsible for selling almost a quarter billion dollars of Latin American bonds to the American public during the 1920s, could observe that "The theory of collecting debts by gun boats is unrighteous, unworkable, and obsolete."[16] The United States sought other, less offensive ways to exercise its political power. One example of such a strategy was the 1923 treaty signed with Central American Republics, by which they all agreed not to recognize a government gaining power through violence. This treaty was meant to encourage political change through orderly processes but, in fact, set up a mutual protection association of dictators then in power.

Overall, the United States was unwilling to abandon its option to intervene, even though events in the 1920s were proving intervention to be increasingly expensive and unsuccessful. In addition to maintaining troops in Haiti, the United States intervened to put down a revolt in Nicaragua in

1927. During the next four years, the Marines, whose number at times exceeded 5,000, engaged in guerrilla warfare with the followers of the popular rebel leader, Augusto Sandino. During the sixth Pan American Conference in 1928, the United States was denounced for its activities in Nicaragua and Haiti and for its refusal to renounce its policy of intervention.

Aside from the problems of United States trade, investment, and political policy in Latin America, the potential for a far more serious and basic challenge to United States hegemony over Latin America was slowly developing as a result of the internal social changes occurring within Latin American societies. The expansion of the capitalist mode of production in agriculture disrupted traditional rural societies and reduced many peasants to the status of landless laborers. Also, early forms of industrialization created the nucleus of an urban working class. As a result, throughout the first third of this century the dominance of Latin American social and political life by the traditional landed, export-oriented oligarchies was beginning to be challenged by the emergence of mass-based political movements demanding a greater share in the wealth and political life of the nation. The specific causes, characteristics, and pace of development of these new emerging groups, and the response of the ruling elites varied greatly from country to country. Overall, the export-based, traditional societies of Latin America were undergoing fundamental social change.

These changes manifested themselves earliest and most spectacularly in Mexico, where the 1910 revolution succeeded in mobilizing the peasant population and destroying much of the structure of the old social order. Less spectacular, but just as much a harbinger of change, were developments in countries such as Chile and Argentina that saw the emergence of national labor movements and the election with labor support of presidents who promised social reforms and a greater voice for these new groups in the nation's political life. Similarly, Uruguay, before World War I, began the construction of a modern social welfare state based on the model of Switzerland. Even in a more traditional society like Peru, the government found it necessary to institute a program of governmental paternalism to mollify the increasingly politically active peasant and working class groups. Of course, one should not overestimate the political self-awareness or organization of these new groups and the nature and meaningfulness of the early reforms. Nor should one underestimate the complexity of the social and political dynamics involved. Often the social and political demands of the groups were formulated and controlled by members of the small and weak urban middle class, who then tended to use the popular strength of these mass groups to reach their own accommodations with the traditional oligarchies. Throughout Latin America during the 1920s, there were numerous reforms and social legislation and programs, a good portion of which were financed with loans from North American banks. The general aim of such efforts was the control of the political development of these young mass-based movements and the containment of whatever political threat they posed to the established order. Given the rudimentary nature of these emerging groups and the ability of the various governments, due to the prosperity of the 1920s, to satisfy their initial demands, these groups did not, as yet, represent a serious threat to the structure of power in these societies.

For the United States, a potentially disruptive element in these new movements was the sense of economic nationalism they began to develop and espouse. Contrary to the traditional political nationalism of the landed ruling oligarchies, these groups began to merge their demands for social change and political power with demands for greater control over the nation's resources and economic life. Thus the 1917 Mexican constitution vested all subsoil rights to the Mexican people, a move which directly threatened British and American oil companies in Mexico. In Chile, legislation was passed which reserved certain lines of business, such as insurance, for nationals, and reserved to the state the ownership of all oil deposits. An extreme example of an early form of popular Latin American nationalism was the Alianza Popular Revolucionaria Americana (APRA), founded in 1924 in Peru. This movement envisioned a self-sufficient society that, rejecting the materialist capitalist world, would be based on the communal values of pre-Colombian Peruvian society. During the 1920s, the economic nationalism of these new popular movements was only crudely articulated with vague goals. It, nonetheless, indicated a growing critical awareness on the part of the masses of the extent to which Latin American economic and social life was governed by external forces and factors over which the Latin American nations as a whole had little control.

The depression and the subsequent disruption of world trade threw the Latin American nations into economic turmoil. With prosperity fast fading, the problems and contraditions inherent in United States–Latin American relations were clearly revealed. Trade between the United States and Latin America declined drastically. Between 1929 and 1932, the total value of United States trade with Latin America dropped 73 percent, from $2,080 million to $574 million. The flow of United States capital likewise dried up, and total United States investment in the region declined 19 percent between 1929 and 1936. With world demand for their products falling, Latin American countries were unable to earn the foreign exchange necessary to buy needed imports. Moreover, they were also unable to service the vast loans floated during the 1920s. Between 1921 and 1931, bonds with a face value of $1,935 million were floated by Latin American governments on the United States bond market. At the beginning of 1935, approximately $1,189 million of these bonds were in default.[17]

With their export-based economies disrupted, many Latin American countries entered a period of political and social crisis. In the 2 years following the crash of the stock market in New York, 1930 and 1931, six Latin American countries, Argentina, Brazil, Bolivia, Chile, the Dominican Republic, and Panama, experienced military take-overs or extra-constitutional changes in government. In general, among Latin American nations, there was a movement away from the nineteenth century liberal parliamentary model of government and toward stronger forms of authoritarian control. Moreover, the depression brought into clear light the extent to which Latin American economies were heavily dependent on foreign markets and foreign sources of capital, an awareness that stirred a nationalist resentment.

Many of the changes in government were in response to, some on behalf of, the increasingly militant labor movements that were joined by sectors of the middle class, both demanding reforms and national economic policies designed to lessen the control of foreign interests and factors over the national economy. Thus, in Brazil, labor laws were demanded to improve the condition of workers and increase the portion of wealth, through increased wages, produced by foreign-owned firms which would stay in the country. In addition to such laws, tariffs and other import controls were demanded to keep out imports and thus provide incentives for national production. In Colombia, the government passed laws imposing control and restrictions on foreign businesses, and recognized the right of labor to strike. Even in Chile, where the disruption caused by the depression brought to power a conservative government committed to maintaining the existing power structure, it was felt necessary to place some controls on foreign business. In general, by seriously disrupting the export economies upon which the traditional Latin American power structure was based, the depression accelerated the development of mass-based popular movements that were becoming more militantly nationalist and demanding greater participation and control over national life. Moreover, in those countries where the traditional elites were able to maintain power, governments began to find it necessary to depart from traditional laissez faire economic policies. They began to exercise greater control over the direction and development of the economy, and to espouse notions of economic nationalism.

Similar to its response on the domestic level, the response of the Hoover Administration to the changes wrought by the depression in inter-American relations was confused and contradictory. On the one hand, Hoover's Secretary of State, Henry L. Stimson, attempted to deal with the more visible causes of Latin American complaints by committing the United States to a policy of removing the United States occupation troops in Haiti and Nicaragua, and replacing them with local national military forces that had been trained by the United States. The administration also dropped the policy instituted during the Wilson era of recognizing only constitutionally empowered governments, a policy condemned by Latin American governments as a form of indirect intervention. The United States returned to the more traditional policy of recognizing governments based on effective control over their territory. Moreover, the administration tried to put some distance between itself and the economic involvement of its citizens by warning United States citizens and investors in Latin America that they should not expect automatic United States protection if their safety or property were endangered.[18]

Yet, despite all these measures designed to impress Latin Americans of the good intentions of the United States, the Hoover Administration failed to pass the litmus test by its unwillingness to renounce its right of intervention. Moreover, whatever good the administration hoped to accomplish in the political realm was negated by United States actions in the economic realm. The 1930 Smoot-Hawley Tariff, the result of intensive log-rolling in Congress, raised tariff rates to their highest point in history. Most of the major Latin American products were placed on the higher tariff lists, thus effectively closing off United States markets to many Latin American products. Many Latin American governments retaliated by putting up their own tariff barriers against United States products.

The coming to power of Franklin D. Roosevelt in 1933 marked a significant shift in United States hemispheric relations and the development of a whole new approach toward Latin America. Although, in the election, discussion of foreign policy was overwhelmed by the problem of the depression, it became apparent that, once in office, the new administration, just as it was willing to experiment in order to deal with the domestic problems of the depression, was also willing to try new departures in order to regain the ground lost in Latin America due to the disruption of world trade and unpopular policies of the past administrations. The new Latin American policy—termed the "Good Neighbor Policy" after Roosevelt's vague inaugural pledge to follow the "policy of the good neighbor" in foreign affairs—was aimed at removing the cause of many of the Latin American complaints about the United States and reopening the channels of trade between the two continents.

The specific elements of the new policy were revealed by Roosevelt's Secretary of State, Cordell Hull, at the seventh Pan American Conference in Montevideo in December 1933. To the amazement and gratification of the representatives of the other American states, Hull agreed to sign a proposed convention that prohibited the intervention by one state into the affairs of another. A few days later in Washington, Roosevelt emphasized the change in policy by stating in a speech that "the definite policy of the United States from now on is one opposed to armed intervention."[19] Moreover, the administration, to demonstrate its good intentions, moved up the date for the withdrawal of American troops from Haiti and Nicaragua. Thus, with little fanfare, the unilateral right of the United States to intervene in the affairs of other American nations—a principle that was the major point of contention in inter-American affairs—was renounced.

Along with the renunciation of intervention, Hull reversed another long-standing United States policy by proposing, at the Conference in Montevideo, the mutual reduction of tariffs through negotiations of liberal reciprocity agreements based on mutual trade concessions. This proposal, aimed at undoing the harm of the tariff barriers erected by past Republican administrations, was warmly received by other American nations, although the actual implementation of the proposal through the negotiation and signing of actual trade agreements would take a number of years.

These two principles—nonintervention and trade reciprocity—formed the basis of the Latin American policy during the first term of the Roosevelt Administration. This initial formulation of the Good Neighbor Policy was primarily negative in nature, representing a pledge not to intervene or to engage in economic warfare. As noted by Laurence Duggan, one of the administration's Latin American policy makers during the Roosevelt era, the years 1933–1936 were devoted primarily to "clearing away deadwood" accumulated from past administrations.[20]

The policy of trade reciprocity seemed a natural policy for the new Democratic Administration. As both Roosevelt and Hull were grounded in the Democratic Party's long tradition of free trade, they had no philosophical or political commitments to high tariffs. Yet, more in line with the New Deal experimentation, the opening of foreign markets through reciprocal trade agreements was regarded by the new administration as one possible method among a number of different methods that formed part of the overall efforts of the New Deal to stimulate domestic production, get rid of the agricultural surplus, raise prices, and lead the country toward economic recovery. However, the overall policy of reciprocal trade failed both to increase inter-American trade or stimulate domestic production. By the end of the 1930s, there was little evidence that trade with those Latin American countries which had signed reciprocal trade agreements had increased any more than trade with those nations with whom no agreement existed.

Yet the reciprocal trade policy had a significance far greater than being just another New Deal measure that did not work. The policy was noteworthy in that it was the first expression of a modern economic internationalism, or an awareness that the United States economy was intimately tied to the international economy and that prosperity at home would depend on a "constructive interaction" between the economies of the United States and other countries. No longer did the flag simply follow the dollar, or were tariffs simply thrown up to protect some domestic producers, or foreign markets regarded primarily as outlets for surplus goods unable to be sold domestically. Rather, international markets were beginning to be seen as an integral element in the American economy. Moreover, just as the depression had shown that the stability of both the domestic and international economy could not be entrusted to undirected market forces, some degree of international economic planning was necessary, which required the government to become more involved in international economic matters by defining, formulating, and pursuing both short and long term objectives regarding the United States' position and activity in the world market. Until the depression, tariff levels were primarily an expression of domestic politics, while with the New Deal they became elements in international economic diplomacy. The Trade Agreements Act of 1934, the legislative implementation of the reciprocal trade program, gave the President the power to use tariffs as a tool in international economic planning by allowing him to alter existing tariff levels by as much as 50 percent. The reciprocal trade agreements with Latin America were the beginning of an increasingly sophisticated understanding of the interrelationships between the domestic economy and international political and economic policies. As the government developed and pursued new international policies based on this understanding, it would often come into conflict with specific individual business interests. Yet such conflicts did not overshadow the fact that the end goal was to provide for domestic prosperity by insuring the United States access to ample raw materials, and that there existed a stable and secure international environment for the orderly expansion of United States economic power and activity. Although the reciprocal trade agreements were not a notable success in the 1930s, by the end of the decade they were supplemented with more creative measures of international economic planning such as the organization of the Export-Import Bank.

The pledge of nonintervention was that aspect of the Good Neighbor Policy that received the most attention. Some commentators saw the pledge of nonintervention as proof that the imperialistic policies of the United States were an aberration which was corrected by the enlightened leadership of Roosevelt. Yet it is questionable how radical a departure the pledge of nonintervention really was. As recognized by every Secretary of State since Hughes, military intervention was costly, ineffective, and counterproductive. The Good Neighbor Policy was based, in part, on a realization that military intervention actually hindered the effective employment of American military and economic power.[21] Moreover, given the domestic crisis which the United States faced in the early 1930s, it was questionable whether the nation could expend the energy, effort, and resources in actively asserting itself militarily throughout the hemisphere. Given the major symbolic significance that the issue of intervention had assumed in Latin American public opinion, there was little to lose and much to gain in renouncing a policy which was generally recognized to be ineffective and unenforceable.

Yet, if the United States foreswore force, what other means of control could it exercise? Fortunately, the Latin American situation was such that, during the first years of the Roosevelt Administration, with one exception, there was little serious challenge to the United States position in the hemisphere. As United States business activity was stagnant, the types of situations that prompted United States involvement in the past did not occur. In these first few years, the challenge of mass-based nationalist movements, or the challenge of foreign intrusion, both of which were to occupy administration policy makers after 1936, had yet to appear or make a significant impact.

The one exception to this was the events in Cuba in 1933–1934. They were noteworthy as an early test of the administration's resolve not to use force. The administration was not entirely successful in handling the Cuban crisis, as it was criticized for unilaterally intervening, although in an indirect manner. However, due to the Platt Amendment, the clause in the Cuban constitution that gave the United States the right to intervene in Cuban affairs, United States intervention in Cuba was generally regarded by other Latin American countries as being less offensive. More important though, the United States learned some very significant lessons from the Cuban experience in the more sophisticated methods of exercising its political will in Latin America, methods which became more refined as more experience was gained.

Having contributed to the fall of the increasingly unpopular and ineffective Cuban dictator, Gerardo Machado, in August 1933, the United States ambassador to Cuba, Sumner Welles, especially appointed by Roosevelt to end the political unrest on the island, was irked to see the new United States supported president replaced after only 1 month, first by a military junta and then by Dr. Ramón Grau San Martín. The new president, a nationalist intellectual, had the support of militant labor, student, and peasant groups, and made moves to initiate labor and land reforms and enact measures to control foreign firms in Cuba. Welles urged Roosevelt to withhold recognition of the Cuban regime and intervene with armed forces to overthrow Grau San Martín. The call for armed intervention was also taken up by United States business interests fearful of attacks on their property. The administration, taking a somewhat wider view of the situation, tried to avoid being stampeded into action. As Hull advised threatened businessmen in Cuba, "I am telling people who have property there to let it be injured while the Cubans are establishing a government themselves. Because should the Cubans themselves establish a government, the outbreaks will gradually cease, business will return to normalcy, and the Americans will recover their losses."[22]

Yet the United States was intensely interested in the type of government that the Cubans would establish for themselves, and was not willing to let events follow their own course. While not directly intervening, the United States sent warships to Cuba with instructions to appear off the Cuban Coast and to protect American life in case of imminent danger. Moreover, the United States took the position that the new government lacked popular support. Welles, for example, argued that Grau San Martín's supporters consisted chiefly of "a small group of young men who should be studying in the university instead of playing politics and . . . a few individuals who joined them from selfish motives."[23] The United States held that the Cuban government was unable to maintain its rule over the island, citing among other things the fact that groups of Cuban laborers had seized sugar mills and attempted to set up workers' soviets. On this basis, the United States refused to recognize the new regime. Meanwhile Ambassador Welles was encouraging Cuban military leaders, many of whom—such as Colonel Fulgencio Batista—initially supported the regime, to overthrow Grau San Martín. They followed his advice and replaced the President with one more to the liking of the United States in early 1934. The United States quickly withdrew the warships and recognized the new government, which then proceeded to disband the labor unions and repress all opposition. The United States moved to stabilize the regime politically and economically. To give the new government a nationalist aura, it allowed Cuba to repeal the Platt Amendment to the Cuban constitution, while allowing the United States to maintain its naval base on the island. To help the regime economically, the United States reduced the tariff on Cuban sugar and increased the amount which could be exported into the United States under the quota system. The end result of the Cuban experience was that an impending social revolution in Cuba was suppressed, United States business interests were protected, and the United States maintained control, all without incurring the liability of armed intervention. The United States successes in Cuba demonstrated the benefits of a more sophisticated understanding of political change and a more sophisticated manner of exercising North American political will in the region. Sumner Welles moved on to become one of the principal architects of United States–Latin American policy during the Roosevelt Administration.

Overall, the Good Neighbor Policy represented a new approach in Latin American policy aimed at dealing with the problems that the social and political changes in Latin America created for American dominance. Much in the same way that the New Deal was proclaimed in its day by both friend and foe as marking a radical, if not revolutionary, departure from the political and economic basis of American capitalism, Roosevelt's Good Neighbor Policy was hailed in its time as a radical reversal of United States policy in Latin America. With the Good Neighbor Policy, imperialism was seen as finally and absolutely liquidated. Substituted in its stead were policies based on respect and cooperation with all the nations of the hemisphere.

However, just as with the New Deal, with time, the discontinuities in Roosevelt's policies gradually begin to lose their significance, and their continuities with past policies, practices, and goals, both at the international and domestic levels, become more compelling. Roosevelt's achievements lie not with dismantling capitalism or liquidating imperialism, but with creatively transforming them in order that they be able to successfully confront modern challenges.

Notes

[1] J. Lloyd Mecham, *A Survey of United States-Latin American Relations* (Boston: Houghton Mifflin, 1965), p. 93; Federico G. Gil, *Latin American-United States Relations* (New York: Harcourt Brace Jovanovich, 1971), pp. 150–151.

[2] United Nations, Economic Commission for Latin America, *External Financing in Latin America* (New York: United Nations, 1965), p. 14–15; J. Fred Rippy, *Globe and Hemisphere* (Chicago: Henry Regnery, 1958), pp. 30–36; U.S. Department of Commerce, Bureau of Foreign and Domestic Commerce, *Statistical Abstract of the United States 1936* (Washington, D.C.: Government Printing Office, 1936), pp. 446–447; Donald W. Baerresen, Martin Carnoy, and Joseph Grunwald, *Latin American Trade Patterns* (Washington, D.C.: The Brookings Institution, 1965), p. 20.

[3] Joseph S. Tulchin, *The Aftermath of War—World War I and U.S. Policy Toward Latin America* (New York: New York University Press, 1971), pp. 116–117.

[4] Ibid., pp. 155–205; Leslie Bennett Tribolet, *The International Aspects of Electrical Communication in the Pacific Area* (Baltimore: Johns Hopkins Press, 1929), pp. 41–57; F.J. Brown, *The Cable and Wireless Communications of the World* (London: Sir Isaac Pitman and Sons, 1927), pp. 17–22. An excellent and detailed account of United States cable policy and practice up to the mid 1920s is found in George Abel Schreiner, *Cable and Wireless and Their Role in the Foreign Relations of the United States* (Boston: Stratford, 1924).

[5] U.S. Department of State, *Papers Relating to the Foreign Relations of the United States 1915* (Washington, D.C.: Government Printing Office, 1924), pp. 24–25; ibid., *Papers Relating to the Foreign Relations of the United States 1916* (Washington, D.C.: Government Printing Office 1929), pp. 5–10, 976–977.

[6] Unsigned State Department Memorandum, June 16, 1919. Latin American Radio file, Box 2731, *BFDC*.

[7] Gleason L. Archer, *History of Radio to 1926* (New York: The American Historical Society, Inc., 1938; reprint edition with addendum, New York: Arnor Press,

1971), pp. 227, 233–239, addendum, pp. 1, 2–4; Radio Corporation of America, *Annual Report 1920*; E.E. Bucher, "Radio and David Sarnoff," David Sarnoff Library, Princeton, New Jersey, Vol. II, pp. 339–340; Tribolet, *The International Aspects*, pp. 57–69.

8 International Telephone and Telegraph Corporation, *Annual Report 1930*; U.S. Congress, Senate, Interstate Commerce Committee, *Study of International Communications, Hearings before a Subcommittee of the Committee on Interstate Commerce*, 78th Congress, 1st session, 1945, Part 2, pp. 248–249; J. Fred Rippy, *Latin America and the Industrial Age* (New York: G.P. Putnam and Sons, 1947), pp. 177–187. Most of the Latin American telephone companies acquired by ITT were originally established in the 1880s and 1890s by North American and British telephone interests. See J. Fred Rippy, "Notes on the Early Telephone Companies of Latin America," *Hispanic American Historical Review* 26:1, 1946, pp. 116–118.

9 Kent Cooper, *Barriers Down* (New York: Farrar and Rinehart, 1942), pp. 1–80; Joe Alex Morris, *Deadline Every Minute* (Garden City: Doubleday, 1957), pp. 102–111. Emily S. Rosenberg, *Spreading the American Dream* (New York: Hill and Wang, 1982), pp. 97–99; Mary A. Gardner, *The Inter-American Press Association: Its Fight for Freedom of the Press, 1926–1960* (Austin: University of Texas Press, 1967), pp. 3–5.

10 "Foreign Markets," *Moving Picture World*, 7 January 1922; Gaizka de Usabel, "American Films in Latin America: The Case History of the United Artists Corporation, 1919–1951" (Ph.D. dissertation, University of Wisconsin, 1975), pp. 1–7.

11 U.S., Department of Commerce, Bureau of Foreign and Domestic Commerce, *Advertising Methods in Cuba*, by J.W. Sanger, Special Agent Series No. 178 (Washington, D.C.: Government Printing Office, 1919); U.S. Department of Commerce, Bureau of Foreign and Domestic Commerce, *Advertising Methods in Chile, Peru, and Bolivia*, by J.W. Sanger, Special Agent Series No. 185 (Washington, D.C.: Government Printing Office, 1919); U.S., Department of Commerce, *Advertising Methods in Argentina, Uruguay, and Brazil*, by J.W. Sanger, Special Agent Series No. 190 (Washington, D.C.: Government Printing Office, 1920).

12 *Advertising Methods in Argentina, Uruguay and Brazil*, pp. 34–35.

13 U.S., Department of Commerce, Bureau of Foreign and Domestic Commerce, *Broadcast Advertising in Latin America*, Trade Information Bulletin No. 771 (Washington, D.C.: Government Printing Office, 1931).

14 U.S., Department of Commerce, Bureau of Foreign and Domestic Commerce, *Advertising in Brazil*, Trade Information Bulletin No. 838 (Washington, D.C.: Government Printing Office, 1943), p. 10; "Advertising: American Sales Plug into Other Nations' Air," *Newsweek*, 14 March 1936, p. 44.

15 United Nations, *External Financing in Latin America*, p. 14; United Nations, Department of Economic and Social Affairs, *Foreign Capital in Latin America* (New York: United Nations, 1955), p. 15.

16 Quoted in Lloyd C. Gardner, *Economic Aspects of New Deal Diplomacy* (Madison: University of Wisconsin Press, 1964), p. 51; Rippy, *Globe and Hemisphere*, p. 56.

[17] *Statistical Abstract 1936*, pp. 446–447; United Nations, *External Financing in Latin America*, p. 32. Samuel Flagg Bemis, *The Latin American Policy of the United States* (New York: Harcourt, Brace and Company, 1943), pp. 333–336.

[18] Edward O. Guerrant, *Roosevelt's Good Neighbor Policy* (Alburquerque: University of New Mexico Press, 1950), p. 105.

[19] James W. Gantenbein, editor and complier, *The Evolution of Our Latin American Policy* (New York: Octagon Books, 1971), p. 165.

[20] Laurence Duggan, *The Americas: The Search for Hemisphere Security* (New York: Henry Holt and Company, 1949), p. 70.

[21] Edwin Lieuwen, *U.S. Policy in Latin America—A Short History* (New York: Frederick A. Praeger, 1965), pp. 61–82; Gardner, *Economic Aspects of New Deal Diplomacy*, p. 47.

[22] Quoted in Bryce Wood, *The Making of the Good Neighbor Policy* (New York: Columbia University Press, 1961), p. 76.

[23] Quoted in David Green, *The Containment of Latin America* (Chicago: Quadrangle Books, 1971), p. 15.

CHAPTER 3

THE MEDIUM: THE DEVELOPMENT OF NORTH AMERICAN SHORTWAVE BROADCASTING UP TO 1936

Paralleling the rise to dominance of the United States in Latin America was the invention and development of radio communication. Indeed, these two developments are so interrelated that one could perhaps argue that, just as Britain's global dominance in the nineteenth century was based on naval power and cable communications, United States dominance in the twentieth century was based on air power and radio communication. As noted in the previous chapter, the United States went to great lengths to insure that hemispheric radio communications remained under its control.

In the 1920s there occurred, roughly simultaneously, two important developments in radio communication. The first was the discovery of the immense usefulness of the upper portion of the radio spectrum—the shortwaves—for long distance radio communication. The second was the development of radio broadcasting as a new and mass-based form of radio communication. In Britain these two developments were pursued separately, and shortwave communication technology was immediately incorporated into the plans of the British Marconi Company to build a worldwide point-to-point radio communication network, linking the far-flung British Empire with London. In the United States, however, these two developments were closely intertwined, and many of the early applications of shortwave communication were in the field of broadcasting. Throughout the 1920s, the United States pioneered and dominated the field of international shortwave broadcasting, primitive as it was at that time.

Much of the interest and activity in shortwave broadcasting during the 1920s was motivated by the desire to develop a system of program exchanges among the broadcasting systems of various countries. However, alternative technologies were developed which made such program exchange methods obsolete. No longer necessary to the United States domestic broadcasting system, and lacking an immediate or even potential commercial application, American shortwave broadcasting by the mid 1930s became a technology without a purpose.

Early Development of Shortwave Radio Communication

Although many of the earliest attempts in the transmission and detection of radio waves before the turn of the century were conducted in the upper portion of the radio spectrum, experimenters concerned with developing radio as a means of long distance communication found that higher frequencies tended to fade as distance increased. Thus, while Marconi's initial experiments were in the range of 300,000–150,000 kHz (1–2 meters), he quickly found that such shortwaves were unable to go beyond a few hundred yards. Further experiments supported the notion that longer waves, or lower frequencies, achieved greater distances and that shortwaves were useless for all but the shortest distances. In theoretical terms, it was argued that, the higher the radio frequency, the greater the absorption by the atmosphere. Continued experiments and growing experience in radio communication seemed to prove this to be the case.

It was this understanding of the nature of radio waves and the radio spectrum that dominated the development of radio communications until the early 1920s. Much of the effort in radio research during this period went into developing more effective transmitters and receivers. Very little attention was given to an exploration of the radio spectrum itself, as it was generally thought that its important characteristics had been determined. Thus, the initial effort after World War I to develop reliable and commercially profitable international radio communication by the British Marconi Company and RCA was based on longwave technology.

Yet, the basic technical strategy of longwave long distance communication—lower frequencies coupled with higher power equaled greater distances—created insurmountable limitations to the expansion of long distance radio communication. Long distance stations equipped with huge and costly Alexanderson alternators were connected to extensive aerial antenna systems often measuring 10 miles in length. These stations "pushed a signal through by brute force."[1] The problem of interference was immense. The transoceanic stations built after World War I attempted to avoid interference by going to increasingly longer wavelengths, with some stations operating as low as 13.7kHz (21,820 meters). As the low end of the usuable radio spectrum is 10 kHz, the expansion of longwave radio communication was severely restricted by the limited numbers of available channels.

In the early 1920s, however, successful attempts by American and European radio amateurs in using shortwave frequencies to transmit transatlantic radio messages suggested that radio researchers and experimenters had vastly underestimated the potential of the upper portion of the radio spectrum for long distance communication. The success of the amateurs was an ironic comment on the level of knowledge of the radio spectrum at the time. As amateur interference in commercial and military radio communication was one of the earliest problems in radio communication, most countries passed legislation that regulated amateur radio activity. A common feature of most legislation was the restriction of amateur radio use to frequencies generally above 1,500 kHz (200 meters). These higher frequencies were considered to be useless for commercial or military communication. After the war, radio amateurs, many of them having received radio training during wartime military service and being equipped with high quality military surplus radio equipment, began exploring the possibilities of high frequency radio communication. In February 1921, a small group of American amateurs attempted to transmit prearranged high frequency signals across the Atlantic to British amateurs. The effort failed due to interference and the poor quality of British receiving equipment. In December of that year, the major American amateur organization, the American Radio Relay League, organized another attempt at high frequency transatlantic transmission. This attempt was a success, and British amateurs were able to pick up American signals quite clearly. In December 1922, another organized transatlantic test resulted in 316 American amateur stations being heard in Europe. It was equally important that, for the first time, European amateur signals were heard in the United States. In November 1923, two way communication was achieved between a group of French and American amateurs. Through such transmissions it was quickly discovered that the higher the frequency—or the shorter the wavelength—the greater the distance achieved. By the winter of 1923, two way radio communication was being established by radio amateurs all over the globe, utilizing frequencies as high as 60,000 kHz (5 meters).[2]

The success of the amateurs astounded the radio world. There was no scientific theory that could explain such an accomplishment. Indeed, accepted understandings of the radio spectrum indicated that such distances were impossible. Amateurs, however, were discovering and exploring the reflection characteristics of the inosphere. Until the amateur tests, scientists did not know the effect of the ionosphere on radio communication; many even doubted its existence. Until then, all long distance radio communication was based on ground waves which traveled along the surface of the earth. Because of the specific characteristics of the lower frequencies, the distance of the ground wave transmission increased as power increased and frequency decreased. This resulted in the trend toward more powerful and lower frequency stations.

Shortwave radio communication is based on an entirely different principle of radio wave propagation. Shortwave transmission depends on skywaves, or those radio waves which do not follow the surface of the earth, but are directed upward. The groundwave of a shortwave signal travels only a very small distance, often only a few miles—a phenomenon that led early radio engineers to dismiss the long distance capability of shortwaves. The skywave of the shortwave signal, however, is transmitted upward, bounces off the ionosphere, travels back to earth, bounces back toward the ionosphere again and finally returns to earth. This type of skywave propagation pattern allows shortwave signals of very low power to travel immense distances and to be received thousands of miles away while receivers within 10 miles of the transmitter may not pick up anything at all. Later developments in directional beam antennas allowed the shortwave signal to be channeled in one direction, much as one could focus a light beam, thus increasing signal strength and decreasing interference. Previous attempts by radio engineers and scientists to use shortwaves no doubt resulted in long distance transmission. However, as the characteristics of the ionosphere were not understood, nobody bothered to look for these signals thousands of miles away. Early reports by radio operators of picking up long distance radio signals on frequencies above 1,000 kHz (or below 300 meters) were dismissed or attributed to freak occurrences.[3]

Development of Shortwave Communication by Marconi

With the success of amateur shortwave transmission, attention was focused on the radio spectrum and the potential for a vastly expanded number of radio channels which the shortwaves promised. Although the American amateurs discovered the usefulness of shortwave transmission and began to explore it in a rudimentary way, it was Marconi who realized the commercial possibilities of shortwave transmission and who began to explore its use as an alternative to the costly high powered, low frequency, long distance radio communication then in use.

Starting in the spring of 1923, Marconi began a series of tests designed to explore the range, reliability, and other transmission characteristics of shortwave communication. Overall, the tests left little doubt that shortwaves could become the basis of worldwide commercial long distance radio communication. There was an added impetus to Marconi's development of shortwaves. At the time, the British Marconi Company was competing with the British Post Office for a contract to build, own, and operate an imperial radio network designed to link the British colonies and possessions with London. The Post Office was committed to an expensive longwave high power system, although its past record in operating longwave government stations was not impressive. The major advantage held by the Post Office was that it would guarantee government ownership and control of the imperial radio network. Marconi initially proposed a long-wave system of imperial communication based on the latest improvements in longwave technology and privately owned and operated by the Marconi Company. However, the success of the shortwave tests completely altered the picture. If the Marconi Company built the costly longwave system, it would be obsolete after the introduction of shortwave and the Company would lose its investment in its already built longwave stations. Yet, to propose a system based on shortwave would be risky. While the practicality of a shortwave system was proven to the satisfaction of the Marconi Company, the engineering and planning aspects were far from complete. If the Marconi Company asked for a delay in order to completely explore the characteristics of shortwave transmission and to perfect a system, the clamor on the part of the colonial governments, impatient with waiting for a radio link with London, would no doubt give the advantage to the Post Office.

Based on these considerations, the Marconi Company took a gamble, and in the spring of 1924, proposed to the government a plan for an imperial radio network based on shortwave technology. Given the government's skepticism over the new shortwave technology, and its disinclination to have the entire system controlled by private interests, a contract was negotiated and signed in July 1924 between the government and the Marconi Company designed to meet the government's doubts and fears. While the Marconi Company would build, own, and operate the shortwave stations in the colonies, the British shortwave stations would be built by the Company and turned over to the ownership and control of the Post Office, the Company receiving a patent royalty based on the traffic revenue of the British stations. The Marconi Company would be free to develop shortwave services from any part of the Empire, including Britain, to any place outside the Empire, thus giving it control of the profitable European and transatlantic traffic. Suspicious of the reliability of shortwaves, the British government made stringent contractual requirements for both the schedule of construction and the level of technical performance of the British stations. Moreover, the Marconi Company was not to realize any profit from the construction of the British stations, the individual maximum cost of which was limited to £35,120 (compared to the £500,000 cost of the longwave station the Post Office was building at Rugby). Any profit on the British stations would come solely from the patent royalties on future traffic revenues.

Given the then-current popular understanding of shortwaves as a very unreliable and limited communication medium, many politicians and financiers saw the contract for the British imperial radio stations as "a colossal joke on the autocratic Marconi Company."[4] Staking its fortunes on shortwave, and faced with a challenge that would end in either control of a world radio system or its own ruin, the Marconi Company concentrated all its energies and resources in developing the shortwave system. Both the development of the engineering design and the actual construction of the stations proceeded apace, often being only a matter of a few days from the perfection of an engineering detail to its incorporation into station construction. Confounding earlier predictions of failure and financial ruin, the Marconi Company was able to meet all its deadlines and, on October 18, 1926, turned over to the Post Office the first shortwave station designed to transmit and receive from the Marconi station in Canada. For a period of 1 week the Post Office conducted tests in which the station easily surpassed the technical specifications and traffic requirements of the contract. Commercial service between Canada and Britain was then opened, followed the next year by the opening of shortwave service between Britain and Australia, South Africa, and India, thus bringing to fruition the imperial network. The Marconi Company also proceeded to incorporate shortwave into its regular service with countries outside the Empire. By 1929, 10 of its 16 transmitting wavelengths, and 56 of its 94 receiving wavelengths, in London were shortwaves.[5]

The Development of Shortwave Radio in the United States

In contrast to its development in Britain, the development of shortwave in the United States did not proceed in as straightforward a manner. In Britain, shortwave technology was developed and applied primarily in response both to the political needs of the British government to maintain contact with its far flung colonial empire and to the technical and commercial exigencies of the Marconi Company as it attempted to establish predominance in British communications. In the United States, however, the forces and factors behind shortwave development were far more complex and diverse.

As the discovery and early development of shortwave in the United States occurred simultaneously with the development of broadcasting, many of the early efforts in shortwave application were made in the field of broadcasting. One of the major figures in these early efforts was Frank Conrad, the radio engineer who, with the development of the Westinghouse station, KDKA, in East Pittsburgh in late 1920, is generally credited with originating broadcasting. An enthusiastic radio amateur who kept abreast of the shortwave transatlantic tests, Conrad began experimenting with shortwave radio broadcasting in early 1922. Simulcasting regular KDKA programs over a shortwave transmitter, he was able to reach places as far away as Boston with a signal strength and clarity far surpassing the transmissions on the regular frequencies. Beginning in 1923, Conrad began transmitting regular KDKA programs to Cleveland via shortwave. There they were picked up by a Westinghouse relay station and rebroadcast over regular medium frequencies. These experiments were encouraged and supported by Westinghouse, as the company saw in shortwave radio a potential medium for interconnecting radio stations throughout the country into a national network. To further test the potential of shortwave, another relay broadcasting station was built in Hastings, Nebraska, in the fall of 1923 for the purpose of rebroadcasting KDKA programs.

A major factor behind Westinghouse's interest in shortwave was the then growing struggle between the American Telephone and Telegraph Company (ATT) and the RCA, General Electric, and Westinghouse companies for control of American broadcasting. Earlier, in order to overcome the patent conflicts among themselves that had obstructed the development and commercial exploitation of radio communication, these companies negotiated cross-licensing agreements for the radio patents held by each company. As part of this overall settlement, the companies agreed to divide the field of radio communication and the manufacture and sales of radio equipment among themselves. ATT obtained the rights over the field of telephony, and General Electric, Westinghouse, and RCA the rights over the manufacture and sales of radio equipment, along with rights to the building and operating of radio stations. However, since these agreements were made before the sudden and rapid development of radio broadcasting in 1920–1921, they contained no provisions specifying which company had control over this new field. ATT argued that broadcsting was a form of telephony over which it had sole rights. It built the New York radio station, WEAF, for the purpose of implementing its conception of broadcasting—"toll broadcasting," as it was then called—by selling time over the air to anyone who cared to buy it. ATT acknowledged the right of the radio companies to build and operate radio broadcasting stations. RCA opened station WDY in New Jersey in 1921 and later, in 1923, took over Westinghouse's New York station, WJZ. General Electric opened station WGY in Schenectady, New York in 1922. And Westinghouse operated station WBZ in Springfield, Massachusetts, along with its Pittsburgh station, KDKA. However, the telephone company argued that under the various cross-licensing agreements, such stations could not be operated for profit.

An important advantage that ATT had was its control over the long distance telephone lines. Initially, radio stations provided their own individual programming; however, it quickly became obvious that the individual programming costs could be drastically reduced while the program quality increased through the creation of radio networks. The only feasible method to connect stations at that time was interconnection via telephone lines.

Making arrangements with other locally owned radio stations, the telephone company proceeded to construct a radio network over which WEAF programming could be relayed via long distance telephone lines and then rebroadcast. The first permanent interconnection occurred in July 1923, and by the end of 1924 a special coast-to-coast network broadcast of over 20 stations was achieved. ATT would not allow any of the radio stations of RCA, General Electric, or Westinghouse to make use of the telephone lines for interconnection without its prior approval. Thus, while these companies were free to operate broadcasting stations, they could not do it on a commercial basis, nor could they hope to establish any type of national network based on the use of telephone lines.[6]

It was in the context of this conflict between the radio companies and ATT that shortwave broadcast experiments at interconnection were conducted first by Westinghouse and then later by General Electric. Shortwave radio was seen as a means of circumventing ATT's control of the long distance telephone lines and establishing interconnection among radio stations. However, while the shortwave rebroadcasting tests conducted throughout 1923–1925 were generally successful, they could not match the lack of static, reliability, or clarity of the ATT transmissions. Shortwave was a technology that was still very little understood. While ATT by the end of 1924 had developed a reliable and effective system of interconnections, the radio companies' efforts at shortwave interconnection were still very much experimental.

Also working against the development of shortwave, as a method of interconnection, was the fact that the radio companies and ATT were attempting to come to some type of settlement regarding their differences. Throughout 1925 and the first half of 1926, negotiations were being conducted. ATT's insistence on the exclusive control over commercial broadcasting activity and its control of the telephone lines used for interconnection had brought the company a great deal of negative publicity that, as a government monopoly, it could ill afford. In 1926, ATT and the radio companies signed an agreement under which ATT withdrew from the field of broadcasting and agreed to lease long distance telephone lines to the radio companies for the interconnection of radio stations. The National Broadcasting Company (NBC) was formed, owned jointly by RCA, Westinghouse, and General Electric. NBC was to take over and operate the broadcasting properties of the telephone company along with those of the radio companies. With the radio companies now given use of the telephone lines, the commercial rationale for developing shortwave as an alternative method of interconnection was no longer present. The use of telephone lines as the primary form of station interconnection was subsequently written into government radio regulations. In 1929, the Federal Radio Commission prohibited the use of shortwave transmission as a form of station interconnection, except in cases where telephone line interconnection was not available or feasible.

The Beginning of United States International
Shortwave Broadcasting

Although shortwave did not find an immediately successful domestic application, it was apparent that it had the potential for reliable international broadcasting. Early experiments in the use of shortwave for international broadcasting were undertaken in conjunction with experiments in domestic shortwave interconnection.

The possibility of international shortwave broadcasting between Great Britain and the United States was first raised and discussed in 1922 by Frank Conrad with a representative of the British radio manufacturing company, Metropolitan Vickers, who was visiting the Westinghouse radio plan to investigate Westinghouse's broadcasting activites. Although shortwaves at that time were still an untested medium, and no definite plans were made, it was decided that, if warranted by progress in shortwave development, international broadcasting tests between Westinghouse and Metropolitan Vickers would be arranged.

By the fall of 1923, Conrad's shortwave tests had reached a point where he felt it possible to test the long distance broadcasting capabilities of shortwave. Together with constructing the rebroadcasting transmitter at Hastings, Nebraska, Conrad arranged for Metropolitan Vickers to construct a shortwave receiver at the company's plant in Manchester. After numerous preliminary tests, the first shortwave transatlantic radio broadcast was arranged for the evening of December 31, 1923. The broadcast was transmitted at a frequency of 3,200 kHZ (94 meters) from KDKA to the shortwave receiver at Manchester, and then relayed by telephone lines to the Metropolitan Vickers' station and to the seven other British Broadcasting stations. The program consisted of New Year's greetings and remarks from Westinghouse officials, followed by musical selections. The same program was also successfully rebroadcast over the Westinghouse Hastings station. This success was followed by other experimental attempts during the next 2 years, with Westinghouse successfully transmitting programs for rebroadcasting to stations as far as Australia, South Africa, and Argentina.

Interest in international shortwave radio broadcasting was also evident at General Electric. In January 1924, General Electric constructed a shortwave transmitter in Schenectady which rebroadcast the programs of the company's station WGY over shortwave. These programs were heard as far as South Africa. Over the next 2 years, General Electric continued to expand its shortwave broadcasting activities by devoting more money to shortwave research and equipment and by using more frequencies. By 1926, General Electric had built five shortwave transmitters at its plant in Schenectady as part of its shortwave effort.

Although during the 1920s the programs of Westinghouse's station KDKA and General Electric's WGY dominated international broadcasting and were received and often rebroadcast by radio stations throughout the world, the major motivation behind such activity was scientific. As shortwave radio communication was a startling innovation which overturned prior conceptions' about the nature of radio communication, a great deal of research and testing had to be done in order to explore the characteristics of the shortwaves and to determine the possibilities for commercial exploitation. As the propagation patterns of the shortwaves were radically different from those of longwaves, engineers at Westinghouse and General Electric relied on the reports of the shortwave reception of KDKA and WGY programming in order to determine the characteristics of the radio waves. General Electric, for example, did extensive research on broadcasting simultaneously on different high frequencies.[7]

General Electric and Westinghouse's activity in shortwave broadcasting was primarily experimental and part of their overall plan to develop and market shortwave radio equipment. However, RCA, the other major radio company, regarded the development of shortwave radio communication and broadcasting from its position in international radio communication and national broadcasting. In spite of the success of the Westinghouse and General Electric tests, RCA was very reluctant to incorporate shortwave in its international communications business or in its later experiments in international program exchanges. Although David Sarnoff, General Manager and later President of RCA, expressed interest as early as 1920 in the possibilities of the use of the shortwave portion of the spectrum for long distance communication, Sarnoff and RCA placed their faith in longwave technology.

RCA's reluctance over shortwave was based on doubts about shortwave's value and reliability as a commercial communications medium. In 1923, RCA began experimenting with shortwave by transmitting transatlantic commercial messages simultaneously over long and shortwaves. Although engineers at RCA were able to achieve longer distances with higher frequencies, they were not able to achieve levels of reliability necessary for commercial traffic. To these doubts about the reliability of shortwave were added concerns over the potential threat shortwaves posed to RCA's vast current and planned investments in longwave technology. Communication based on longwave technology was used between the United States and the more important European nations, whose traffic volume and need for year-round, all-hour reliability warranted the investment in the huge highpowered stations. Initially RCA saw shortwave as complementing longwave transmission by serving as an inexpensive communication medium with countries whose volume of radio traffic and reliability requirements did not justify the heavy investment and use of the extremely limited longwave channels. Many of the experimental shortwave transmitters built and operated by RCA in 1924 and 1925 were for potential communications with Pacific and South American nations.

The announcement in the summer of 1924 of plans of the Marconi Company to build an imperial radio network based on shortwave raised the threat that shortwave would not merely complement longwave transmission but, indeed, make such transmission obsolete. In signing the contract with the British government, Marconi predicted that, because of superior characteristics, shortwave would put longwave stations out of business. With such statements, whatever doubts RCA officials had about the technical capabilities of shortwave were heightened by their concern over public confidence in the company. Over the next 2 years, public statements by RCA officials and technicians discounted the threat of shortwave to RCA's longwave investments. Sarnoff, returning from a trip to England at the end of the summer of 1924, where he inspected Marconi's shortwave experiments, issued a press release noting that he had seen nothing "which justified any claims that the present high powered longwave stations employed in commercial transoceanic communication will be supplanted by lower powered shortwave stations."

It was in this climate of doubt and concern over the effect shortwave would have on its commercial business and investment that RCA began its first attempts at international broadcasting. Although, prior to 1924, RCA officials tended to give little thought to international broadcasting, Conrad's 1923 New Year's Eve broadcast to Britain, and his subsequently widely publicized successes during the first half of 1924 in sending KDKA programs to stations all over the globe, gave RCA the impetus to consider the possibilities of international broadcasting. By June 1924, Sarnoff was promising the public that international radio broadcasting would be accomplished within the next year.[8]

Sarnoff and RCA's notion of international broadcasting was far different than the activities of Westinghouse and General Electric. While Conrad and the engineers at General Electric were engaged primarily in transmitting American programs abroad, Sarnoff was far more interested in bringing foreign radio programs to the American public. This was to be accomplished through a highly organized system of program exchanges arranged with foreign broadcasting organizations. Through such a system, radio programming in Europe and other parts of the world would become available to the American radio listener. A not insignificant aspect in RCA and Sarnoff's sudden interest in the possibilities of international broadcasting was the struggle between ATT and the radio companies for control of

American broadcasting. If RCA was able to develop a successful system of international program exchanges, this would give the radio companies a great advantage in establishing a dominant position in American broadcasting, as ATT was barred under the various licensing agreements from engaging in any form of international radiotelephony.

Yet, despite Conrad's successes and Marconi's advocacy of shortwave, such a method of broadcast transmission was regarded with skepticism by RCA. While Conrad had succeeded in transmitting KDKA programs halfway around the globe via shortwave, such transmissions were experimental. Moreover, it was one thing to transmit shortwave programs abroad; it was another to receive and rebroadcast them within the United States. So far, there had been no successes in reception within the United States of foreign shortwave broadcasting signals.

Instead of shortwave, RCA turned to international superpower transmission as the solution. This strategy involved the transoceanic transmission of broadcast signals over regular broadcasting frequencies, but at very high power. While most standard home receivers on the opposite shore would be unable to pick up the signals, the especially designed and supersensitive receiving equipment of the broadcasting companies would receive them and rebroadcast them over regular frequencies at standard power. This strategy was part of the plan for domestic superpower stations proposed by Sarnoff at the Third Radio Conference in Washington, D.C. in October 1924, as an alternative to the ATT-dominated networking system of radio program distribution.

The first attempt at superpower transoceanic transmission was on March 12, 1925 and involved a program exchange between the British Broadcasting Corporation (BBC) and RCA's New York station WJZ. While the BBC was able to pick up and rebroadcast the American program, WJZ was unable to successfully receive and retransmit the British program. Another attempt a week later was more successful, with WJZ broadcasting the sounds of Big Ben and 2 hours of music from the Hotel Savoy ballroom in London. RCA officials, buoyed by this success, again arranged for a program exchange with the BBC which would occur that winter. However, when this program exchange was attempted on December 31, 1925, the broadcasts were plagued with static and generally judged not to have been successful.[9]

The Commercial Adoption of Shortwave in the United States

The next year, 1926, marked, in many ways, the end of the experimental era of American radio broadcasting. Radio broadcasting was no longer an amateur affair but a national form of popular entertainment. That year the lax federal regulatory regime, erected under the 1912 Radio Act, collapsed in the face of a series of legal challenges, paving the way for the Radio Act of 1927, the creation of the Federal Radio Commission, and the structure of contemporary broadcasting regulation. With the settlement between ATT and the radio companies and the formation of NBC, the basis of the industrial structure of American broadcasting was set.

During this year, RCA was also reevalauting its activities in international broadcsting. Experimental longwave transmissions from Europe—sometimes successful, sometimes not—were losing their popularity. It was evident that superpower transmission over standard frequencies had not met expectations. As Sarnoff noted in the summer of 1926, "The day is gone when the people of the United States will listen to Europe for the novelty of doing so. The listeners are no longer interested in how they get their air programs, but in what they get."[10] If RCA was to incorporate international programming into its regular broadcasting, it would have to develop a far more satisfactory technology.

By this time, RCA was abandoning its resistance to shortwave and was coming to the conclusion that this new technology had the potential of revolutionizing international point-to-point communications. In October 1926, the Marconi Company successfully completed and inaugurated the imperial shortwave radio network conclusively demonstrating that shortwaves were able to provide reliable and efficient long distance radio communication. By the beginning of 1927, RCA had put into operation 15 experimental shortwave transmitters and conducted an extensive program of research in order to develop reliable transatlantic transmission. Such efforts proved successful. In August 1927, RCA moved its shortwave activities from experimental status to commercial operation by announcing that it would inaugurate a commercial shortwave service between London and New York.[11]

RCA's new commitment to shortwave was further demonstrated in May 1928, when it applied to the Federal Radio Commission for 55 of the 74 new point-to-point shortwave channels which the United States claimed under the new world allocation assignments made the previous year by the International Telegraphic Radio Conference. Due to the heavy competition for the new shortwave channels, however, RCA received only 15 of the requested 55 channels. Still, together with its existing shortwave channel assignments, RCA had a total of 65 transoceanic point-to-point shortwave channels, 28 more than its major competitor in international point-to-point communications, the ITT-backed MacKay Company. Although RCA made numerous denials about the obsolescence of longwave, it was clear that the days of the Alexanderson alternator were numbered. One reflection of the impact of shortwave on RCA's international operations, and on international radio communicaions in general, is the fact that in 1926, before the introduction of shortwave, RCA operated 62,400 miles of radio circuits. By 1932, after the adoption of shortwave, RCA's radio circuits had increased by 163,950 miles.[12]

Paralleling RCA's move into transoceanic point-to-point shortwave communication was the company's abandonment of the superpower strategy of international broadcasting and its attempts to develop shortwave as a reliable international broadcasting medium. With the assistance of Westinghouse and General Electric, RCA, through its broadcasting subsidiary NBC, began to devote its efforts toward developing shortwave to a level of reliability where international program exchanges could become a regular part of NBC's activities and programming. In November 1927, RCA conducted its first public attempt at a shortwave program exchange when it tried to pick up and rebroadcast Armistice Day services from the BBC. The attempt, however, was not successful. RCA realized that such shortwave program exchanges would require far more testing and research than previously thought. Rather than continue to make its failures at international program exchanges a matter for public comment, RCA discontinued broadcasting its shortwave programming attempts. During the next 2 years, NBC conducted numerous private tests in international program exchange in cooperation with the BBC. While the results of such tests were never publicly reported, NBC officials periodically announced that the tests were proceeding smoothly and that international program exchanges would be accomplished in a matter of months. As part of its shortwave experiments, NBC began to simulcast WJX programming over an RCA shortwave transmitter.[13]

During this period, the Federal Radio Commission was engaged in the process of writing regulations for international broadcasting. The 1927 International Telegraphic Radio Conference allocated six bands between 1,500 kHz and 23,000 kHz (200 and 13 meters) for international broadcasting. In February 1929, after a detailed study of the shortwave broadcasting technologies and practices among the stations already engaged in such activity, the Commission issued regulations governing American international broadcasting. Underlying these regulations was a conception of international broadcasting as primarily a form of relay broadcasting, or "the transmission on high frequencies over long distances of broadcast programs from one broadcasting station to another such station which rebroadcasts the program to the public on the regular broadcasting frequency of the receiving station." Because the Commission defined shortwave as an experimental service, putting it in the same category as the early experimental activity in television and aviational radio communication, it would grant licenses only to those seriously engaged in improving the technique of the art. The initial licenses were granted for 6 months, with longer licenses granted at the renewal at the discretion of the Commission. While broadcasting of commercials was to be allowed as part of the simulcasting of regular programming, shortwave stations could not be operated for profit. The Commission assigned 27 channels. In general, the notion of international broadcasting as program exchanges between broadcasting organizations was built into these regulations through the requirement that relay broadcasting stations were to transmit and receive programs via shortwave. Although starting in the early 1930s, international broadcasting became less a system of program exchanges and more a system of direct shortwave broadcasting, these rules would be the basis for the federal regulation of shortwave for the next 7 years. Over the next 8 months, the Commission issued licenses for twelve existing shortwave broadcasting transmitters and construction permits for four more.[14]

As the legal structure of American international broadcasting was being cast in Washington, rapid progress was being made in developing shortwave program exchange methods. On February 1, 1929, NBC finally succeeded in an attempt to rebroadcast a British program over the regular NBC network. Over the next months, programs from England, Holland, and Germany were received and rebroadcast over the network. These broadcasts were still considered to be experimental in nature, and rarely were the radio engineers and network officials able to plan more than a week in advance. In late 1929, RCA engineers, however, were in the process of completing a study begun in 1927 of the shortwave propagation characteristics over the North Atlantic that enabled them to predict the transmission patterns with far more accuracy than previously possible, thus allowing for greater program planning. On Christmas Day 1929, NBC successfully presented a multi-nation program exchange. Using the Westinghouse transmitter in Pittsburgh and the General Electric transmitters in Schenectady, NBC broadcast programs in the morning to Britain, Holland, and Germany. In the afternoon, through RCA's shortwave receiver station at Riverhead, Long Island, NBC picked up and rebroadcast programs from these same countries. Given the degree of detailed coordination required and the possible danger of fading and static, these transmissions were judged to be outstanding successes.[15]

NBC's efforts were beginning to be matched by its recently formed rival, the Columbia Broadcasting System (CBS). Through its purchase of station WABC in New York in 1928, CBS acquired a shortwave transmitter operated by the station. In October of the next year, notifying the Federal Radio Commission of its plans for rebroadcasting tests with Europe, CBS asked for additional channels and an increase in power from 50 to 200 kw. CBS maintained another shortwave outlet through the shortwave facilities of radio station WCAU in Philadelphia, a CBS affiliate owned individually by one of the members of the CBS board of directors. In 1929, CBS, acting on behalf of WCAU, requested the Commission grant the Philadelphia station a transoceanic broadcasting license for experimentation with shortwave.[16]

By the beginning of 1930, after years of tests and half successful attempts, the international exchange of radio programs via shortwave came of age. This new era was inaugurated in late January 1930 with the proceedings of the London Five-Power Naval Conference being transmitted to the United States and rebroadcast over the NBC and CBS networks. This broadcast was quickly followed by others. In March, broadcasts from the Byrd Expedition in Antarctica were heard by American listeners. Also in that month, excerpts from a performance in Dresden of the opera *Fidelio* were rebroadcast throughout the United States. CBS inaugurated a series of radio talks by foreign personages which eventually included Leon Trotsky, Pope Pius XI, the Prince of Wales, and George Bernard Shaw. Speeches to the American people were also received and rebroadcast from the President of Argentina and the Premier of Japan. International program exchange was regarded as the outstanding broadcasting event of 1930. By 1931 it had become a standard part of American broadcasting. In that year, NBC rebroadcast 159 international programs, and CBS 97. While the bulk of these programs were from Europe, programs were received from places as diverse as Brazil, Japan, Chile, Palestine, and Siam.[17]

Initially, these programs were transmitted to the United States in a variety of ways, sometimes via the shortwave transmitters of the foreign broadcasting organizations, as in the case of the British and German programs, at other times by RCA's point-to-point shortwave transmitters, and even, occasionally, by ATT's recently developed transoceanic radio telephone circuits. However, as RCA developed its shortwave technology, it perfected methods of shortwave program transmission to the United States. Through the RCA Communations Corporation (RCAC), the RCA subsidiary formed in 1929 to handle the company's international communications activities, RCA began to offer foreign program transmission service to all American broadcasting companies in 1932. By 1933, RCAC transmitted approximately 127 hours of foreign programs to United States broadcasting companies.[18]

Thus, in the early 1930s, the goal which motivated the broadcasting companies' involvement in shortwave broadcasting—the bringing of foreign programs to American listeners—was achieved. Ironically, once this was achieved, the broadcasting companies lost much of their interest in broadcasting American programs abroad. For example, in 1931, while NBC received and rebroadcast 159 foreign program transmissions, equaling 73½ hours, it only transmitted 24 programs to countries outside the United States, a total of 11½ hours. As William Paley, President of CBS, noted at that time, the major flow of international program transmission was from other countries into the United States.[19]

A major reason behind this lack of interest on the part of the major broadcasting companies in sending American programs abroad was that the system of program exchanges that had motivated the broadcasting companies to develop a shortwave reception and transmission capability never really was successful or became the basis of international broadcasting. During the 1920s, the system of program exchange was based on the technical necessity of cooperation with various foreign broadcasting organizations. The technology for point-to-point program transmission developed by RCAC in the early 1930s, however, freed American broadcasters from a reliance on the shortwave transmitters of foreign broadcast organizations. Such a transmission service allowed American broadcasters to select what foreign programs and events they wanted to transmit, and made it possible to tailor those programs to suit American tastes and the programming requirements of the American broadcasting companies. For example, through such technology, the rise of the American foreign broadcasting correspondent was made possible. Moreover, as national systems of broadcasting developed, the incompatibility among systems—from basic organizations and goals to type of programming—became more pronounced. As many of the European systems were state-owned and noncommercial, many of the heavily commercialized products of American radio that were oriented toward wide popular tastes were regarded as unsuitable for European listeners. Adding the language barrier, it was nearly impossible to organize a system of regular program exchanges.

Despite the apparent lack of usefulness and purpose, NBC and CBS, however, regularly renewed their shortwave licenses and continued to operate the transmitters they had built or acquired. The shortwave transmissions consisted largely of simulcasts of regular network programming, with little effort to develop any type of special programming for foreign audiences or to study the reception patterns of their shortwave signals systematically.

In addition to the shortwave transmitters of Westinghouse, General Electric, and the broadcasting networks, there were a number of other broadcasting companies involved in shortwave broadcasting. Paul Crosley, owner and operator of WLW in Cincinnati, Ohio, obtained a license from the Commerce Department in 1924 for a shortwave transmitter operating at 100 watts of power. In 1930, Crosley requested, and in 1933 was granted a power increase to 10 kw by the Federal Radio Commission, making it the most powerful shortwave station operating in the United States at that time. Yet, despite such increased power, Crosley showed little interest in developing any special type of foreign programming during this period, and most of the programming consisted of simulcasts of regular WLW fare.[20]

The one shortwave broadcaster interested in international programming was Walter S. Lemmon, who formed and managed the World Wide Broadcasting Corporation, which operated a shortwave educational station in Boston. He was a radio enthusiast and inventor who developed a single dial tuning mechanism. Lemmon became interested in international broadcasting while serving as a radio officer on the U.S.S. George Washington in Brest Harbor, during President Wilson's visit to Europe for the Peace Conference. He tried to interest the United States government in building an international longwave broadcasting station, but although President Wilson responded favorably to this idea, nothing ever came of it.

In 1929, Lemmon was General Manager of the New York shortwave station, W2XAL, owned by the Aviation Radio Corporation (AVCO). AVCO was investigating the possibility of manufacturing shortwave receivers, and planned to use W2XAL as a means of inciting interest in shortwave broadcasts abroad and advertising its receivers. The company was also interested in developing a program exchange system with other countries in order to supply foreign programs to nonnetwork United States radio stations. Such plans, however, did not materialize. In June 1931, having sold his single dial tuning patent to RCA for $1 million, Lemmon bought the radio station from AVCO, moved it to Boston, and changed its call letters to W1XAL. Initially, the station broadcast about 10 hours a week, and much of the programming consisted of simulcasts of the programs of Boston station WEEI.

The major purpose of Lemmon's station was to broadcast noncommercial, high quality cultural and educational programming to foreign countries. In 1934, he formed the World Wide Broadcasting Foundation as the programming arm of the World Wide Broadcasting Corporation, the legal owner of the station. Drawing upon the educational resources of the Boston area, he broadcast noncredit university courses, lectures, language lessons, and other programs of public interest.

He solicited and received financial support from both his listeners, who were concentrated in Europe and Great Britain and who could become members of Lemmon's World Wide Listener's League, and from the business community. In addition to owning and managing W1XAL, Lemmon was also employed by the International Business Machine Corporation (IBM). A major supporter of World Wide's activities was IBM's president, Thomas J. Watson, who served on the board of directors of the World Wide Broadcasting Foundation. In spite of such prestigious backers, finances were always a problem, and, even by late 1935, World Wide's special programming was limited to 2 hours daily.

A number of other minor shortwave broadcasting stations were licensed and put into operation in the late 1920s and early 1930s. These stations were generally owned by regular medium wave stations, operated at low power, and had programming which consisted primarily of simulcasts of the regular station's programming. A shortwave transmitter was licensed to the Wonderful Isle of Dreams Broadcasting Company, owner and operator of WIOD in Miami, Florida. WCFL, owned by the Chicago Federation of Labor, had a 500 watt shortwave transmitter, over which was simulcast the station's regular programming. Also in Chicago, the NBC affiliate, WENR-WMAQ, owned and operated a shortwave transmitter with programming consisting entirely of broadcasting material from the NBC network.[21]

In applying for shortwave broadcasting licenses in the late 1920s and early 1930s, both the major and minor broadcasting companies generally expected that shortwave broadcasting had a commercial future. However, by 1933, it was becoming obvious that such expectations were not being met. American shortwave broadcasting did not fill any conceivable function or role in the commercial broadcasting system, nor did it offer any special advantages to the companies with shortwave transmitters. Indeed, it seemed that the shortwave activities were beginning to become a burden. In 1930, both Westinghouse and General Electric applied to the Federal Radio Commission for permission to sell commercial time on their shortwave broadcasts. Noting that they had developed the state of the art of shortwave broadcasting to the point where it was almost 100 percent reliable, the radio companies stated that they were not interested in making money on their shortwave activities. They only wanted to recoup some of their investment in shortwave and have their continuing shortwave broadcasting activities become self-supporting. The Commission, feeling that additional shortwave research was necessary and wishing to preserve the experimental nature of shortwave broadcasting, denied the request.[22] In any event, it was questionable how successful shortwave advertising would have been at this point. With the growing depression curtailing American export trade and with very little knowledge about foreign radio audiences available, there did not seem to be much of a market for export advertising over shortwave. The other broadcasting companies expressed no interest in developing shortwave broadcasting as an export advertising service.

As other nations began to develop extensive shortwave broadcasting systems, the United States lost its leading position in the field of international boadcasting. In 1936, according to one estimate, the United States received three times as much shortwave programming from abroad as it transmitted. Ironically, the increase in shortwave broadcasting from other nations caused a growth in interest by the American public in shortwave reception and a boom in the sales of shortwave or all wave receivers, which first appeared on the American market in 1933. Yet, the number of licensed shortwave transmitting stations actually decreased from 13 to 12 between 1931 and 1932, and remained stable for the next 5 years.[23] Although there was not much to gain from shortwave transmission other than some small public relations advantages, the broadcasting companies were not prepared to liquidate their investment in shortwave. Given the growing interest in the development of commercial services in the high frequency region of the spectrum, the broadcasters' shortwave licenses might prove to be valuable, if not for shortwave broadcasting, then at least for future bargaining purposes with the Federal Communications Commission.

Although the United States pioneered and dominated the field of international shortwave broadcasting during the 1920s, by the mid-1930s, the development of such broadcasting was at a standstill. The major impetus behind the shortwave activities of the United States broadcasters in the 1920s was, not so much the desire to broadcast American programs abroad, as it was to import foreign programs via shortwave for domestic broadcast transmission. Initially, such importation was based on a system of international program exchanges that required United States broadcasters to develop both shortwave transmission and reception capabilities. However, as alternative technologies were developed for program importation, the importance of transmitting American programs abroad declined.

In comparison to other countries, where shortwave broadcasting was developed with larger political purposes in mind, in the United States shortwave was developed and operated as an adjunct to the domestic commercial broadcasting system. The private commercial domestic broadcasters were largely responsible for determining the scope and uses to which shortwave broadcasting would be put. However, after having developed international shortwave broadcasting, the broadcasters could not find any immediate compelling use for it. It was a technology and a practice that did not seem to have any commercial application. Nonetheless, the broadcasters continued to maintain their control over it.

It was at this point that an interest in shortwave was beginning to develop among policy makers and officials in Washington. As shortwave did not seem to have any immediate commercial use, perhaps a more appropriate application would be in the field of international politics. The political use of American shortwave was particularly appealing to those policy makers concerned with the position of the United States in Latin America. Both in the context of Roosevelt's Good Neighbor Policy and, more importantly, the growing threat to United States hegemony posed by Germany and other nations, shortwave broadcasting could play an important role in United States–Latin American relations.

If the private broadcasters could not develop any significant use for shortwave, then perhaps the government could. This, however, would require a major change in the traditional relations between private broadcasters and the government. As the next chapter shows, it was not a change that would be accomplished easily.

Notes

[1] W.M. Dalton, *The Story of Radio*, 3 vols. (London: Adam Hilger, 1975), I:101.

[2] Stanley Leinwoll, *From Spark to Satellite—A History of Radio Communication* (New York: Charles Scribner's Sons, 1979), pp. 107–112.

³ A.W. Ladner and C.R. Stone, *Shortwave Wireless Communication*, 3rd ed. (New York: John Wiley and Sons, 1936), p. 17.

⁴ Dalton, *The Story of Radio*, II:147.

⁵ This account of Marconi's development of shortwave is substantially based on W.J. Baker, *A History of the Marconi Company* (London: Meuthen & Co. Ltd., 1970), pp. 204–255; R.N. Vyvyan, *Wireless over Thirty Years* (London: George Routledge & Sons, 1933), pp. 74–77, 82–94; H.M. Dowsett, "Commercial Short Wave Wireless Communications. Part I: The Empiradio Beam Services," *The Marconi Review* 13 (October), 1929, pp. 14–30; H.M. Dowsett, "Commercial Shortwave Wireless Communications. Part II: The 'Via Marconi' Services," *The Marconi Review* 14 (November), 1929, pp. 1–15; and Ladner and Stone, *Short Wave Wireless Communication*, pp. 10–23.

⁶ Erik Barnouw, *A Tower in Babel: A History of Broadcasting in the United States to 1933* (New York: Oxford University Press, 1966), pp. 64–74; H.P. Davis, "The Early History of Broadcasting in the United States," in *The Radio Industry: The Story of Its Development* (Chicago: A.W. Shaw & Company, 1928), pp. 189–226; W.W. Rodgers, "Is Short-wave Relay Broadcasting a Step toward a National Broadcasting System," *Radio Broadcast* 3 (June), 1923, pp. 119–122; Gleason L. Archer, *History of Radio to 1926* (New York: The American Historical Society, 1938; reprint ed., New York: Arno Press, 1971), pp. 306–308; The most detailed and comprehensive account of the dispute between ATT and the radio companies can be found in Gleason L. Archer, *Big Business and Radio* (New York: The American Historical Society, 1939), pp. 3–276; see also N.R. Danielian, *A.T.T.—The Story of Industrial Conquest* (New York: The Vanguard Press, 1939), pp. 121–134; and W. Rupert Maclaurin, *Invention and Innovation in the Radio Industry* New York: Macmillan, 1949), pp. 111–131.

⁷ W.W. Rodgers, "Broadcasting Complete American Programs to England," *Radio Broadcast* 4 (March), 1924, pp. 359–364; *New York Times*, 2 January 1924, 19:4; Michael Kent Sidel, "A Historical Analysis of American Short Wave Broadcasting 1916–1942" (Ph.D. dissertation, Northwestern University, 1976), pp. 71–89.

⁸ H.E. Hallbord, L.A. Briggs, and C.W. Hansell, "Short-wave Commercial Long Distance Communication," *Proceedings of the Institute of Radio Engineers* 15:6 (June 1927), pp. 467–499; *New York Times*, 11 July 1924, 1:2; 30 August 1924, 10:3; 20 June 1924, 5:4.

⁹ Archer, *History of Radio*, pp. 350–351; *New York Times*, 19 October 1924, IX:17:1; 27 October 1924, 16:1; 13 March 1925, 23:6; 25 March 1925, 23:6; 18 July 1925, 8:1; 26 August 1926, 4:3.

¹⁰ Ibid., 26 August, 1:2.

¹¹ Hallbord et al., "Short-wave Communication"; *New York Times*, 5 August 1927, 36:6.

¹² U.S., Federal Radio Commission. Second Annual Report (1928), p. 30; U.S., Congress, House, *Report on Communication Companies*. House Report No. 1273, 73rd Congress, 2nd Session, 1934, Part III, No. 4, p. 4193.

¹³ *New York Times*, 13 November 1927, 24:3; 24 April 1928, 18:6; 11 May 1929, 22:5; Sidel, "A Historical Analysis," p. 100.

¹⁴ Federal Radio Commission, *Second Annual Report* (1928), p. 72; *Third Annual Report* (1929), p. 99; U.S. Department of Commerce, *Radio Service Bulletin* 144 (March 30, 1929), p. 16.

[15] "Voices Across the Sea," *Scientific American* 142 (May) 1930, pp. 356–357.

[16] *New York Times*, 16 October 1929, 26:4. *United States Daily*, 8 May 1929, IV:563:3; Sidel, "A Historical Analysis," p. 110.

[17] *New York Times*, 19 January 1930, VIII:15:1; 26 January 1930, VIII:16:1; 12 March 1930; 26:3; 17 March 1930, 30:6; 28 December 1930, IX:8:1; Orrin E. Dunlap. *Radio and Television Almanac* (New York: Harper & Brothers, 1951) pp. 93–96; Barnouw, *A Tower in Babel*, pp. 248–249; U.S., Congress, Senate, *Commercial Radio Advertising*, Senate Document No. 137, 72nd Congress, 1st Session, 1932, pp. 18–21.

[18] William A. Winterbottom, "The World Comes to America Via Radio," *Broadcasting*, 15 June 1934, p. 31.

[19] *Commercial Radio Advertising*, ibid; *New York Times*, 9 August 1931, IX:9:6.

[20] Sidel, "A Historical Analysis," pp. 111–112; Lawrence Wilson Lichty, "'The Nation's Station,' A History of Radio Station WLW," 2 vols. (Ph.D. dissertation, Ohio State University, 1964), I:59–60; *New York Times*, 8 April 1927, 18:6.

[21] *United States Daily*, 7 July 1931, VI:1013:6. Sidel, "A Historical Analysis," pp. 112–117, 121–125.

[22] *Broadcast Advertising*, November 1930, p. 38; *New York Times*, 19 October 1930, X:11:1; 22 March 1931, 16:2; Sidel, "A Historical Analysis," pp. 140–141; *United States Daily*, 4 April 1931, VI:285:2.

[23] Silas Bent, "International Broadcasting," *Public Opinion Quarterly* I (July) 1937, p. 120; Sidel, "A Historical Analysis," p. 127; U.S. Federal Radio Commission, *Sixth Annual Report* (1932), p. 6; U.S. Federal Communications Commission, *Third Annual Report* (1937), pp. 34–35.

CHAPTER 4

THE UNITED STATES, LATIN AMERICA, AND SHORTWAVE, 1936–1939

Up to the early 1930s, the United States government remained uninterested in the use of shortwave broadcasting as an instrument of foreign policy. However, starting with the Roosevelt Administration and the formulation of the Good Neighbor Policy, an interest was shown by the government in the commercial and political use of shortwave radio broadcasting. Initially, the development of a program of shortwave broadcasting to Latin America was seen as forming closer ties between the United States and Latin America. Such broadcasting would play a role in the construction of an inter-American system of political and economic relations organized around the goals and interests of the United States. However, with Germany beginning to threaten the dominant position of the United States in the hemisphere in the latter part of the decade, the administration began to regard as urgent the development of shortwave as a method of countering German threats.

Whatever political plans the administration had for shortwave were greatly complicated by the fact that the shortwave stations were in the hands of the commercial broadcasters. Moreover, traditional relations between the government and the broadcasting industry seemed to preclude direct government involvement in broadcasting. Rather than radically change these relations, the administration instead sought an accommodation with private broadcasters. Shortwave would remain in private hands, but would aim at achieving the administration's goals in inter-American relations.

The Development of an "Activist" Good Neighbor Policy

The Good Neighbor Policy as formulated and implemented during Roosevelt's first term was devoted primarily to "clearing away deadwood" accumulated from past administrations. The two major aspects of this new policy renunciation by the United States of its claim to the right of unilateral armed intervention and trade reciprocity were aimed at removing the ostensible causes of many of the Latin American complaints about the United States, and reopening the channels of trade between the two continents. As such, this initial formulation of the policy was negative in nature, representing a pledge not to intervene or engage in economic warfare.

In the years immediately following the 1933 Montevideo Conference (see p. 32), the United States took steps to implement its new policy direction. As the Caribbean was the scene of the most active involvement and intervention by the United States into Latin American affairs, it was here that the new policy of the Good Neighbor found its initial realization. In August 1934, completing a process of disengagement begun during the Hoover administration, the last detachment of United States Marines was withdrawn from Haiti. Negotiations were also begun that, in 1941, would lead to the United States relinquishing control over Haitian government finances and the return to that country of control of its customs receipts. In addition to the withdrawal of troops from Haiti, the United States began negotiations with Panama, Haiti, and the Dominican Republic, with the intention of renouncing prior treaty rights of intervention in the internal affairs of these countries. Also, in January 1934, the United States abandoned the special recognition policy, in force since 1907, by which any new government in the five Central American republics that came to power by extra-constitutional means was refused recognition by the United States. These actions, together with a new willingness by the United States to negotiate reciprocal trade treaties, seemed to present convincing evidence to many that this country was sincere in its desire to turn away from its former imperialist methods and goals and to develop a new policy based on respect for the sovereignty and self-determination of Latin American nations.

However, on closer inspection it becomes clear that such actions did not mean that the United States was any less concerned about Latin American affairs, or any less committed to pursuing and protecting its own national self-interest and goals throughout the hemisphere. The Roosevelt Administration's response to the revolutionary situation in Cuba demonstrated that it was intensely concerned with the course of events in Latin America. By no means was the United States abdicating its presumed leadership and dominance in hemispheric affairs. What was occurring was the abandonment of old, ineffective methods and techniques of control and the search for newer and more sophisticated ones which would match the increasingly complex process of political and social change in Latin America.

The development of a new policy and a new system of relations between the United States and Latin America, of course, would take time and be the product of much trial and error. However, even as the United States was renouncing its rights of intervention at Montevideo and withdrawing the Marines from Haiti, some of the broad contours of the Good Neighbor Policy as an active instrument designed to insure United States hemispheric dominance began to emerge. In December 1933, in the same speech in which he declared United States opposition to the policy of armed intervention, Roosevelt also declared that the maintenance of constitutional governments "is not a sacred obligation devolving upon the United States alone." He stated:

> The maintenance of law and the orderly process of government in this hemisphere is the concern of each individual nation within its own borders first of all. It is only if and when the failure of orderly processes affects the other nations of the continent that it becomes their concern; and the point to stress is that in such an event, it becomes *the joint concern of a whole continent in which we are all neighbors.* (Emphasis added)[1]

This emphasis on collective action and inter-American security was also reflected at the Montevideo Conference, where attempts were made to deal with the problem of strengthening the regional security structure. The outbreak of war the previous year between Bolivia and Paraguay over the disputed Chaco region, and the possibility of a border dispute between Peru and Colombia escalating into war, revealed the inadequacies of the hemispheric peace-keeping and arbitration system. The United States actively supported a move at the Montevideo Conference for all American nations to sign and/or ratify all current inter-American arbitration treaties, in an attempt to both reduce conflict within the hemisphere and encourage collective settlements of disputes between American nations. Although such actions and statements were not particularly important in themselves—the arbitration treaties were never ratified by all the American nations—they are significant as early expressions of a developing new conception on the part of the United States of the structure of hemispheric affairs and relations. Involved in such a newer conception was a broader definition of what the important United States interests and objectives were in the hemisphere.

In the early years of the Roosevelt Administration, the United States goals were oriented primarily toward keeping the region open for trade, particularly since production for foreign markets was considered a necessary element in domestic economic recovery. The administration would not have its actions in the hemisphere tied to the specific interests of United States investors in the region, but took into account the broader interests of United States capitalism as a whole. While the administration was sympathetic to the plight of United States holders of defaulted Latin American bonds, the amount of which exceeded $1 billion, it tended to regard this as a private matter and would not let it interfere with larger

United States goals in the region. Overall, the Roosevelt Administration was successful in establishing as a fundamental principle of the Good Neighbor Policy that there were national interests of the United States in its relation with Latin America different from and superior to the private interests of any one sector of the business community or any individual company.[2]

It soon became apparent, however, that United States hemispheric hegemony were being threatened from other quarters. In Germany, with the new Nazi government in power only 9 months, Propaganda Minister Joseph Goebbels issued a secret directive in September 1933 detailing plans for an extensive propaganda campaign aimed at the Americas. This campaign's purpose was to mobilize support in the German-American communities for the aims and goals of the new German government. A broader goal was to cultivate public opinion in favor of Germany and its current foreign policy goals (e.g., revision of the Versailles Treaty, regaining of former German colonies, and German rearmament). In general, the German government hoped to neutralize any opposition that the American governments might have to German foreign policy aims.

In the United States, the campaign was not notably successful. In Latin America, however, the prospects for failure were not as well assured. Although there was less German migration to Latin America than North America, German immigrants to Latin America formed tight communities and sought to maintain their separate ethnic identity, resisting assimilation into the local cultures. Moreover, many of the Latin American Germans were recent arrivals who had fought in World War I, and they found the revanchist elements of the Nazi appeals attractive. The first country-wide Nazi party outside Germany was organized in Paraguay in 1932, and, over the next few years, parties were organized in other Latin American nations. Soon many of the local German newspapers acquired a pro-Nazi character. It was evident that the Nazi government was successful in dominating the politics of the local German communities. The Nazi government attempted to influence wider public opinion through such tactics as having local German businessmen and traders in Latin America place their advertising en bloc in papers which proved either editorially inoffensive or pro-German. Moreover, many of the financially weaker Latin newspapers gratefully accepted the free services of the Nazi-organized world news agency.

Although it was not until the latter part of the decade that the Roosevelt Administration became seriously concerned about such propaganda activities, Germany's other main interest in Latin America, the acquisition of raw materials for German industry in return for German manufactured products, was quickly noticed by the United States. In the fall of 1934, a German trade delegation toured South America, studying trade and marketing conditions, and was able to conclude trade agreements with Argentina, Brazil, Chile, and Uruguay. Typically, these agreements were based on barter arrangements in which Latin American nations, lacking the necessary foreign exchange, traded raw materials for finished German products. The United States expressed concern over such agreements, as they tended to create exclusive bilateral trade ties between Germany and the various Latin American nations. This resulted in a situation in which German trade partners in Latin America were unable to buy as much from other countries. Although such barter arrangements were not as successful as Germany had originally hoped, by 1938 Germany had practically regained the place she had held in Latin American trade before 1913, replacing Great Britain as the second major supplier of goods to Latin America after the United States.[3]

To this threat of German penetration into the Western Hemisphere was added the growing possibility of another general war in Europe into which the American nations would be drawn. In autumn 1935, Italy invaded Ethiopia and started an aggressive war that proved the League of Nations to be an impotent guarantor of world peace. Earlier, Hitler had announced German's withdrawal from the League of Nations, its rejection of the restriction of the Versailles Peace Treaty, and the expansion and rearming of the German military. The response within the United States to such events was a growing anti-war sentiment reflected in the passage of the Neutrality Act of 1935.[4]

It was in the context of the disturbing European situation that, in January 1936, Roosevelt proposed a special inter-American conference "to determine how the maintenance of peace among the American republics may be best safe-guarded."[5] Aside from keeping peace among American nations, the more important goal of Roosevelt and Secretary of State Hull in calling this conference was their desire to make the neutrality policy of the United States a hemispheric policy. In the event of a general war in Europe, Roosevelt wanted to insure that no American nation would become involved.[6] Meeting in Buenos Aires in December 1936, the Inter-American Conference for the Maintenance of Peace represented a significant step in the evolution of an activist Good Neighbor Policy. The importance of this Conference was attested to by Roosevelt's trip to Argentina to address the opening session. Among the measures discussed and approved by all the delegates was one that expanded and reaffirmed more emphatically the nonintervention pledge approved at Montevideo in 1933. This measure stated in part that the American nations "declare inadmissable the intervention of any one of them directly or indirectly, and for whatever reason, in the internal or external affairs" of any American state.[7]

In exchange for this unequivocal renunciation of unilateral intervention, the United States gained a far more effective and important policy instrument in the formulation of the principle of collective intervention embodied in the "Convention for the Maintenance, Preservation, and Re-Establishment of Peace," generally known as the Consultative Pact. This pact provided that (a) in the event that the peace of the hemisphere was menaced from any source, (b) in the event of war between American states, or (c) in the event of a war outside the Americas which might menace the peace of the American republics, the American nations would consult with one another for the purpose of deciding appropriate actions in order to secure and safeguard the peace of the hemisphere.

The pact did not go as far as Roosevelt and Hull wished in providing for positive measures against the danger of foreign wars. It did not oblige the contracting parties to do anything more than consult, nor was any machinery set up to invoke consultation. Nonetheless, the recognition of the collective concern and common interest of each American republic in the security of all was a significant achievement for the Roosevelt Administration. In essence, it represented the "Pan-Americanization" of the Monroe Doctrine. Up to this point, the United States had the unilateral responsibility of achieving its objective of keeping non-American states from intervening or having influence in hemispheric affairs. However, with the formulation of the Consultative Pact, such responsibility was collectively assumed, at least in theory.

In contrast to past United States policy in Latin America, the Good Neighbor Policy in its activist construction was grounded on the idea that the countries of the Western Hemisphere constituted an inter-American system based on broad notions of political and economic reciprocity and collective hemispheric solidarity and action. A major assumption underlying this conception of inter-American relations was the mutuality and harmony of interests among the American states, particularly between the industrialized United States and the non-industrialized, raw material-producing Latin American nations as a whole. While the system was based on the principle of equality of all American nations, it was, nevertheless, a system which was to become defined and dominated by the interests and goals of the United States. In return for the renunciation of intervention and discriminatory trade practices on the part of the United States, later supplemented with loans and economic aid, the Latin American nations would pledge their cooperation in achieving and protecting what the United States saw as its important hemispheric objectives.

The Consultative Pact signed at Buenos Aires was only the first step. As the decade continued, and with the growing threats of Nazi penetration and a general European war, the structure of the inter-American system took more definite shape. In November 1938, following the Munich Crisis, Roosevelt proposed a defensive alliance of American nations against external aggression be considered at the Eighth Inter-American Conference meeting the next month in Lima, Peru. The Conference, when it met, did not go as far again as Roosevelt wished, largely due to the opposition of Argentina. Nonetheless, it agreed upon proposals extending the scope of the Buenos Aires Pact. Although it was not until the actual outbreak of war in Europe and the fall of France in 1940 that the American nations seriously began to organize a common hemispheric defense program, the actions taken at Buenos Aires and Lima were important in reflecting the new conception of hemispheric relations on the part of the United States and in laying the groundwork for war-time collaboration between the United States and Latin America.

While hemispheric solidarity and defense through the "Pan-Americanization" of the Monroe Doctrine was one important objective of the United States, another major and closely related set of goals was the continuing access and control by the United States of Latin American raw materials and the maintenance of Latin American markets for United States manufactured goods. The latter was to be achieved through the expansion of liberal hemispheric trade policies—a matter which was on the agenda both at Buenos Aires and Lima—and the negotiations of bilateral reciprocal trade agreements. It was in the context of these objectives that the expansion of German trade in Latin America through barter agreements was viewed as threatening to United States interests.

It was in the maintenance of, access to, and control of Latin American raw materials that the Good Neighbor Policy received its severest tests and ultimately achieved its greatest successes. While the United States government could pledge nonintervention and noninterference in the internal affairs of Latin American countries, it could not deny that much of the control of Latin American economic resources was in the hands of United States interests. While much of the previous United States policy had been directed toward limiting, as far as possible, European economic and financial interests in Latin America, thus gaining control of the region's resources, in the 1930s rising economic nationalism presented another, more serious threat. The programs of the growing mass-based popular nationalist groups throughout Latin America could only proceed if the nations were able to gain full control of their own economic resources.

The first major challenge to United States economic control came in March 1937, when the Bolivian government, charging tax fraud and other illegal action, annulled the Bolivian petroleum concessions of Standard Oil and confiscated its properties. The United States government's response was cautious and in keeping with its Good Neighbor image. It regarded the expropriations as legal, and the main issue the amount of compensation to be paid to the oil company. The administration urged the oil company to take the matter to the Bolivian courts and exhaust all local remedies before applying to the United States government for assistance. A far more serious challenge occurred the next year, when Mexico expropriated the properties of foreign oil companies. This action was particularly dangerous because, in contrast to the Bolivian case, it was part of a revolutionary nationalist program being implemented by a popular, constitutionally elected government representing a revolutionary tradition going back 20 years. An ominous development occurred when Mexico, in response to a boycott by protesting American and British oil companies, reluctantly turned to Italy, Germany, and Japan to take up the slack in her oil exports. Such an action raised the dangerous possibility that, given Germany's growing econonic and propaganda campaign in Latin America, Latin American economic nationalism might find a useful ally in the Axis plan for the Americas. Both Brazil and Argentina seemed particularly vulnerable to Nazi blandishments.

Faced with the need to control Latin American resources on the one hand, and the need to cultivate hemispheric cooperation and solidarity in the face of the increasingly threatening world situation on the other, the Roosevelt Administration had to evolve a new response to the militant nationalist demands. If the United States was to maintain its dominance in the hemisphere without destroying its Good Neighbor image, it would have to find some way to insure its position "without," in the words of one historian, "either antagonizing or giving too much free rein to Latin American nationalists."[8]

Although it was a product of a number of years of trial and error, the administration's response to this seeming dilemma was succinctly articulated by Roosevelt in 1940. Outlining United States policy toward Latin America to a group of newspaper editors, Roosevelt noted that it was a legitimate desire for Latin Americans to want to control their economic resources. Many Latin American nations could look forward to gaining control of foreign businesses in their nations by eventually buying into them, a plan he called "an option on the equity." Aptly summarizing his administration's policy toward Latin American economic nationalist demands, he concluded, "That is a new approach that I am talking about to these South American things. Give them a share. They think they are just as good as we are, and many of them are."[9] By granting concessions to the demands of Latin American nationalism and assisting in the economic development of the region, the Roosevelt Administration hoped to channel nationalist energies toward paths more conducive to United States interests and dominance in the hemisphere.

An important element in this new approach was the development of a program of loans, economic aid, and planning assistance to Latin American. Such a program sought to keep German and other European investments and influence in the region to a minimum. But, more important, by having the power to select the projects to be funded and the type of technical assistance to be given, the United States would play a very important role in shaping the nature and direction of Latin American economic development. Starting in 1938, the Export-Import Bank, founded in 1934 for the primary purpose of assisting United States export trade, began to make loans to Latin American countries based on broader political consid-erations. That year Haiti received a $5.5 million loan for road construc-tion and other public works; it was generally believed that the loan was made to forestall a German loan to that country. In 1939, a $15.8 million loan was made to Chile to assist in the industrialization program of that country's government. Nicaragua also received a $2 million loan, and Paraguay a $3.4 million loan, for construction purposes. With the begin-ning of the European war, with Latin American raw materials and defense cooperation becoming all the more important, loans to Latin American countries increased dramatically. Whereas total loans to all foreign coun-tries from the Export-Import Bank between 1934 and 1939 totaled $61.4 million, between September 1, 1939 and December 7, 1941, the Bank made loans to 16 Latin American countries totalling $229 million, the largest being $45 million to Brazil for the construction of a steel mill.[10] The use of such loans and other economic assistance proved an effective instru-ment in achieving United States defense objectives in the region and modi-fying nationalist demands. By the end of 1942, all Latin American nations except Chile and Argentina had either declared war or had cut off rela-tions with the Axis powers. In August 1941, Bolivia signed an economic assistance pact with the United States, and, in January 1942, the Bolivian government entered into an agreement with Standard Oil regarding com-pensation for the expropriated oil parties. Needing Mexican cooperation in the war effort, the Mexican oil controversy was settled amicably with compensation to the oil companies decided upon by a joint United States–Mexican arbitration committee.

Overall the policy of "giving them a share" represented a sophisticated and effective response to the demands of Latin American nationalists. Through such a policy, the position and power of the United States in Latin America was not only maintained, but strengthened. As one com-mentator, assessing the results of war-time United States economic assistance, loans, and planning aid for Latin America, concluded, "If any-thing, the 'new' Good Neighbor Policy gave the United States an ever in-creasing dominance in inter-American relations on economic issues because of this power of the purse. The United States called for hemi-sphere planning, initiated some itself, and thereby extended its control over the ideas coming from Latin America. Though this is a harsh analysis, it is essentially accurate."[11]

The Origins of Cultural Diplomacy

Closely intertwined with efforts to develop hemispheric solidarity and deal with the rising challenge of Latin American economic nationalism, were attempts by the United States to devise policies dealing with inter-

American cultural relations as an important component of the overall
Good Neighbor strategy. Such attempts at cultural diplomacy represented
a radical departure from past United States foreign policies and practices.
Prior to the Good Neighbor Policy, the United States government took little, if any, interest or effort in the promotion or dissemination of cultural
products, practices, or ideas overseas. What little activity did exist in the
way of cultural promotion and exchange was sponsored by private individuals, foundations, or educational institutions. Thus, for example, the
Institute of International Education, founded in 1919 and funded in large
part by the Carnegie Foundation, was largely responsible for many of the
international student and faculty exchanges taking place in the inter-war
years. The arts were considered to be a matter for private philanthropy,
and education a matter for the states; thus the Federal Government had
little direct role or responsibility in the shaping of American culture.
Moreover, there was often an implicit assumption that the superiority of
American democratic culture spoke for itself, as witnessed by the fact that
the government had to erect immigration quotas to regulate the flow of
foreigners to this country. Given these factors, the government felt little
need or incentive to develop any type of international cultural programs.

Aside from its form of constitutional government and its public school
system, both very influential models in the nineteenth century, the United
States generally had very little cultural impact on Latin American life
prior to World War I. While the Pan American Union was involved in the
exchange of information between the United States and the Latin American countries, generally such exchanges were primarily for trade or diplomatic purposes. Overall, while the Latin Americans tended to recognize
the material progress and economic power of the United States, they looked
to Europe as the source of cultural values and models. Influential Latin
American intellectuals and writers such as José Enrique Rodó and Manuel
Ugarte depicted the United States as a crass materialistic country brutally
working its will throughout the hemisphere by naked force. According to
this view, the power and materialistic character of "the Colossus of the
North" represented a dangerous threat to the higher spiritual values upon
which Latin American culture, and all Romance cultures in general, were
based. The armed interventions and interference of the United States in
Latin America, and the popular media image of the United States drawn
from the influx of movies from the north after World War I, did little to
alter this opinion.

The popular image of Latin America fared no better in the United-
States. Given the constant reports of tyrannical rulers, revolutions, and
marauding bandits, there developed a general indifference, if not actual
contempt, for Latin American society and culture. As one commentator
noted, "The region and its people remained to the northern republic a

profitable place to trade with, an interesting field for explorers and geographers, a continent for pioneer engineers, a romantic land for footloose soldiers of fortune, [and] a vast and challenging field of Protestant missionary competition."[12]

In line with its lack of a cultural policy prior to the Roosevelt Administration, the government did very little in the way of promoting cultural and educational exchanges between the two continents. The lack of interest even extended to refusing to cooperate with private groups involved in such activity. Very rarely did United States ambassadors or consular officials go out of their way to extend any assistance to United States exchange scholars in the the region.

However, starting with the Montevideo Conference and the early formulation of the Good Neighbor Policy, there were indications that such indifference to culture as an instrument of foreign policy was ending. While the United States delegation maintained the general policy of not approving conventions or recommendations which would involve the federal government in educational or other areas traditionally not in its domain, it did exhibit a more active interest in the expansion of cultural ties between the two continents, and approved a number of recommendations on cultural matters, one of which called for the development of an inter-American system of radio broadcasting. Secretary of State Hull, later in a Washington address reporting on the achievements of the Conference, expressed the developing new attitude about the importance of cultural matters when he declared, "The delegates realized that a crisis had been thrust upon the New World and that it was absolutely incumbent upon the Conference to sound a new note, to broadcast a new spirit, and to proclaim a new day in the political, economic and cultural affairs of this hemisphere."[13]

In the period following the Montevideo Conference, the administration began to examine more closely the possibilities and advantages that a program of cultural diplomacy had to offer toward the achievement of the larger goals of the Good Neighbor Policy. Moreover, the need for such a program became increasingly apparent as more reports began to be received in Washington about increased Nazi cultural and economic activities.

The initial focus of the administration's cultural interests was on educational exchanges. In a number of public addresses given in 1935 and 1936 devoted to inter-American relations, Assistant Secretary of State Sumner Welles urged colleges and universities to be prime movers in making the Good Neighbor Policy a reality by expanding their courses on Latin America and developing educational exchanges with Latin American universities. A number of universities and private organizations responded by offering fellowships to Latin American students for study in the United States.[14] Still, given the strapped financial resources of American universities at that point, if any great success was to be achieved, the government itself would have to get involved. The Buenos Aires Conference in 1936, along with the proposals for the development of an inter-American security system, represented a significant first step in the development of a United States cultural policy and program. For the first time in history, an American diplomatic delegation included an official cultural advisor, Dr. Samuel Guy Inman, an American educator and Protestant missionary with long experience in Latin America. At the Conference, in marked contrast to past conferences, the United States delegation took a leading role in cultural matters. It proposed and had approved by the Conference the "Convention for the Promotion of Inter-American Cultural Relations," which provided for a student–faculty exchange program to be financed by the governments of the American states. Other binding cultural conventions approved by the United States dealt with government assistance and cooperation in the exchange of artistic exhibits and publications, and the creation in the national libraries of each country a section dedicated to the works of other American countries. Nonbinding recommendations by the United States dealt with such matters as education, libraries and bibliographies, radio broadcasting, and moral disarmament. By signing these statements, the government, without binding itself, endorsed principles upon which it could act as soon as public opinion in the United States advanced adequately to their support.

Five months after the Conference, Roosevelt submitted the cultural conventions to the Senate, which ratified them in July 1937. Not waiting for ratification by the other American states, the State Department set up the Division of Cultural Relations in 1938 to administer the educational exchanges and carry out other activities relating to cultural relations with Latin America. At about the same time, the Interdepartmental Committee on the Cooperation with the American Republics was established under the direction of the State Department to coordinate the activities of the various government departments and agencies in carrying out cultural projects in Latin America.

The actual progress of the cultural programs prior to the United States entry into the war was slow. Funds for the educational exchange were not appropriated by Congress until 1940. It was not until September of that year that the first exchange actually took place. Moreover, compared to the cultural programs and activities of the United States during and after World War II, the early activities were almost negligible. Nevertheless, the larger significance of these early programs far outweighed their initially slight achievements. In proposing and signing the convention on educational exchanges, the United States government was incorporating for the first time a means of developing cultural relations with other countries into its formal foreign policy. In doing so, an essential part of wartime and post-war foreign policy was being firmly established.

To some, the development of these cultural programs and policies represented a progressive step forward for United States diplomacy. Such actions were proof again that this country was abandoning past imperialist practices based on force and intervention, in favor of policies devoted to the development of mutual understanding and respect among American nations.[15] According to this view, many of the past antagonisms and conflicts between the United States and Latin America had been based on mutual misunderstandings and misconceptions. Only when the people of the Americas came into contact and were able to talk with one another would everyone become aware and appreciate, not only the particular achievements and merits of each nation's culture and society, but, more importantly, the underlying bond of common values and ideals that united the nations of the hemisphere. With an understanding and appreciation of both the diversity and similarity among the cultures of the Americas, peace and progress in the hemisphere would be assured.

Without a doubt, many people, including both Latin Americans and high United States government officials, sincerely viewed the development of United States cultural activities in this light. Few people could disagree with the goal of increasing cultural understanding among nations. Thus, both in the United States and in Latin America, this innovation in United States foreign policy was enthusiastically welcomed. Yet, one cannot remove the development of such cultural diplomacy from the larger context and goals of the Good Neighbor Policy. As with the Good Neighbor Policy as a whole, the development of cultural relations as a formal part of foreign policy was in response to the changing situation the United States found in Latin America in the 1930s.

A major immediate factor behind the development of such cultural policies was a defensive reaction against growing German cultural and economic activity. While much of the German activity was initially very low-keyed, by March 1937, Nazi-dominated German communities throughout Latin America felt secure and strong enough to celebrate the "Day of the German People" with public pro-Nazi demonstrations and displays of the swastika. Rapid and open nazification of German community schools throughout the region was also reported. Utilizing shortwave radio broadcasts, educational exchanges, speaker's bureaus, movies, subsidized publication of books, newspapers and magazines, bloc advertising in local newspapers favorable towards Germany. Germany, and to a lesser extent Italy and Japan, developed an extensive campaign to sway public opinion in favor of Axis aims and goals and develop closer ties between Latin American countries and the Axis powers.[16] Much of this activity was aimed at and involved local Latin American German communities. Yet, in the eyes of many United States government officials, many Latin Americans, because of their presumed lack of a democratic tradition, would be strongly attracted to such fascistic appeals. This was particularly threatening to the

United States, given the rising economic nationalism in the region and the large reservoir of anti-United States sentiment. Though there was by no means complete agreement in the United States as to the seriousness of the threat of Nazi propaganda in Latin America, among the policy makers in the Roosevelt Administration the dominant feeling was that something had to be done to combat the growing Nazi penetration of the hemisphere.

Yet, even though this threat loomed large enough in the minds of many concerned with Latin America, it is mistaken to view the development of cultural diplomacy solely as a negative, defensive measure or as a cynical public relations gimmick. The Good Neighbor Policy, in its economic, political, and cultural manifestations, was not developed solely as a response to the Nazi threat, although such a threat did shape some of the specific characteristics of the policy. Cordell Hull, for example, was a strong liberal free-trader who devoutly believed that open and free exchange among nations, whether in goods or in ideas, was essential to human progress. That the development of both trade and cultural exchanges would lead to a greater understanding among nations and to a reduction in international conflict and tensions was not mere rhetoric, but an ideal firmly believed by Hull and others.

Yet, despite this sincere belief in their own positive intentions and understanding of the role and nature of cultural exchanges, it is apparent that these United States policy makers were becoming aware of a lesson learned quickly by every modern empire or imperial system. While an imperial power never absolutely renounces the ultimate sanction of force, it is far more useful, effective, and less costly to rely upon other seemingly noncoercive control measures. That the United States, after having learned the disadvantages of a primary dependence on force, should incorporate in the 1930s measures of cultural diplomacy in its formal policy practices in Latin America, was another sign that this country was coming of age as an imperial and world power. As with any imperial power, the United States found it necessary to construct mechanisms for the dissemination of a world-view which would justify its position of power and dominance. Such a world-view would seek to show that the "true" interest and welfare of all the client states in the imperial system were closely tied to the interests and welfare of the imperial power. Such a world-view would seek to convince the client state that, despite apparent inequalities, the costs and benefits, obligations, and rewards associated with the imperial system as a whole were evenly distributed. Moreover, it was to be shown that only by the client state being a part of the imperial system and accepting the structure of power, could the hope of some future progress, however defined, be realized. Finally, it was a great advantage that those within the imperial center who constructed and disseminated this world-view also sincerely believed in it.

As part of the Good Neighbor Policy, the formulation and application of such a world-view to Latin America took a number of years and only achieved its full development during World War II. An important theme was the common heritage of the Americas and their distinct identity as a whole, as opposed to Europe and Asia. Also stressed was the mutuality and harmony of interests and the interdependence among American states. The division of labor between the United States and Latin America, with the latter producing raw materials and the former producing manufactured goods, was depicted as natural and beneficial to all. Finally, it was assumed that all American states and peoples were bound by their commitment to liberal democracy and individual freedom, the two values which together represented the social ideal for which all American states would strive and protect. Threats to these ideals and values always came from sources outside the hemisphere.

Through the propagation of such a world-view, the structure of power in the Americas would be seen as being justified. The demands of the nationalists would be blunted and modified so as to preserve the dominance of the United States. Overall, the contradictions, conflicts, and inequalities between the United States and Latin America would be veiled.

As with the Good Neighbor Policy and New Deal policies in general, cultural diplomacy represented an innovative redefinition of the role of government. In formulating a policy of international cultural activity, the administration was entering into fields—art, education, music, the media —traditionally considered to be the proper domain of state governments and private interests. Such intervention into the field of culture can be seen, in part, as one aspect of the larger activist stance the Roosevelt Administration took, in general, in the area of cultural production and promotion. Domestic relief measures such as the Federal Art Project, the Federal Music Project, and Federal Writer's Projects, and the Federal Theatre Project were evidence of the major restructuring that was occurring in relations between the government and the cultural spheres of life. As with such domestic projects, the possibility of controversy and charges of government self-propaganda were always present in governmental foreign cultural activities. The government proceeded slowly and cautiously in this new area of cultural diplomacy. The first moves of the federal government were in the area of educational exchanges. Little opposition was voiced. Within the United States educational community, there was a great deal of sentiment in favor of government support of educational exchanges and the development of the exchange program was welcomed.

It was in the area of broadcasting—specifically, shortwave radio broadcasting to Latin America—that the first major debate over the government's efforts in cultural diplomacy first occurred. The relations between private broadcasters and the federal government, although generally hostile and antagonistic during much of the New Deal, were based on a division of control and responsibilities. The federal government had control over the general field of spectrum management and utilization. Private broadcasters were licensed to use portions of the spectrum. Within very broad limits, the management of broadcasting and the direction and control or radio content were left explicitly in the hands of private broadcasters. However, the relations that existed at the domestic level could not simply be extended to the international level. Foreign broadcasting was an activity which had a very close bearing and effect on the practice of foreign policy, which was explicitly in the domain of the federal government. With the federal government moving toward a practice of cultural diplomacy, it was only natural that the administration policy makers saw in shortwave radio, heretofore an activity left solely up to the private broadcasters, a useful method of achieving foreign policy aims. If the federal government was to use shortwave, the relations between private broadcasters and the government needed to be re-assessed and reformulated.

Shortwave Broadcasting and Latin America

Although United States radio and broadcasting companies had developed and dominated the field of international shortwave radio broadcasting in the 1920s, they were unable to develop any immediate practical commercial application for shortwave broadcasting. By the mid-1930s, the field of United States shortwave radio broadcasting had stagnated. Not wanting to relinquish their shortwave licenses, which could prove to be of some value or use, in the future, broadcasters maintained their transmitters and routinely renewed their licenses. The content of United States shortwave broadcasters consisted primarily of simulcasts of regular domestic programming, with little effort to develop any special type of programming for foreign audiences. Although, in their simulcasts, they also broadcast regular network radio commercials, the shortwave service was noncommercial, and the broadcasters could not sell time specifically on their shortwave transmissions.

This state of affairs was in marked contrast to shortwave development elsewhere in the world. Just about the time that United States interest in shortwave was waning, the broadcasting organizations of a number of European countries with colonial empires began investigating the medium with the aim of developing an international broadcasting capability. In 1927, Holland began experimenting with shortwave services to the Dutch Indies, and by 1929 had instituted a regular broadcasting schedule to these islands. Also in 1927, the British Broadcasting Corporation began experimental overseas transmissions, although, due to financial difficulties, it was not until 1932, that a regular service was organized. France inaugurated its regular shortwave service in 1931, and in 1934 Belgium instituted daily shortwave broadcasts to the Belgian Congo.

These shortwave broadcasts were aimed at the colonial possessions of the respective European powers, with the goal of maintaining and strengthening the imperial ties in the face of growing threats by newly emerging nationalists and separatist forces. In general, the broadcasts were in the language of the mother country and were aimed at the small colonial elites. Broadcasts consisted of news and items about the home country, music, and other programs similar to the radio fare available back in Europe. The themes of empire unity and solidarity were stressed. One exception to this general description was the French service, which also carried broadcasts in the major native language of the various French colonial areas, reflecting the French colonial policy of assimilation. Although all the European shortwave services were directed primarily to the colonial possessions, the broadcasts could be heard and tended to attract audiences in other countries. This was particularly true of Latin America, where the French broadcasts were especially popular.[17]

Aside from their larger political function of maintaining and strengthening traditional colonial ties, these shortwave broadcasts were not explicitly political. In contrast, the Soviet Union had recognized early the explicit political potential of radio. It had begun international broadcasting activities as early as 1918, when it broadcast radio telegraphic appeals to German soldiers to mutiny. However, the effectiveness of its international broadcasts was limited, due to the fact they were transmitted on long and medium waves. It was not until the mid-1930s that the Soviet Union developed an effective shortwave capability.

The purpose and nature of Germany's shortwave activity represented a new development in international broadcasting. Although experimental broadcasts were made from the German short wave transmitter at Zeesen, a small village near Berlin, as early as 1927, regular shortwave service was not inaugurated until the Nazis' assumption of power. German shortwave broadcasts were aimed at German immigrant communities in other nations. Such broadcasts, as noted earlier, were part of a larger effort organized by the Propaganda Ministry to gain control over German elements in other countries and sway public opinion in general in favor of Nazi Germany. The first broadcasters began in April 1933 and consisted of daily 2-hour programs of news and talk in German and English, and of musical selections directed toward North America. The next year, broadcasting services were expanded with the use of new directional antennas and special programming aimed at Africa, the Far East, and South America. In 1935, shortwave services and programs for South Asia, Australia, and Central America were added.

As the largest number of German emigrants lived in the Western Hemisphere, North and South America were of particular importance to the German progaganda effort. Special efforts were made to appeal both to

Latin American German and native audiences. In 1935, the Nazis organized a special broadcasting department for developing programming and services for South and Central America. By fall 1936, Nazis were broadcasting approximately 42 hours a week—6 hours daily—of special programming to Latin America. Aside from musical selections which comprised over half of the transmission line, the bulk of the programming consisted of news and talks in German aimed at the German-speaking community in the region. Also included in the total weekly programming were 2½ hours of news in Spanish and Portuguese, an amount which comprised a little more than one-fifth of the total non-musical programming.[18]

Although United States shortwave broadcasters made little effort to provide special programming for foreign audiences, the few efforts which were made were generally intended for Latin American audiences. Westinghouse's first foreign language broadcast, made in March 1924, was in Spanish and was aimed at Latin American audiences. Although little information remains about early Westinghouse foreign language shortwave broadcasters, most likely they were comprised of talks concerning current events followed by appropriate musical selections. In 1927, General Electric began a brief nightly newscast in Spanish. Two years later, Westinghouse began to broadcast Department of Agriculture reports on wool and livestock prices to Latin America over its shortwave transmitter. In 1931, General Electric began special broadcasts of closing New York Stock Market prices to Latin America, where they were often reprinted in local newspapers. Also, Latin American ambassadors to the United States were occasionally invited to speak over General Electric's shortwave broadcasts during special programs commemorating the national holidays of the individual Latin nations. Although minor and sporadic in nature, these early attempts at special foreign programming do reveal that United States broadcasters were inclined to view Latin America as a major audience for their services, based on the close economic ties between the two continents. General Electric, for example, in its unsuccessful attempt to get permission from the Federal Radio Commission in 1930 to sell advertising on its shortwave service, noted that it had built up a sizeable audience in Central and South America. In applying for a shortwave license in 1930, the Isle of Dreams Broadcasting Company told the government that it wanted to use the shortwave transmitter to relay programs to Central and South America and predicted that the service would "aid in promoting good will and commerce between these countries."[19]

The interest of the United States government in Latin American shortwave broadcasting also dates back to the late 1920s and early 1930s. Like the shortwave broadcasters, the government's efforts in this area were sporadic and generally uninformed by any larger sense of purpose, direction, understanding, or appreciation of the possibilities of shortwave radio broadcasting. The first major activity by the government in hemi-spheric shortwave broadcasting revolved around the disposition and use of the so-called Pan American frequencies. In 1929, the Navy Depart-ment, alert to the future value of the shortwave spectrum, registered five unused frequencies (6120, 9550, 11730, 15130, and 21500 kH) with the Bureau of the International Telegraph Union at Berne. Later, feeling that the newly developed medium of shortwave radio might be of some use and value to the Pan American Union's work, President Hoover, over a 4-year period, assigned the use of these Navy frequencies to the Pan Ameri-can Union. One of these five frequencies was then temporarily assigned to CBS for its shortwave activities. Although the Pan American Union made no use of these frequencies, these assignments were reconfirmed by Roose-velt in December 1933 in a routine general allocation of all government frequencies.[20]

Later that month, at the inter-American conference in Montevideo, the Director of the Pan American Union approached Secretary Hull, head of the United States delegation, and asked him to present a resolution noting the existence and availability of these frequencies and their potential in "promoting better understanding among American republics by broad-casting...music and addresses on cultural and intellectual lines." The resolution would recommend that the American governments develop shortwave facilities in order to make use of these Pan American frequen-cies, and that the Pan American Union be directed to formulate a plan for the allocation of time over these frequencies to the various countries. Hull, unacquainted with the subject, wired the State Department, asking for information and direction. The State Department, in its reply, noted that these frequencies were unused. It had been the Department's plan, given the approval of the Navy Department and the necessary appropria-tion, to buy transmission equipment (estimated cost around $50,000) for broadcasting use by the Pan American Union. While the Department in-dicated that such a resolution would be in line with Department policy, it was concerned about the type of inter-American programming to be broadcast, particularly given the current war between Paraguay and Bolivia. The shortwave station the State Department was initially contem-plating would broadcast programs "confined to music." It suggested that Hull see that the resolution contain language insuring that Pan American broadcasting "would tend to build up rather than destroy friendly rela-tions among the American Republics."[21]

Changing the language in line with such considerations, the delegation proposed the nonbinding resolution, and the Conference approved it on December 24, 1933. The resolution recommended that the American gov-ernments utilize the Pan American frequencies as soon as possible for the broadcasting of inter-American radio programs containing "the music of

the several countries and addresses on their cultural and intellectual life."
The Pan American Union was instructed to take the steps necessary to
bring about the utilization of these frequencies.

After the Conference, officials of the Pan American Union contacted
American governments about their possible use of the Pan American frequencies. A number of governments—Mexico, Bolivia, Ecuador, and the
Dominican Republic—replied that they had shortwave broadcasting transmitters and were interested in any plans for the development of some type
of Pan-American broadcasting system. However, like many of the nonbinding resolutions approved at the inter-American conferences, the idea
of a Pan American broadcasting system was strong on good intentions and
very weak on implementation. Overall, the idea was vague and ill-formed
and much confusion surrounded the possible implementation of the resolution.[22]

For example, Secretary Hull, back in Washington, requested that the
Federal Radio Commission study the resolution and provide some information and guidance as to the possible nature and organization of a system
of Pan-American broadcasting. Based on its reply, it was apparent that the
Commission regarded the Pan American frequencies and any Pan American broadcasting as the sole property and activity of the United States
government. The station would be based in Washington, D.C. It would be
Pan American in the sense that it would broadcast programs to Latin
America "of a Pan-American nature." Examples of such programs were
the events and activities of the Pan American Union in Washington,
speeches by high United States government officials, and concerts by
United States military bands and noted private orchestras. The Commission felt that such Pan American broadcasts would only take up a small
amount of time. When not broadcasting to Latin America, the station and
the frequencies could be used to broadcast programs over shortwave to audiences in the United States. Examples of such programs the Commission
considered appropriate for this station were ones dealing with "the aims,
functions and policies of government," "debate and discussion about current governmental problems, interpretation and obeyance of laws," and
"the rationalization of public life by the development of a new type of
statesman and a new type of voter."[23] In its consideration of a Pan American station and Pan American broadcasting, the Commission totally
omitted any consideration of broadcasting by the other American republics to the United States or the possibility of inter-American program exchanges. Also the suggestion that the shortwave station could also be used
for domestic broadcasting much in the same way as a medium wave station reflected a misconception about the nature of shortwave radio. The
Commission succeeded in combining an ignorance of shortwave radio
broadcasting with a patronizing and imperialistic attitude toward the role
of radio in hemisphere affairs.

Due to such confusion and disagreement as to the role, nature, and control of any proposed Pan American broadcasting, the resolution approved at Montevideo was never carried out, and after a time the Pan American Union gave up trying to organize some kind of inter-American use of the Pan American frequencies. Nonetheless, this episode demonstrates that, as early as 1933, the federal government was interested in the construction of a radio station and saw radio broadcasting as playing a role in the Good Neighbor Policy. However, confusion as to the specific purpose and organization of such broadcasting obstructed the implementation of the Montevideo resolution. Moreover, the Navy Department, as the most likely operator of the station, was not enthused about getting into the broadcasting business. After a while, plans for a government station were put aside.[24]

The Montevideo radio resolution apparently had little impact on the private broadcasters who paid little attention to it and continued their shortwave activities unchanged. The growth of German and other nations' radio broadcasting to Latin America also provoked little response or concern among the private broadcasters. For example, in the summer of 1934, the *New York Times* reported that both German and French shortwave broadcasters heard in Latin America contained material which promoted the sales of these countries' goods. Such broadcasts consisted of music and entertainment interspersed with talks or items which praised the quality and workmanship of various French and German products. Officials from NBC responded with promised plans to match such trade promotion: "If it is to be a battle of music and words, we will be in the thick of the fight." However, despite such vigorous words, neither NBC nor any other shortwave broadcaster changed its programming in any way to counter the German and French promotional broadcasts.[25]

Thus, through the first part of the decade, while both the government and private broadcasters expressed interest in shortwave broadcasting to Latin America at various times, overall, very little was done. While the broadcasters made a number of technical improvements in line with the experimental nature of their activity and licenses, the United States was steadily losing its position in international shortwave. By 1938, the two 40 kw transmitters operated by General Electric and Westinghouse, the most powerful in the United States, were being dwarfed by the eight 50 kw transmitters operated by Germany and the five 50 kw transmitters operated by Great Britain.[26]

In 1936, there began to emerge a new government interest in shortwave radio, this time on the part of the Commerce Department's Bureau of Foreign and Domestic Commerce. The Bureau, which was charged with the promotion of United States foreign trade, saw in shortwave a possible method of increasing trade with Latin America. Concerned with the aggressive promotional techniques used by Nazi Germany to expand its

Latin trade, techniques which included extensive mail and newspaper advertising along with shortwave radio promotion, the Bureau urged American exporters to match such efforts.

As noted in Chapter II, the Bureau was very active in developing information about advertising possibilities and practices in foreign markets. It was particularly interested in the use of broadcast advertising, a field which the United States pioneered, as a means of foreign trade promotion. As an aid for United States exporters, it issued a series of reports in 1932 dealing with the possibilities of broadcast advertising in Asia, Africa, Europe, and Latin America.[27] By the mid-1930s, it was evident that United States exporters were beginning to utilize advertising on the local broadcast media in various foreign markets. According to one estimate, foreign broadcast advertising by United States exporters in 1935 totaled more than $10 million, a 700 percent increase over the amount spent the previous year, and roughly one-tenth of United States domestic radio advertising sales. The next year the amount doubled. Latin America was seen as a particularly good place for radio advertising. With the exception of Radio Luxembourg, which grossed over $1 million from United States advertisers in 1935, European stations either banned or severely restricted all radio advertising. Outside Shanghai, the possibilities of radio advertising in Asia were limited. "In contrast," reported *Business Week* in 1936, "Central and South America are wide open to exploitation, and the high rate of illiteracy makes radio the only effective direct-to-consumer advertising medium. Loudspeakers in public squares help spread the advertising gospel."[28]

Most of the foreign radio advertising was arranged by New York agencies specializing in such matters. Much of the actual production was done in New York, where recorded transcriptions were made and sent to agency representatives in foreign markets, who then placed the advertisements on local radio stations. Alternatively, in cities such as Buenos Aires, where there was a large pool of local talent and suitable production and studio facilities, the agency representative would arrange for live local commercial production. In 1935, Broadcast Abroad Inc., one of the major agencies specializing in such foreign radio advertising, served as the United States representative and had advertising contracts with 47 radio stations in 16 Latin American and Caribbean countries. Among the commercials heard on local Latin radio were advertisements for companies and products such as Parker Pen, Quaker Oats, Standard Oil, Ford Motor Company, Heinz Ketchup, Listerine, Oxydol, and over 50 other products and companies.[29]

While it was apparent that United States exporters were developing the potential of Latin American radio advertising, the Bureau of Foreign and Domestic Commerce was also interested in exploring the possibilities of shortwave radio as a means of promoting United States exports in Latin America. In the summer of 1936, the Bureau took the first step by sending advance schedules of United States shortwave broadcasts to United States embassies. These schedules were prepared by the Radio Manufacturers Association, which was interested in popularizing United States shortwave programs overseas as a means of expanding markets for shortwave sets. The Bureau distributed the schedules to the commercial attachés in the various embassies, instructing them to distribute them to local newspapers. Along with the schedules was a booklet showing the use that United States newspapers made of similar program material on foreign shortwave broadcasts. The response to these advance schedules was so great that the Bureau quickly expanded the service and sent schedules to whoever requested them. Among those receiving schedules were Latin American educators, businessmen, journalists, and government officials. The shortwave broadcasting companies, however, were not very happy about the Bureau's activities. Given the advance time period necessary for distributing the schedules overseas, the stations found that they had to commit themselves to a shortwave broadcasting schedule weeks in advance. They were thus obligated to plan and formalize their shortwave services to a greater degree than previously required.[30] Although this would seem to be a minor irritation to the broadcasters, it would be, as shall be shown, the first step in a long series of events in which the government, either directly or indirectly, forced the shortwave operators to expand their service and take their shortwave activities more seriously.

By 1935, the worsening European situation began to worry the Roosevelt Administration and, as noted above, one of the main purposes of the specially called inter-American conference in Buenos Aires in December 1936 was to devise measures to protect the Western Hemisphere, and the United States' dominant position within it, from the threatening world situation. The extent of German radio and other cultural activities was beginning to be regarded as serious and threatening to United States interests.

At the Buenos Aires conference, in line with the new United States-supported emphasis on cultural matters, a number of resolutions dealing with inter-American radio broadcasting were considered. One major resolution recommended the establishment of the Pan American radio hour, a shortwave broadcasting program in which all the American nations would participate. The Pan American hour would "comment upon all happenings of importance occurring in the nations of the continent. . . announce Government dispositions of major importance. . . take advantage of national independence anniversaries. . . and provide knowledge concerning various aspects of different countries, such as statistical reports, geographical, historical, folklore and other information." The resolution represented another, yet far more modest, attempt to organize an inter-American system of broadcasting exchanges and to use the radio as a means of developing closer ties among the American republics. In contrast to the earlier attempt at Montevideo, the implementation of this resolution was more successful. A number of Pan American Hour programs were organized by the Pan American Union and aired over private United States shortwave broadcasting stations in 1937 and 1938. Generally, however, such programs tended to consist of United States government officials and educators speaking to Latin American audiences on Latin American subjects.[31]

Aside from reaffirming and expanding the interests of the United States government in hemispheric radio, another important outcome of the Buenos Aires conference was that it gave United States broadcasters an opportunity to become acquainted with the Latin American radio situation, and to consider seriously the development of shortwave services directed primarily toward Latin American audiences. John Royal, NBC's vice-president in charge of programs, and Paul White, CBS's director of special events, both left for the Buenos Aires conference in November 1936 to arrange special broadcasts of the conference proceedings for transmission to the United States. This was the first time that representatives from a major United States broadcasting organization visited South America. As part of their trip, they toured and inspected the broadcasting facilities in major Latin American countries, including Brazil, Argentina, Mexico, Chile, and Uruguay. They found Latin American broadcasting practices "backward," the most serious faults being the lack of precise timing in programming schedules and an underdeveloped broadcast advertising industry. Nonetheless, they were impressed with the growth and potential of Latin American radio, and a number of special program exchanges were arranged between the major Latin American stations and the two United States networks.[32]

In one sense, this trip by Royal and White represents the real beginning of United States shortwave broadcast activity in Latin America. During the next year, 1937, all the major United States shortwave broadcasters began major improvements in their service to Latin America. NBC and CBS installed directional antennas and more powerful transmitters, especially for transmissions to Latin America. In March, CBS hired a full-time Spanish speaking announcer to organize special broadcasts to Latin America, and, in May, it set up its shortwave operations as a separate department with its own staff. In July, NBC began having its regular network musical programming, which was broadcast to Latin America introduced by Spanish and Portuguese announcers. In August, General Electric began construction of a new 100 kw shortwave transmitter in Schenectady especially designed for transmission to Latin America. In October, Westinghouse announced that it was reorganizing its shortwave activities and altering the design of its transmitters in order to provide stronger and improved shortwave service to Latin America.[33]

The new interest in Latin American broadcasting could be explained in part by the fact that recent developments and innovations in shortwave technology—the use of high power transmisison and directional antennas —made north–south transmission feasible. Previously, atmospheric disturbances at the equator often interferred with transmission to Latin America. Added to this were the growth of Latin American radio audiences, the relatively unregulated nature of Latin American broadcasting, and the availability of shortwave sets, all of which suggested that there were numerous opportunities to be explored for the commercial exploitation of Latin American broadcasting. Moreover, in 1936 the Federal Communications Commission, as part of an overall investigation and allocation of services in the high frequency of the spectrum, rewrote existing regulations on shortwave, putting them more in line with actual international shortwave broadcasting practice. Rather than being termed as an experimental relay service, the Commission reclassified shortwave broadcasting as the experimental transmission of broadcast programs for direct international public reception.[34] Thus, the broadcasters were able to develop this service as direct international broadcasting without any fear of government objection.

However, in themselves, such factors do not explain the sudden new interest in shortwave. Government regulations still prohibited the sale of commerical time on shortwave transmissions. Moreover, the characteristics of the Latin American shortwave audience were largely unknown, making the service useless to advertisers who put their advertising dollars in local Latin American radio stations. More important than the possibility of the immediate commercial exploitation of shortwave was the broadcasters' fear that the federal government, in becoming more and more concerned about Nazi propaganda in Latin America, would build its own shortwave stations to counter it. For example, *Broadcasting*, in reporting the trip by Royal and White to Latin America in November 1936, devoted a large amount of space to altering broadcasters to the ominous possibility that, at the Buenos Aires conference, Secretary Hull might propose the construction of a government-owned shortwave station in Washington for the purpose of broadcasting programs in Latin America. The magazine hinted that such a proposal was alive and being actively considered by the State Department, something for which there is no evidence.[35]

Whatever fears the broadcasters had about the State Department were greatly aggravated by Federal Communications Commissioner George Henry Payne, an old line Progressive Republican and staunch critic of the broadcasting industry. In a speech in early January 1937, Payne described the important need for a government shortwave station to broadcast to

Latin America in order to promote better understanding and relations between the United States and Latin America. Such a station, according to Payne (incorrectly), had been proposed at the 1933 Montevideo Conference, and afterwards there had been plans to build such a station. However, Payne charged that attempts to build the station were continually being frustrated by "unscrupulous and misguided captains in industry." He accused the broadcasters, "a selfish minority whose only object is to exploit the public with commercial nostrums for their own financial enrichments," with seriously endangering the national interest by secretly obstructing attempts by the government "to defend itself over the air from the attacks of foreign or unfriendly agencies." He claimed he had "complete documentary evidence. . . including the names of the persons and organizations involved" to back up his charges of almost treasonous behavior on the part of the broadcasters. Payne threatened that, "unless constructive steps are taken by the industry to clean up some of the flagrant violations of public confidence and support, Congress itself will be obliged to take an active hand in the matter."[36]

Whatever evidence Payne had of a conspiracy by broadcasters to sabotage a government station, he never revealed it. Payne was correct in noting that the broadcasters objected to a government station. One, of course, would expect such opposition, given the industry's general position that the government should stay out of broadcasting as much as possible. However, such an objection was intensified by the greater fear that a government shortwave station would be the first step in a government takeover of broadcasting. Such a fear reflected the state of government–broadcasting industry relations during much of the 1930s. While the industry called for and welcomed government regulation in the 1920s as a means of rationalizing private control of the field, such regulation was carried out under pro-business Republican administrations. The depression and the New Deal totally unsettled the close relations which had existed between government and business. The government assumed an activist role in the affairs of business in order to achieve solutions to the social and economic problems of the depression. Of course, the New Deal reforms were essentially conservative, in that they left untouched the basic structure of United States capitalism while defining a more activist role for the government in the maintenance and protection of that structure.[37]

Yet such assessments are made only with the benefit of hindsight. To the businessman and private broadcaster of the time, who evaluated New Deal policies in the context of the past policies of Harding, Coolidge, and Hoover, the actions of the New Deal were radical, if not revolutionary. Moreover, the direction the Roosevelt Administration would take was, to the businessman, always unpredictable. Even as late as 1938, after the New Deal had passed its apogee, a moderate governmental reoganization proposal was defeated in Congress due to the strong opposition of business-men and conservatives who felt it gave the President unprecedented and almost dictatorial powers.

Given the suspicions and mistrust of the business community and, alter-natively, the President's penchant for pointing to selfish and greedy capi-talists as the major cause of the depression, there was little wonder that broadcasters saw in any talk of a government station a larger conspiracy to take over domestic broadcasting altogether. Moreover, that in the winter of 1936–1937 such talk was emerging again was particularly ominous. In the November election, not only did the President receive the largest plu-rality in history, but his party held almost four-fifths of the seats in Con-gress. There was no telling what new outrages and attacks against business Roosevelt would commit in his second term.

A Proposed Government Shortwave Station and the Formulation of Government Policy on Shortwave Broadcasting

It was not long before the talk about a government station took more defi-nite form. On February 3, 1937, less than a month after Payne's attack on the broadcasters and their presumed obstruction of a government station, Representative Emanuel Celler, Democrat of New York, introduced legis-lation calling for the construction of a government shortwave radio sta-tion. The bill appropriated $750,000 for a shortwave radio station to be built in Washington, D.C. and operated by the Navy Department using the Pan American frequencies. The station was to transmit programs for reception in Latin America; $100,000 was to be appropriated annually to the United States Commissioner of Education who would produce the pro-gramming. General policies of the station would be determined by a nine-member advisory board consisting of the Secretary of State, the Director General of the Pan American Union, the Chairman of the Federal Com-munications Commission, and five other individuals appointed by the President.

In drawing up the legislation, Celler was assisted by Commissioner Payne, and it was evident that much of Celler's concern and knowledge of this issue came from Payne. He repeated Payne's earlier argument that such a station had been proposed and approved at Montevideo, that spe-cial frequencies had been set aside by the President for the station, and that the station would have been built except for the strong and secret op-position from the private broadcasters.

In making the argument on behalf of a government station, both Celler and Payne were engaging in some fanciful reconstruction of past events. As noted above, the Pan American frequencies had been first set aside by

President Hoover and one temporarily assigned to CBS for its shortwave use. Roosevelt, in an Executive Order dated December 2, 1933, had reconfirmed the Pan American allocations as part of a more general allocation plan for all government frequencies. There is no evidence that there was any special intention or purpose behind the reconfirmation of the Pan American frequencies. Moreover, the contention that these frequencies were set aside in order to be used by a government station in accordance with the Montevideo resolution is belied by the fact that the Executive Order was issued before the Montevideo Conference even began and, also, before the Director of the Pan American Union approached the United States delegation with the suggestion for the resolution. Thus, it was incorrect to state that Roosevelt, in pursuance of the Montevideo resolution, had set aside five frequencies for a government station. Both Celler and Payne were attributing far more planning and conscious effort to the earlier discussions within the State Department about broadcasting to Latin America than the evidence suggests existed. Moreover, in presenting this account, Celler consistently stated that the Montevideo Conference took place in December 1932, not 1933. This, of course, could be a minor slip of the tongue. Nonetheless, putting the conference back a year made his account internally consistent.

However, it was not the juggling of the historical record that disturbed the broadcasters. Celler, in repeating Payne's earlier speech almost word for word, noted that private broadcasters feared that a government shortwave station would lead to a government takeover of domestic broadcasting. To such fears he responded, "That is ridiculous. . . . One Pan American shortwave station, set up in pursuance of the treaty, in an unassigned channel, on a non-competitive basis, will not in the slightest militate against private initiative. It will not lead to government monopoly."

Yet, despite such reassurances, Celler also argued that the station could be used for broadcasting to United States audiences as well. Drawing from the earlier 1934 Federal Radio Commission report to Hull on Pan American broadcasting, Celler declared that such a station could also broadcast to over 2,000,000 shortwave sets in the United States. Domestic broadcasts would consist, echoing the Commission's earlier words, of programs dealing with "Aims, function, and policies of government. . . interpretations and obeyance of laws. . . the relationalization of public life."

Under this bill, when the government was not using the broadcasting station, private companies could use it as long as their programming was non-commercial and "controlled and censored by the Commissioner of Education." In addition, all private stations throughout the country could rebroadcast any programs of this station over regular frequencies. Apparently, Celler felt that such proposed cooperation between the government and private broadcasters would allay any fears of a government takeover. According to Celler, this station was not meant to pose a threat to private enterprise and, therefore, there was no reason to oppose it. Yet in a manner not calculated to still their doubts, Celler demanded that private broadcasters "must now cease their opposition, else they will get their fingers burned."

In presenting this legislation, Celler argued that it was in line with administration policy and furthered administration goals. In the area of foreign policy, the station would create "good will between this and other nations...eradicate international misunderstanding...[and] develop two-way trade between the United States and other nations by propagandizing for our own products, indicating to foreigners the worth-while-ness of our goods, and encouraging importation of our goods."[38] The threat of the Nazi radio propaganda to United States interests in Latin America was mentioned only in passing, reflecting the fact that the concern and knowledge of such radio activity was not yet widespread. Over the next year, however, in part due to Celler's proposal, more attention would begin to be paid to the extent and seriousness of Nazi broadcasting to the region.

The response by the broadcasting industry was predictable. At its annual convention in June, the National Association of Broadcasters passed a resolution expressing its opposition to the Celler bill and urging all members to work for its defeat.[39] Yet the private shortwave broadcasters no doubt realized that the Celler bill touched upon a real problem. With the increasingly disturbing world situation, government concern over the decline in the United States position in international broadcasting would grow greater, not lessen. While the fear on the part of the broadcasters over a government takeover of domestic broadcasting was real, it was hard to deny that the government, as part of its constitutional powers in the field of foreign affairs, had a legitimate interest in maintaining this country's position in the field of international broadcasting. In addition to opposing the Celler bill, private shortwave broadcasters, as noted above, began to upgrade their shortwave services in order to forestall government action.

The response of the administration to the Celler bill was not as clear as that of industry. In presenting the bill, Celler indicated that he had encouragement from individuals in the State, Interior, and Agriculture Departments, the Federal Communications Commission, and the Pan American Union. Moreover, he declared that the construction of a government radio station had the support of the President, the Secretary of State, and others in the administration. Later in July, Celler reported that Hull had recommended to the President that the administration support the bill.[40] Overall, Celler attempted to project his bill as having strong administration backing.

In fact, the administration response to his bill was evasive. Although the administration favored increased shortwave broadcasting to Latin America, something that would fit into its larger political and economic goals in the hemisphere, the administration was not particularly happy that Celler had taken the initiative on the issue of shortwave broadcasting. Yet, the administration could not oppose the bill without offering an alternative. Rather than reflecting the administration's wishes, the Celler bill had the effect of forcing the administration to confront the issue of this country's declining position in international broadcasting. Yet, the legislation proved to be very useful. By the response and reaction to the bill from the broadcasting industry, Congress, and other important sectors, the administration was able to gauge the strength of support and opposition to the measure, and the various options on the issue, without having to commit itself prematurely.

The development of an administration policy and position on shortwave broadcasting proceeded slowly throughout 1937 and early 1938. Overall, the process of development revealed the different sets of concerns, viewpoints, and interests over the issue that existed within the administration. In February 1937, partially in response to the Celler bill and partially in response to the growing Nazi activity in Latin America that he had observed while attending the Buenos Aires conference the previous December, Secretary Hull solicited comments from United States embassies in Latin America regarding the reception of United States shortwave broadcasting to the region. Typical of the responses Hull received was the one from the United States Minister in Bolivia:

> I am forced to the admission that the powerful shortwave stations in Europe have practically dominated the air in South America. . . . The European governments have been expending very large sums of money to this end. . .[and] very little, if anything, has been done by our privately owned broadcasting stations to meet, in the public interest, this competition from Europe.
>   . . . I am not suggesting that our government should go into the broadcasting business for I believe that the present American programs have a definite appeal to a large audience on the continent—if they could be consistently received. Practically every radio sold in Latin America is built to cover the shortwave bands, and the great majority are of American manufacture. This valuable market, in which we have such preeminence, is worth an effort to retain, but I already notice that broadcasts from Germany, given in German and Spanish, speak of the high quality of German radio receivers, recommending the purchase of a German-made set if full value of the quality of the transmission is to be obtained. Likewise, recent broadcasts from the same source have extolled the virtues of German-made cars, and their economy in gasoline.
>   . . . There is nothing wrong with American radio programs as far as their appeal to Latin American listeners is concerned; the problem is to get these

programs heard here in competition with those that come from Europe. This end can be accomplished only by the outlay of larger sums of money than the United States broadcasters are prepared to consider without the prospect of some commensurate return to their stockholders.[41]

Shortly thereafter, Hull wrote to Secretary of Commerce Daniel Roper asking his advice on this matter, noting, "The question of the reception of broadcasts from the United States in Latin America is a matter of great interest to this Department, and I shall appreciate any action which you believe your Department can take with a view to improving such reception."

Roper responded that the lack of reception was due to the inadequacy of the shortwave transmission equipment. He noted that the best way to insure an improvement in equipment was to allow the companies to pursue such broadcasting on a commercial basis. Observing that there was currently some discussion within the Federal Communications Commission to allow shortwave broadcasters to sell commercials on their shortwave transmissions, Roper concluded, "I understand the situation is being developed along appropriate lines and feel that it should be encouraged as one which will be helpful not only to American business, but to the international relations of our country as a whole."[42]

That the State Department was willing to defer to the Commerce Department in this matter was not surprising. At this point, the German broadcasts to Latin America were not yet openly hostile to the United States. Although the newscasts and radio talks reflected a Nazi view of the world, most of the news and programs tended to cultivate Latin American opinion by painting a glowing picture of the new order in Germany. An important component of these broadcasts was the promotion of German goods. While Secretary of State Hull and the State Department were no doubt concerned with the growing Nazi activity in Latin America, they tended to regard the Nazi and other European shortwave broadcasts to Latin America primarily in terms of their effect on the United States' trade with the region. They were concerned that broadcasts from the United States were losing out to the more powerful transmissions from Europe. As this was a matter concerning private United States companies and foreign trade promotion, the State Department turned to the Commerce Department for guidance.

In formulating Department policy on shortwave, Roper turned to the Business Advisory Council. The Council, a semi-official government body formed in 1933, was comprised of representatives of major United States corporations and was organized into committees and subcommittees dealing with different areas of business and commerce. Overall, the Council acted as a major forum for discussion of the major issues between business and government, and it served as the major conduit for the opinion of the business community into the policy making of the Department of Commerce and the New Deal as a whole. Overall, it was the businessmen's voice in the New Deal.

In March, Roper asked the Council to advise him on the entire question of shortwave radio broadcasting in Latin America. The matter was referred to the Council's Committee on Foreign Trade, headed by William Dickerman, President of American Locomotive Company. Initially, in line with Roper's thinking on the matter, the Committee took the position that the best way to improve the United States' position in shortwave, and to use shortwave to improve trade with the region, was to allow shortwave broadcasters to sell commercial time on shortwave broadcasts. The committee recommended against the construction of a government station. However, in July Dickerman met with representatives of General Electric, Westinghouse, CBS, NBC, and other shortwave broadcasting companies. The general consensus among the broadcasters was that they were not yet prepared to sell advertising time on shortwave. They knew very little about the Latin American audience, its size and tastes in radio programs. Given the lack of information, there was little demand by exporters for such advertising service. The broadcasters would offer such commercial service when they had developed a sufficient knowledge and coverage of the Latin market and when there was sufficient demand for the service.[44]

As a result, in July 1937, based on the Committee's report, the Council informed Secretary Roper that, while much progress had been made, "international shortwave broadcasting has not been developed sufficiently to warrent commercial programs that will reflect credit upon the United States or upon the companies which may be engaged in broadcasting." The Council urged the Department to "continue its program in investigation as to the commercialization of shortwave broadcasting." The Bureau of Foreign and Domestic Commerce was asked to gather as much information as possible regarding shortwave reception, listening habits, program tastes, and size of audience.

In line with the Council's recommendation, the Bureau sent a detailed questionnaire to all commercial attaches in Latin America. This was the first comprehensive attempt by either business or government to study the shortwave situation in Latin America. By October, the survey was completed and the results released to the private broadcasters and later to the public. The survey showed that shortwave programs from the United States were as popular, if not more popular, than the European programs. However, the reception from the United States was generally poor, and the powerful European stations, particularly the German stations, were increasingly interfering with United States broadcasts. The general conclusion drawn from the survey was that the United States was quickly losing out to German and other European shortwave programs in Latin America. The major problems, according to the survey, were the lack of power on the part of the United States stations and an inadequate number of frequencies on which to broadcast.[45]

Aside from the activities of the Department of Commerce, there were other indications that the government, rather than being committed to the idea of a government radio station, was leaning toward the interests of the private broadcasters. In September, acting upon the recommendation of the Interdepartmental Radio Advisory Committee, comprised of representatives of government departments using the radio frequencies allocated to the government, the Federal Communications Commission added the four unused Pan American frequencies to the international broadcasting band, making them available for assignment to private broadcasters. Their assignment, however, would be temporary, and they could be withdrawn and cancelled without notice. These frequencies were registered with the United States but had been unused since 1929. There was concern that at the upcoming International Radio Conference to be held in Cairo the next spring, several nations, particularly Germany and Italy, would demand that these frequencies be forfeited by the United States for nonuse and reassigned to those countries which were very actively engaged in international broadcasting. Thus, it was felt necessary that the frequencies be made use of as soon as possible. Rather than build a government station which would make use of these frequencies, the administration decided, for the time being, to let the private broadcasters have them. The Pan-American Union acquiesced in this move. Following the reassignment, General Electric, NBC, and World Wide Broadcasting all applied for these new frequencies. In hearings on the new allocations, the broadcasting companies noted the growing dominance of German shortwave in Latin America and argued that additional frequencies were needed if they were to do an adequate job in broadcasting to the southern continent. Because of World Wide's educational broadcasts to Latin America and Westinghouse's proposed plan of experimental shortwave broadcasting, the Commission awarded each of these broadcasters two of the four available frequencies. Within a month, both companies were using these frequencies for broadcasts to Latin America. In spite of such actions, private broadcasters still feared that the federal government was deeply committed to a government shortwave station and that such a station was the entering wedge of government intervention in broadcasting. In early spring 1938, *Broadcasting* reported that the proposed government shortwave station was the first step in a government plan to build a series of superpower stations aimed at domestic audiences.[46]

Proponents of the government radio station were also concerned about the administration's true intentions. Fearful that the Commission's action in making the Pan American frequencies available meant a lack of administration support for a government station, Celler, in November 1937, wrote the President, asking that he openly support his bill. More than a month later, after having sought the advice of Frank McNinch, Chairman of the Federal Communications Commission, Roosevelt responded in a brief note that he was studying the matter.[47]

Additional pressures were placed upon the administration to publicly take a stand on the issue of a government radio station when a bill similar to Celler's was introduced in the Senate in January 1938 by Senators Dennis Chavez of New Mexico and William McAdoo of California. The station proposed in the Senate bill would broadcast only to Latin America and would be built in San Diego, California. The station would be operated by the Department of State and would be designed to "strengthen the spiritual, political, and historical ties among the United States and the nations of the Western Hemisphere." Given the prestige of McAdoo, a powerful Democratic figure in the Senate, this bill represented a far more serious attempt than the Celler bill to have the government build a station.[48]

Roosevelt, growing concerned about German radio activity in Latin America, wanted something done, but he was not yet committed to any type of direct government intervention and involvement. After a cabinet meeting in February, he met privately with the Secretaries of State, Commerce, Interior, and Agriculture, and the head of the Export-Import Bank, and discussed ways in which Axis radio propaganda in Latin America could be countered. Secretary of the Interior Harold Ickes later described that discussion as "hazy," indicating Roosevelt's ideas on the matter were not yet well formulated. Nonetheless, the bills in Congress were making progress and hearings were scheduled on them in May. The administration, while very concerned about shortwave activity, was being asked to take a position on the matter of a government station.

Rather than being forced on this matter, Roosevelt, in late February, appointed an interdepartmental committee to examine the entire problem of international broadcasting. The Interdepartmental Committee to Study International Broadcasting was comprised of representatives from the Departments of State, Commerce, Interior, and Agriculture, and the Export-Import Bank. It was chaired by McNinch, and among the issues it was to study was the extent and seriousness of Nazi radio broadcasting in Latin America. Based on its investigation, it was to recommend to the President an appropriate course of action. In March, the Committee met with the representatives of the private shortwave broadcasting companies to learn of their operations and plans. In late April, McNinch met with the President to discuss the Committee's progress and noted to the press that its report and recommendations would be issued shortly. Although there was no official word, it was strongly expected that the Committee would recommend a government station to the President.[50]

As the Interdepartmental Committee was to recommend administration policy on shortwave, action on the Celler and Chavez bills was halted pending announcement of government policy. Nonetheless, as they had already been previously scheduled, committee hearings on these bills were held in mid-May. On May 12, hearings opened before a subcommittee of the Senate Interstate Commerce Committee on the Chavez-McAdoo bill. Chairing the hearings was the noted isolationist, Senator Homer T. Bone of Washington. Given the fact that the Interdepartmental Committee was still conducting its investigations, representatives from the State, Commerce, and Navy Departments were very reluctant to reveal anything of the administration's thinking on the matter. The only individuals appearing on behalf of the bills were the sponsors and some private individuals, such as Dr. Samuel Guy Inman, who were concerned with expanding cultural relations between the United States and Latin America. Appearing in opposition to the bill were the president of the National Association of Broadcasters and representatives from NBC, CBS, Westinghouse, and General Electric. Chavez and other proponents of the bills argued that a government station was necessary both to the development of closer inter-American cultural relations and as a defense against the growing Axis cultural and economic penetration into the region. While they recognized and appreciated the efforts of the private radio companies, they felt that only a noncommercial government-operated station could effectively promote the national interest on the international airwaves. Moreover, as the current private shortwave service was not able to offer any advertising, the proponents of the bill doubted the commitment and ability of the broadcasters to expand and improve their shortwave service with little hope of financial return. Overall, the ability of the shortwave broadcasters in pursuing and achieving the foreign policy goals was doubted.

Representatives from the shortwave broadcasting companies responded by describing their involvement and commitment to shortwave radio in great detail. For example, Frank Mason, the NBC vice-president in charge of international broadcasting, illustrated his discussion of NBC's efforts with two large volumes of exhibits which contained charts, graphs, and statistics showing the expansion of NBC special programming to Latin America. For example, in May 1938, NBC was programming 7 hours a week of news in Spanish and Portuguese to Latin America. Mason noted that NBC had set up a special International Division and proclaimed that NBC had 1,800 people involved in producing 54,531 programs totalling 19,842 hours for transmission to Latin America. That almost all of these programs were simulcasts of regular network programs, and that the 1,800 figure was the number of employees NBC had involved in regular network program production, was glossed over. All the other broadcasters made similar arguments, pointing to the expansion of their facilities and special programming to Latin America. On the question of commercial operation, the broadcasters felt that, while at some future time they would explore the possibility of selling advertising on shortwave, for the present they were satisfied in operating their shortwave stations as a noncommercial public service.

With regard to Nazi propaganda, the broadcasters acknowledged that there was a growing public concern about the effect such Nazi radio activity was having in Latin America. However, they noted that they had not seen any hard evidence either that Nazi broadcasts were being openly anti-United States, or that they were having any effect on, or causing any threat to, United States interests in the region. Much of the German material was, in the words of the CBS representative, promotional programs "proclaiming the beauty of Germany, and the quality of their products, and the splendid type of their merchandise." They argued that the best antidote to such broadcasts was not the construction and operation of a government station, something which borrows "the technique of dictator countries in which radio is the instrument of the central government, designed to serve the will and prejudice of the individual ruler."[51] Rather, private shortwave broadcasts not subject to government control of censorship and which present "an honest picture of life in the United States" would be far more effective in cultivating Latin American friendship and countering Nazi radio activity. Moreover, the broadcasters indicated their willingness to cooperate in any reasonable way with the government with regard to special programming in the region. They also proclaimed their openness in cooperating with the government in presenting domestic radio programs that would help further the aims of the Good Neighbor Policy. Thus, in the fall of 1937, CBS began broadcasting the program *Brave New World*, which was produced by the Federal Radio Workshop of the U.S. Office of Education and consisted of "dramatic episodes woven about the lives of statesmen, educators, poets and artists of Latin America from the days of the Conquistadores to the present."[52]

Overall, the broadcasters were fairly successful in making the argument that the purpose and goals of the Good Neighbor Policy in Latin America could be better served by private shortwave broadcasting stations, and that Nazi radio propaganda in Latin America was neither effective nor threatening to the interests of the United States in the region. They found a sympathetic listener in Senator Bone, who was suspicious that any government shortwave radio station would represent a growing involvement by the United States in world affairs. As he noted at the end of the hearings, "God was good to this Nation, and put two great oceans between us and people who might cause us trouble." Bone was convinced that most of the German programs consisted of harmless "chamber of commerce boosting."[53]

The hearings in the House on the Celler bill began a few days later. Overall, there were a repeat of the Senate hearings, with the same witnesses from the broadcasting companies presenting the same arguments and evidence. Representative Celler was the only witness to testify in favor of his bill. The Chairman of the Naval Affairs Committee, presiding over the hearings, was irked that no one from the administration appeared to testify for the bill. He continually asked Celler that, if he had all the administration support he claimed, where was it? Celler responded that there was an Interdepartmental Committee studying the matter. He promised that its report would be issued in a few days and that it would favor the construction of a government station. Moreover, he claimed he had been informed by the President that the members of the Interdepartmental Committee were going to testify on this bill.[54]

Unfortunately, Celler totally misjudged administration backing. The day after Celler testified, McNinch, Chairman of the Interdepartmental Committee, met with the President. After the meeting, McNinch announced that, rather than issue a report at that time, the Committee had been instructed by the President to study the matter further in order to investigate certain important phases of international broadcasting which, for lack of time, the Committee had not been able to study. The additional investigation would require several more months; thus, the reports would come out in the fall at the earliest. This being the case, McNinch and other members of the Committee would not be available to testify on any matter dealing with the proposals for a government radio station.[55]

The McNinch statement and the President's position must have come as a slap in the face to Celler. In any event, the administration's silence on this matter effectively killed any serious consideration of either the Celler or Chavez-McAdoo bills.

The administration's action, or lack of action, was most likely due to a number of factors. The response by the broadcasting industry and the shortwave broadcasters was strongly unified and effective. In the words of one critic of the industry, the broadcasters "put their publicity departments and spare vice-presidents to grinding out copy to sell the public and the Congress on the idea that they were doing a good job and that a government station would be a national calamity."[56] In addition to seeking to mobilize public opinion, they also quickly upgraded their services. The account of their shortwave activity presented at the hearings was impressive, even though most of the improvements in programming were superficial and put into effect only a few months before the hearings. Moreover, their transmitter power was far less than that of the European transmitters. Nonetheless, after the broadcasters' testimony, it was difficult for anyone to argue that they were not taking their shortwave activity seriously. The proponents of a government station were not successful in convincing anyone that the broadcasters were not serving the national interest. Moreover, within Congress there was not much support for the legislation.

Within the administration itself, there was no strong support for a government station. The Department of War and Navy, while not objecting to the station, felt it was a waste of money and that such broadcasting should be left to private companies. The Commerce Department actively opposed the construction of such a station, arguing that, if the government found it necessary to broadcast special programs to Latin America, it could make arrangements with the private broadcasters.[57]

Given this state of affairs, the administration declined to take a position on the Celler and the Chavez-McAdoo bills. The delayed, much awaited report of the Interdepartmental Committee, which was to reveal publicly the administration's position, was never released. Indeed, there is some question as to whether there ever was a report. Public mention of the Committee and its expected report became less frequent, and by 1939 the Committee seems to have become inactive. In any event, no general policy statement was ever issued by the administration on shortwave broadcasting.[58]

Yet, the lack of a formal administration policy was itself a policy decision. By neither openly supporting congressional efforts on behalf of a government station nor offering alternatives, the administration gave de facto support to the continued development of shortwave broadcasting by private interests. Further indications of the government's rejection of direct involvement in favor of private interests were given in November 1938, when the Interdepartmental Committee on Cooperation with the American Republics issued its report to the President. This Committee, formed the previous May and consisting of representatives from 13 government departments and agencies, including the Federal Communications Commission, was charged with formulating a program designed "to render more effective" the relations between the United States and Latin America. Its reports offered over 70 proposals for projects to be undertaken by the various departments and agencies. On the part of the Federal Communications Commission, the report enumerated three projects—international radio broadcasting, the elimination of radio interference, and technical assistance in radio communication—as part of a broad program of cooperation with Latin America. None of these proposals suggested the construction of a government radio station. Regarding international broadcasting, the report noted the existence of the Interdepartmental Committee to Study International Broadcasting and stated that its report would be released soon. Meanwhile, as part of its investigation of the matter, members of that Committee were "engaged through informal conferences with the American radio industry, in continuing efforts to develop further cooperation with Latin America and to raise the standard of programs transmitted abroad, especially to Latin America."[59]

That the government was now encouraging private broadcasters to expand and upgrade their service to Latin America was most evident in the activities of the Department of Commerce. In November 1938, the Foreign

Trade Committee of the Business Advisory Council issued its final report on international broadcasting. The report recommended "that the American government, our educational and business institutions and all others interested in improving international understanding should extend every possible assistance and cooperation to the American shortwave broadcasters, and in particular help them improve their services in three respects, namely Programs, Power and Publicity." The Committee recommended that improvements in programming and power could be best accomplished by either allowing commercial advertising on shortwave or by providing governmental subsidies to the private broadcasters, or both. It also recommended that the Department of Commerce expand its activities in publicizing overseas United States shortwave programs.[60]

Working closely with both the Business Advisory Council and with the private shortwave broadcasters was John H. Payne, head of the Electrical Division of the Bureau of Foreign and Domestic Commerce. Payne developed a very close working relationship with the private broadcasters, and it was evident that the Bureau was offering more than just passive encouragement. Describing his relationship with the private broadcasters in a June 1938 letter to the commercial attache in Buenos Aires, Payne wrote:

> As you know, I am keenly interested in the shortwave situation and feel strongly, as you do, that it is very important that this country should get more frequencies and more representative broadcasts on the ether. I have been frequently in touch with the broadcasting companies and feel they are responding in large measure.
>
> It may interest you to know that seven of the nine United States organizations doing shortwave broadcasting sent officials of their companies to meet with me in New York last December.... The two organizations which were not represented have the two least active stations and so it was not so important that they were not with us. Each time I go on business trips, I make a point of seeing these broadcasters and encouraging them in doing a better job. As you know, they get no compensation for this work, except as their names become better known throughout the world. They are not yet permitted to sell advertising services on these shortwave stations. Incidentally, the organizations preferred that our meetings would not be publicized in any way.[61]

Payne felt that only with shortwave broadcasting on a self-supporting basis could the United States commercial and political aims in Latin America be realized. Thus, he was very much interested in developing both Latin American shortwave audiences and advertiser demand for the service. He was constantly writing to the private broadcasters, relaying to them information received from commercial attachés in Latin America and offering suggestions and advice as to how the broadcasters could improve their service. He wrote to Frederick Willis of CBS, upon the latter's appointment as director of that network's shortwave service in January 1939:

> May I add my congratulations on your new assignment involving additional
> activities in connection with the shortwave broadcasting operations. . . . As
> you know, I have been particularly interested myself in encouraging the im-
> provement of shortwave broadcasting by United States broadcasters, and
> thus this announcement is of especial interest. I would like to assure you of my
> desire to cooperate in any way where our facilities—particularly in other
> countries—might be useful.

Based on the correspondence from the broadcasters to Payne, it was evident that their plans and ideas about shortwave broadcasting, and its
possible commercial exploitation, were very undeveloped. As the shortwave director at Crosley Broadcasting Corporation wrote Payne in early
1940, "Offhand, it would seem that most of us are still working in the dark
as far as international broadcasting is concerned."[62]

While Payne and the Department of Commerce were actively encouraging the commercial private broadcasters to expand their activities, the
one noncommercial broadcaster, Walter Lemmon of World Wide Broadcasting Corporation, was also expanding his shortwave activities into
Latin America. A major financial backer behind such activities was the
Rockefeller Foundation. In 1935, the Foundation appropriated $25,000 to
World Wide for the development of international educational radio,
allowing Lemmon to expand his World Radio University programming,
which consisted of lectures and language lessons. The next year, a 2-year
$40,000 grant was made to supplement the previous grant. In 1937, with
an additional $12,820 from the Foundation, World Wide began a series of
special broadcasts to Latin America. This series, done in cooperation with
the Pan American Union, was an attempt to realize the creation of the Pan
American Radio Hour called for in the resolution at the Buenos Aires Conference. The first broadcast, on October 29, 1937, began with a short
speech by Secretary of State Hull, followed by Lemmon and the Ecuadorian
ambassador in Washington. Later programs consisted of special talks on
inter-American topics, along with Latin American music. In 1938, the
Rockefeller Foundation made a $100,000 grant to World Wide to increase
its Latin American programming. By May 1938, the station was beaming
educational programs to Latin America 5 days a week, and in June 1939,
4½ hours a week of new programming were added. The motive behind
the broadcasts, according to one description, was "the drive towards international amity, the breaking down of prejudices, [and] the forgetting of
past wrongs." However, it was not clear how successful these broadcasts
were. As one observer noted, "Endeavoring to live up to its high sounding
name of World Radio University, World Wide's programs were almost
painfully intellectual and patronizing."[63]

Thus, by spring 1939, private broadcasters pointed toward Latin America and were in the process of greatly expanding their services. In order to

further encourage these shortwave broadcasters and provide them with some recompense, if not incentive, the government, in line with its pro-private interest orientation, took the next logical step. Without a formal hearing or any notice, the Federal Communications Commission in mid-May 1939 announced that it was revising the regulations on international shortwave broadcasting in order to open up shortwave channels to commercial programs. Starting on September 15, 1939, broadcasters would be permitted to sell time on their shortwave broadcasts to advertisers interested in reaching foreign audiences. Only products actually available to the foreign audiences would be advertised, and such advertisements could only contain the name of the sponsor and the name and general character of the commodity, service, or attraction advertised. In return for the opportunity to offer advertising, shortwave broadcasters were required to increase their transmisison power to at least 50 kw by July 1, 1940. At this point in time, the most powerful United States transmitters operated at 40 kw. Stations were also required to use directional antennas which would increase their effective radiated power by as much as 10 times. These required technical improvements would, in the words of the Commission, "enable the privately owned United States stations to compete with the government-owned stations of other countries."

The new rules demonstrated that the government had decided to rely totally on private broadcasters to develop United States shortwave transmission to Latin America. In the government's view, with expanded power and financial incentive, shortwave broadcasters would counter the German radio activity in Latin America and also expand trade with the region. As the Commission observed, "South America is subjected to a barrage of transmissions from European stations. . . but it is anticipated that henceforth the United States stations will obtain better coverage in the Latin American republics."[64]

The change in rules caught broadcasters off guard. There is no evidence that they requested such a change, nor were any of them prepared for the new regulations. As *Advertising Age* observed, none of the advertising agencies involved either in broadcast advertising or export advertising "seemed to have any idea of the reason back of this move." It was impossible to determine the size of shortwave audiences and their characteristics or tastes. "As far as *Advertising Age* has been able to determine, there is no present demand for advertising facilities of this character."[65]

Nonetheless, the broadcasting industry welcomed the change. *Broadcasting*, in an editorial titled "Good Neighbor Radio," noted that, in making the change in regulations, the government "proceeds sympathetically along the path decreed for American radio since its inception—namely, that it be conducted by private initiative and enterprise." The magazine observed that proposals for a government station to counter foreign propa-

ganda in Latin America were obviously not the "American way." Fortunately, "cooler heads have prevailed thus far to permit the privately
owned stations to assume the task." Commending the private broadcasters
on their efforts, the editorial concluded:

> Thus far, the impelling motive has been patriotism and an admitted convic-
> tion that they can do the job so well that the Government would have no
> cause to go into the broadcasting field on its own. And even Government,
> eager to develop foreign markets, can hardly begrudge these stations an op-
> portunity to earn at least part of their upkeep while at the same time extend-
> ing the institutional and sales power of radio to the field of foreign trade.[66]

However, if the broadcasters felt that they had won a victory by the
new rules, such a feeling must have been short-lived. When the actual
regulations were made public, the first clause contained the statement, "A
licensee of an international broadcasting station shall render only an international broadcasting service which will reflect the culture of this country
and which will promote international good will, understanding and cooperation." Broadcasters immediately charged that, in drawing up this "culture" rule, the Federal Communications Commission was attempting to
censor international broadcasts. Rather than submit to such presumed
censorship, some of the shortwave broadcasters hinted that they might
turn in their shortwave licenses and shut down their operations. The outcry was widespread, fueled in part by a major campaign organized by the
National Association of Broadcasters which involved sending over 3,000
letters to local broadcasters and opinion makers asking that they oppose
the Commission's action. In terms of the public response to the "culture"
rule, the outcry was not so much about international broadcasting, but
more about what broadcasters feared were the implications of the rule for
domestic broadcasting. It was noted that if the Commission could make
regulations regarding the content of international broadcasts, "it is but a
short step to similar restrictions on standard broadcasting service."[67]

Newspapers joined with broadcasters in denouncing the rule. The *New
York Times*, in an editorial, declared that the rule "might bring about real
censorship... If our international broadcast programs are to be censored
so that they shall not offend this or that foreign government, it is only a
step to the argument that it is at least as desirable to censor our domestic
programs so that they shall not offend our own government." The American Civil Liberties Union petitioned the Commission for a formal hearing
on the new rule, arguing that the phrases, "reflect the culture of this
country," and "promote international good will, understanding and cooperation." were so worded that they "smacked of censorship and with interference in the right of free speech."[68]

Joining the clamor were members of Congress. Senator Burton K.
Wheeler, Democrat of Montana and head of the Senate Interstate Com-

merce Committee, where broadcasting legislation originated, criticized the rule and the fact that the Commission had not held hearings. He hoped that the Commission would seriously contemplate its actions and reconsider the rule. In the House, Clarence McLeod, Republican from Michigan, drew applause when he demanded the resignation of the Commission members, declaring, "We must indict them for what they are—usurpers, law violators, and, worst of all, violators of their solemn oath to uphold the Constitution of the United States." Even Emanuel Celler called upon the Commission to change the rule.[69]

Initially, the Commission indicated that it would not reconsider the rule, but the barrage of criticism had its effect. Hearings on the new rule were scheduled for mid-July. Moreover, there were rumors that the Commission was going to back down. In opening the hearings on July 14, acting Commission Chairman Thad Brown announced that the "culture' rule would be suspended pending further consideration.[70] The Commission then issued a long statement, denying that it had any intention of censoring international broadcasts. They argued that international broadcasting, just as domestic broadcasting, had to serve the public interest. The rule was meant to define the public interest in the area of international broadcasting. In spite of such assurances, during the 3-day hearing broadcasters, civil libertarians, and representatives from the newspapers attacked the rule as a form of censorship. Commission members, on the other hand, felt that the broadcasting industry was using the "culture" rule, which the Commission initially thought would be noncontroversial and innocuous, as the basis for a gratuitous attack on the Commission's work. At the end of the hearing, the Commission said that no action on the rule would be taken until the fall. But as the rule was already suspended, broadcasters considered this a face-saving gesture on the part of the Commission.

On one level, this entire episode can be seen as revealing the climate of mistrust and suspicion between the broadcasting industry and the government which existed during much of the New Deal. The broadcasters were never really sure of the true intentions of the administration regarding the broadcasting industry. No doubt, part of the intensity of the broadcasting industry's response to the "culture" rule can be understood by the fact that this rule was promulgated at a time when the Commission was pursuing its investigation into network monopoly practices. To some, the rule was seen as the first step in a Commission campaign to "grab control of program content in general."[71]

Yet, while the industry as a whole was willing and ready to make an issue of the "culture" rule as part of its overall campaign against what was seen as creeping government interference and control of domestic broadcasting, the shortwave broadcasters had a special cause of complaint that had little to do directly with government interference in domestic broadcasting. The new rules issued by the Commission, while allowing for advertising, nonetheless placed a heavy financial burden on the shortwave broadcasters. They were required to invest in new, more powerful short-wave transmitters. This requirement, coupled with the "culture" rule, made the entire shortwave enterprise commercially unappealing. Broad-casters were afraid that the rule would be applied not only to program content, but to advertising content as well. *Broadcasting* noted that, with new investments in transmitters costing more than $100,000 each, "It is generally felt that the possibility of revenue from shortwave sponsors under the rigid limitations [of the 'culture' rule] are practically nil. . . . Moreover it is felt that domestic network advertisers would want to use the same programs for international broadcasts, rather than tailor new pres-entations at additional expense."[72]

Overall, part of the furor over the "culture" rule reflected the discom-fort the shortwave broadcasters felt at having to expand their shortwave services. No doubt they would have preferred to develop their shortwave broadcasting activities at their own pace, making large new investments in equipment only when they had a definite idea of the commercial poten-tial of shortwave, and some reasonable expectation of financial return. Yet, under these new rules, they most likely felt that they were being rushed into expanding their shortwave service before they were prepared. In a sense, this was the price they had to pay to insure that a government sta-tion would not be built. If the government, rather than building its sta-tion, required the broadcasters to make investments in transmitters, equipment, and programming, then at least the broadcasters wanted as much freedom as possible in developing shortwave as a commercial ser-vice. The "culture" rule defined shortwave broadcasting, first as a political activity meant to assist the administration in achieving its foreign policy goals, and second as a commercial activity meant to make a profit for the broadcasters. While no doubt aware of and in general agreement with the political purpose of shortwave broadcasting, the broadcasters wanted the order of priorities reversed. Their argument was that, if left to pursue their own commercial benefit, broadcasters, in the process, would help achieve the larger foreign policy and trade aims of the government.

The government, at this point, could have reconsidered the option of building a government station. Yet, this was not necessary, as the distance between the shortwave broadcasters and the government on this issue was not great. The broadcasters were willing to go along with the government as long as they were given a reasonable chance to either make a profit or break even. Based on the past evidence of the activity of the shortwave broadcasters and the seeming popularity of their programs with foreign audiences, the government had little reason to doubt, at least at this point, the broadcasters' argument.

The importance of an immediate expansion of United States shortwave activity became all the more urgent in September 1939, when war broke out in Europe. Rather than waste time quibbling about what, in essence, was a very minor matter, the government yielded to the broadcasters. Declaring that "the outbreak of the European war had injected into the problem of international broadcast regulations various additional factors," the Commission quietly suspended the "culture" rule indefinitely in mid-September. A month later, NBC announced that it had signed a contract with its first shortwave commercial sponsor.[73]

Thus, by the fall of 1939, the administration had developed a policy on shortwave which attempted to utilize such broadcasting in achieving foreign policy goals. To comprehend the nature and significance of this policy, one must examine it in terms of what it revealed, at this point in time, about United States–Latin American relations and relations between the government and the broadcasting industry.

As defined by this policy, the major role of shortwave broadcasting was the protection and expansion, first, of the commercial ties, and second, of the cultural ties, between the United States and Latin America. Although, during the period of 1936–1939, the aims and practice of cultural diplomacy were being developed, the administration regarded shortwave broadcasting to Latin America primarily as a commercial weapon. Yet, one should not insist too strongly on this distinction. To many policy makers and trade promoters in government, the expansion of commercial relations implied closer cultural ties. In any event, in shortwave radio there was a close union between trade promotion and cultural penetration.

Closely related to this was the perceived need to counter increased Nazi radio activity in the region. Yet, it was never very clear what, objectively, was the nature of the Nazi radio threat. It was not until the establishment of the Princeton Listening Center in 1939 that any systematic study was done of Nazi radio content. The threat, impact, and effect of Nazi radio broadcasting were unknown. Thus, those concerned with such activity could read into it their own interests, fears, and perceptions of Latin America. Some saw in it a threat to inter-American cultural ties and the possibility of totalitarian fascist states emerging in Latin America. Yet, it was the perception of such radio activity as a commercial threat that tended to dominate government policy on the matter. Perhaps the greatest impact and most significant effect of such broadcasts was that they prompted United States counteraction in the field.

Aside from what it revealed about perceptions of United States interests in Latin America, government policy on shortwave revealed aspects of the relations between the government and the broadcasting industry. On one hand, the policy can be judged as being conservative. Rather than build a government station, the administration left the field to private broadcasters. It is evident that the Commerce Department and the Business Advisory Council played a very active role in the shaping of administration policy on this matter. There was a very close match between the recommendations of the Council and subsequent government actions on shortwave. Yet, as shortwave was defined largely as one method of trade promotion, it was only natural that the Commerce Department, the Business Advisory Council, and the Bureau of Foreign and Domestic Commerce responded to that definition of the issue and helped shape discussion and policy on the matter.

Yet, this was not simply an episode in which private interests dominated. The relationships and developments were far more complex. The single major motivating factor behind the private broadcasters' expansion into shortwave activity after 1936 was not the prospect of financial return, but fear. The spectre of a government shortwave station, and the implications for domestic broadcasting, were enough to galvanize them into action. The broadcasters' response to the Chavez-McAdoo and Celler bills must have been very instructive to the administration. On the one hand, the hearings in those bills showed that the idea of a government radio station provoked the strong unified opposition among the broadcasting industry. Moreover, the idea had little support on Capitol Hill. However, the bill and the hearings also demonstrated how far the broadcasting industry was willing to go to insure that a government station would not be built. In order to forestall government action, the shortwave broadcasters were willing to invest money and time in expanding their shortwave services.

The government, in a sense, exploited this fear. In not taking an official stand on the issue for over a year, it encouraged shortwave broadcasters to continue the expansion of their services. When the government did speak in May 1939, it allowed the shortwave broadcasters to engage in commercial operation, but also required them to increase their power. In a sense, the government's shortwave policy set the broad goals, then, using both the carrot (potential commercial profits) and the stick (the threat of a government station), forced the private broadcasters to achieve these goals. Thus, it was not particularly clear who was manipulating whom, or who "won" and who "lost."

On a broader level, this entire episode tends to discount simplistic explanations of the New Deal, explanations which regard the achievements of Roosevelt either as meaningless or see in the reforms of the New Deal the taming of the crude capitalist spirit and the creation of a liberal social welfare state. Rather, this episode tends to reveal an aspect of the development of a liberal corporate state which was initiated under the New Deal. Actively intervening in the economy, the government developed close relations with the business community in a joint effort to protect and maintain the capitalist system as a whole. This, of course, does not mean that the business community as a whole welcomed the New Deal. The more traditionally conservative capitalists and businessmen, a characterization that describes most of those in the broadcasting industry, tended to oppose the New Deal initiatives as unwarranted intrusions into private affairs. Yet, it is equally mistaken to argue that the New Deal was opposed uniformly by the business community. Many advanced, progressive capitalists and industrialists, like those associated with the Business Advisory Council, welcomed the New Deal and saw close business–government relations and joint planning as necessary to the survival and health of the system as a whole.[74] On the domestic level, the new relationships were revealed in government attempts to rationalize the system of capitalist production by introducing elements of national planning and minimizing the social destructiveness of capitalism. On the international level, the character of the liberal corporate state was revealed in greater government intervention into international economic affairs and attempts to evolve some type of international planning.

In this sense, the government's policy on shortwave was one element in an overall hemispheric policy of economic and political planning designed to strengthen United States interests and dominance. Thus, shortwave broadcasters were not totally free to define and control their activities. Nevertheless, the administration hoped that, by allowing the broadcasters to advertise, a happy marriage between the long term hemispheric goals of the United States and the short term commercial goals of the broadcasters would be consummated. Yet, in spite of such hopes, it would turn out to be a very rocky relationship.

Notes

[1] James W. Gantenbein, editor and compiler, *The Evolution of Our Latin American Policy—A Documentary Record* (New York: Octagon Books, 1971), p. 166; Sumner Welles, *The Roosevelt Administration and Its Dealings with the Republics of the Western Hemisphere*, address read at the Annual Convention of the Association of American Colleges, Atlanta, January 17, 1935, Department of State Latin American Series No. 9 (Washington, D.C.: Government Printing Office, 1935), p. 6.

[2] David Green, *The Containment of Latin America* (Chicago: Quandrangle Books, 1971), p. 21; Samuel Flagg Bemis, *The Latin American Policy of the United States* (New York: Harcourt, Brace and Company, 1943), pp. 337–342; Bryce Wood, *The Making of the Good Neighbor Policy* (New York: Columbia University Press, 1961), p. 167.

[3] Alton Frye, *Nazi Germany and the American Hemisphere*, 1933–1941 (New Haven: Yale University Press, 1967), pp. 21–31, 65–70, 73–74; Joan Raushenbus, *Look at Latin America* (New York: The Foreign Policy Association, 1940), pp. 38–40.

[4] William E. Leuchtenberg, *Franklin D. Roosevelt and the New Deal, 1932–1940* (New York: Harper and Row, 1963), pp. 218–219; Robert A. Divine, *The Illusion of Neutrality* (Chicago: The University of Chicago Press, 1962), pp. 57–121.

[5] U.S., Department of State, *Report of the Delegation of the United States of America to the Inter-American Conference for the Maintenance of Peace, Buenos Aires, Argentina,* December 1–23, 1936, Conference Series No. 33 (Washington, D.C.,: Government Printing Office, 1937), p. 3.

[6] J. Lloyd Mecham, *A Survey of United States–Latin American Relations* (Boston: Houghton Mifflin, 1965), p. 126.

[7] U.S., Department of State, *Report on Buenos Aires Conference,* p. 127.

[8] Green, *The Containment of Latin America,* p. 35.

[9] Quoted in Wood, *The Making of the Good Neighbor Policy,* p. 359.

[10] Edward O. Guerrant, *Roosevelt's Good Neighbor Policy* (Albuquerque: University of New Mexico Press, 1950), pp. 102–103, 167.

[11] Lloyd C. Gardner, *Economic Aspects of New Deal Diplomacy* (Madison: University of Wisconsin Press, 1964), p. 200. The author continues: "Washington still demands reforms in Latin America and then sets the boundaries upon reformist leaders, trying to keep them from becoming revolutionaries; it still gives aid and then demands the creation of a favorable environment for foreign investment, without pausing to see if the two aims are in conflict either generally or specifically."

[12] Bemis, *The Latin American Policy of the United States,* p. 314–315, 322–323.

[13] J. Manuel Espinosa, *Inter-American Beginnings of U.S. Cultural Diplomacy, 1936–1948,* Cultural Relations Programs of the U.S. Department of State—Historical Studies No. 2 (Washington, D.C.: Government Printing Office, 1976), pp. 69–71.

[14] Ibid., pp. 71–73.

[15] Bemis, *The Latin American Policy of the United States,* pp. 313–330; Guerrant, *Roosevelt's Good Neighbor Policy,* pp. 115–127; Mecham, *Survey,* pp. 128–130.

[16] Frye, *Nazi Germany,* p. 77; Samuel Guy Inman, *Democracy versus the Totalitarian State in Latin America,* Pamphlet Series No. 7 (Philadelphia: The American Academy of Political and Social Science, 1938), pp. 14–21.

[17] John B. Whitton and John H. Herz, "Radio in International Politics," in *Propaganda by Short Wave,* ed. Harwood L. Childs and John B. Whitton (Princeton: Princeton University Press, 1942), pp. 8–9.

[18] Ibid., p. 19–31; William G. Harris, "Radio Propaganda in Latin America" (Senior thesis, Princeton, University, 1939), p. 50.

[19] Ibid., P. 179; Michael Kent Sidel, "A Historical Analysis of American Short Wave Broadcasting 1916–1942" (Ph.D. dissertation, Northwestern University, 1976), p. 81–94; *United States Daily,* 20 December 1929, IV: 2841:6; 20 February 1931, VI: 2876:3; *New York Times,* 29 May 1932, VIII: 12:2; *Broadcast Advertising,* November 1930, p. 38.

[20] Howard S. Leroy, "Treaty Regulation of International and Short Wave Broadcasting," *The American Journal of International Law,* 32 (October) 1938, p. 728; U.S., Office of the President, Executive Order #6472, 2 December 1933.

[21] U.S., Department of State, *Papers Relating to the Foreign Relations of the United States 1933,* Vol. IV, pp. 183, 191–192.

22 U.S., Department of State, *Report of the Delegates of the United States of America to the Seventh International Conference of American States, Montevideo, Uruguay, December 3–26, 1933*, Conference Series No. 19 (Washington, D.C.: Government Printing Office, 1934), pp. 49, 279–280; U.S., Interdepartmental Committee to Study International Broadcasting, Report of the Interdepartmental Committee to Study International Broadcastings: Report of the Subcommittee on Programs (Washington, D.C.: Government Printing Office, 1939), Appendix E, pp. 67–68.

23 U.S., Congress, House, Committee on Naval Affairs, *Hearings Authorizing the Secretary of the Navy to Construct and Maintain a Government Radio Station ...And for Other Purposes* (H.R. 4281), hereafter cited as *Hearings on H.R. 4281*, 75th Congress, 3rd Session, 1938, pp. 3474–3475.

24 See Dye to Roper, May 20, 1938, Radio General 1938 file, Box 2724, *BFDC*.

25 *New York Times*, 30 June 1934, 18:1.

26 U.S., Congress, Senate, Committee on Interstate Commerce, *Hearings before a Subcommittee of the Committee on Interstate Commerce on S. 3342, A Bill to Authorize the Construction and Operation of a Radio-Broadcasting Station Designed to Promote Friendly Relations among the Nations of the Western Hemisphere*, hereafter cited as *Hearings on S. 3342*, 75th Congress, 3rd Session, 1938, pp. 55–56.

27 U.S., Department of Commerce, Bureau of Foreign and Domestic Commerce, *Broadcast Advertising in Latin America*, Trade Information Bulletin No. 771 (Washington, D.C.: Government Printing Office, 1931); ibid., *Broadcast Advertising in Europe*, Trade Information bulletin No. 787 (Washington, D.C.: Government Printing Office, 1932); ibid., *Broadcast Advertising in Asia, Africa, Australia, and Oceania*, Trade Information Bulletin No. 799 (Washington, D.C.: Government Printing Office, 1932).

28 "Advertising: American Sales Plug into Other Nations' Air," *Newsweek*, 14 March 1936, p. 44; "Business Broadcasts Abroad," *Business Week*, 29 February 1936, pp. 28–29; "Radio Opportunity in China," *Broadcasting*, 15 August 1936, p. 47; "Latin Radio Moves Forward," *Broadcasting*, 1 December 1936, p. 55.

29 "Broadcasting Abroad, Inc." advertisement, *Broadcasting—1935 Yearbook*, p. 89; "Business Broadcasts Abroad."

30 See "Advance United States Short Wave Broadcast Programs, Week of June 28–July 4, 1936" and other correspondence in Radio General 1936 File, Box 2724, *BFDC*.

31 U.S. Department of State, *Report on the Buenos Aires Conference*, p. 223; See "Pan American Broadcasts to Latin America," *Bulletin of the Pan American Union*, 71 (December 1937), p. 414.

32 "RCA Adds Latin Shortwave Pickup to Sponsorship of Metropolitan Opera," *Broadcasting*, 15 January 1937, p. 19.

33 *Hearings on S. 3342*, p. 101; "NBC Expands Schedule of Shortwave Broadcasts," *Broadcasting*, 1 August 1937, p. 40; "G.E. Boosts Power of Shortwave Unit."; "Westinghouse to Raise Strength of Shortwave Signals by New Beams," *Broadcasting*, 1 November 1937, p. 58.

34 U.S., Federal Communications Commission, *Third Annual Report* (1937), pp. 34–35.

[35] "Closer Ties with Pan-American Nations Seen as Networks Arrange for Pick-ups," *Broadcasting*, 1 December 1936, p. 32.

[36] "Extension of Remarks of Honorable John J. Boylan of New York in the House of Representatives, Monday, April 12, 1937," *Congressional Record*, Appendix, 75th Congress, 1st Session, Vol. 81, p. 817.

[37] Barton J. Bernstein, "The New Deal: The Conservative Achievements of Liberal Reform," in *Towards a New Past: Dissenting Essays in American History*, ed., Barton J. Bernstein (New York: Vintage, 1969), p. 276.

[38] "Extension of Remarks of Hon. Emanuel Celler of New York in the House of Representatives, Wednesday, February 3, 1937," *Congressional Record*, Appendix, 75th Congress, 1st Session, Vol. 81, pp. 135–137.

[39] *Broadcasting*, 1 July 1937, pp. 20, 37.

[40] Celler remarks, February 3, 1937, p. 135; "Secretary Hull Said to Favor Proposed Government Station," *Broadcasting*, 1 August 1937, p. 40.

[41] Norweb dispatch, 4 March 1937, Latin America File, Box 2731, BDFC.

[42] Hull to Roper, 24 March 1937; Roper to Hull, 15 April 1937, ibid.

[43] Draft of Roper letter to Harriman, Radio General 1937 file, Box 2724, BFDC; Zapf to Dickerman, 18 Mary 1937, ibid.; see also "Lifting of FCC Sponsorship Barriers on International Shortwave Discussed," *Broadcasting*, 1 April 1937, p. 32.

[44] Dickerman to Zapf, 20 July 1937, Radio General 1937 File, Box 2724, BFDC; Zapf to Dickerman, 21 July 1937, ibid.; Payne to McIntosh, 23 May 1938, Radio General 1938 file, ibid.

[45] *Hearings on H.R. 4281*, pp. 3491–3494, 3501–3507.

[46] "Shortwave Stymie Ended by FCC," *Broadcasting*, 1 October 1947, p. 22; "Other Nations Said to be Taking Lead in International Shortwave Programs," ibid., 15 November 1937, p. 34; "Promotion of Latin American Good-Will Sought in Shortwave Grants," ibid., 15 February 1938, p. 42; "Foreign Programs on Enlarged Scale," ibid., 1 March 1938, p. 39; "Station Aimed at Pan America," 15 March 1938, p. 19; U.S., Federal Communications Commission, "In the Matter of World Wide Broadcasting Corporation," et al., Dockets 4843, 4844, 4845, February 1, 1938, *FCC Reports*, 5 FCC (1938), pp. 107–116.

[47] Celler to Roosevelt, 16 November 1937, *Franklin D. Roosevelt and Foreign Affairs*, Second Series, ed. Donald B. Schewe (New York: Clearwater Publishing Company, 1979), vol. 7, p. 240; Roosevelt to Celler, 29 December 1937, ibid., p. 519.

[48] *Congressional Record*, 75th Congress, 3rd Session, vol. 83, p. 1260; *Hearings on S. 3342*, p. 1; "Promotion of Latin American Good Will Sought in Shortwave Grants," *Broadcasting*, 15 February 1938.

[49] Harold L. Ickes, The Secret Diary of Harold L. ickes, vol. 2: *The Inside Struggle*, 1936–1939 (New York: Simon and Schuster, 1954), p. 317.

[50] *New York Times*, 27 February 1938, 1:3.; "Federal Station for International Broadcasting Favored," ibid., 1 May 1938, p. 28.

[51] *Hearings on S. 3342*, p. 71, 104, 37.

[52] "New Latin Series Fosters Good Will," *Broadcasting*, 15 October 1937, p. 30.

[53] *Hearings on S. 3342*, p. 104, 156.

[54] *Hearings on H.R. 4281*, pp. 3496–3497.

55 "Bills for Government Radio Station Wither from Lack of Support," *Broadcasting*, 1 June 1938, p. 19.

56 Beth Alene Roberts, "United States Propaganda Warfare in Latin America," (Ph.D. dissertation, University of Southern California, 1943), p. 391.

57 *Hearings on H.R. 4281*, pp. 3481–3482; Dye to Roper, 20 May 1938, Radio General 1938 file, Box 2724, *BFDC*.

58 Apparently, the only document that the Committee produced and that has survived is a report by one of its subcommittees detailing a State Department survey of the content and reception of shortwave programs in Latin America conducted in March 1938 and November 1939. Also included in the report are copies of letters going back to 1931 sent by private individuals to both McNinch and the State Department dealing with United States shortwave programs in Latin America. On the whole, the report represents a compendium of various sorts of information on file in the State Department dealing with shortwave broadcasting. It does not deal at all with the question of a government radio station. Moreover, it was addressed to McNinch after he had resigned from the Federal Communications Commission and went to work for the Justice Department. Although it is not clear why, this report remained classified until 1957. U.S., Interdepartmental Committee to Study International Broadcasting, *Report;* See above, pp. 17–18.

59 U.S., Department of State, Press Release, 3 December 1938, vol. 19, no. 479, p. 385, 391.

60 Culbertson to Dickerman, Business Advisory Council file, box 787, *COM*.

61 Payne to Dunn, 11 June 1938, Radio Argentina 1938 file, Box 2726, *BFDC*.

62 Payne to Willis, 13 January 1939, Radio General 1939, Box 2724, BFDC; Shouse to Payne, 25 January 1940, Radio General 1940, Box 2725, ibid.

63 The Rockefeller Foundation, *Annual Report 1935*, pp. 279–280; *Annual Report 1936*, pp. 278–279; *Annual Report 1937*, pp. 320–322; *Annual Report 1938*, pp. 325–326; Webb Waldron, "Democracy on Shortwave," *Readers Digest*, September 1941, p. 42; Roberts, "Propaganda Warfare in Latin America," p. 382.

64 U.S., Federal Communications Commission, *Sixth Annual Report* (1940), p. 73.

65 "Cenorship Seen in Ruling," *Broadcasting*, 1 June 1939, p. 13; "Program to Latin America Slated to Remain Sustaining," *Advertising Age*, 2 July 1939, p. 17.

66 "Good Neighbor Radio," *Broadcasting*, 15 May 1939, p. 44.

67 "Censorship Seen in Ruling."

68 "Newspapers See Censorship Danger in New International Ruling of the FCC," *Broadcasting*, 1 June 1939, p. 13; "International Censorship Rule to be Given Hearing by FCC," 15 June 1939, p. 16; *New York Times*, 25 May 1939, 24:3.

69 Remarks of Mr. McLeod on Radio Censorship, *Congressional Record*, 76th Congress, 1st Session, vol. 84, p. 8982; "Extension of Remarks of Hon. Emanuel Celler of New York in the House of Representatives—Thursday, June 15, 1939," *Congressional Record*, Appendix, 76th Congress, 1st Session, vol. 84, p. 2692.

70 "FCC Suspends International Ruling," *Broadcasting*, 15 July 1939, p. 17; "FCC Disclaims Intent to Censor; Suspends Rule. . . .," ibid; "Emasculation of 'Censor' Rule by FCC Next Autumn Foreseen," ibid., 1 August 1939, p. 32.

71 "Censorship Seen in Ruling."

[72] Ibid.
[73] "FCC Quietly Inters International Rule as Result of Disturbed World Scene,"
   Broadcasting, 1 October 1939. The rule remained suspended until 1955 when
   the Commission, in a general rule-making procedure, lifted the suspension;
   Douglas A. Boyd, "The Pre-History of the Voice of America," *Public Telecommunications Review* 2:6 (December) 1974), footnote 26; "Foreign Time Sold by
   NBC," *Broadcasting*, 15 November 1939, p. 30.
[74] For a discussion of the involvement of pro-New Deal businessmen and capitalists
   in the policy making process of the Roosevelt Administration see Ronald Radosh,
   "The Myth of the New Deal," in *A New History of Leviathan—Essays on the
   Rise of the American Corporate State*, ed. Ronald Radosh and Murray N. Rothbard (New York: E.P. Dutton, 1972), pp. 146–187.

CHAPTER 5

SHORTWAVE BROADCASTING AND LATIN AMERICA DURING WORLD WAR II

With the commercialization of international broadcasting in 1939, broadcasters attempted to develop shortwave as a profit-making service. Although there were a number of advertisers who experimented with the commercial possibilities of shortwave, it soon became apparent that shortwave's sales potential was very limited. By the end of 1941, for every dollar shortwave broadcasters spent on the operation of their service, they received approximately seven cents in advertising revenue.

Although shortwave held little promise for profit, the increasingly serious world situation in 1940 and 1941 began to highlight the importance of shortwave to the United States government, particularly in terms of protecting its position and interests in Latin America. Government involvement in, and direction of, shortwave broadcasting activities increased. At first, it was voluntary cooperation between broadcasters and the government. Later, these informal relations became more formalized. The process of government involvement and direction reached its logical end point in 1942, when the government took over all broadcasting facilities. Although earlier such a move would have been strongly opposed by the domestic broadcasting industry, close and mutually beneficial wartime cooperation between the broadcasting industry and the government alleviated broadcasters' fears about government desires to take over and control domestic broadcasting. Thus, they no longer feared government control of international broadcasting as an "entering wedge" of control over domestic broadcasting.

The Commercialization of Shortwave

With the new rules allowing commercial shortwave service, broadcasters were given the opportunity of trying to turn a profit on their shortwave activities. The war in Europe seemed to create propitious conditions for the development of commercial shortwave. Because the war was expected to cut off a good portion of the trade between the Americas and Europe, United States exporters hoped to make up for their lost European markets by turning to Latin America. Likewise, Latin American importers were expected to replace their lost European suppliers with sources from the United States. It was expected that this expansion of trade between the United States and Latin America would lead to a large increase in advertising and other sales promotion by United States exporters in Latin American markets.

Of the major commercial shortwave companies (NBC, CBS, Crosley, Westinghouse, and General Electric), NBC took the initiative in developing commercial service. However, like other commercial broadcasters, NBC was greatly handicapped by the lack of detailed information about the size and tastes of the Latin American shortwave radio audiences. Rather than try to sell shortwave to advertisers as a medium for the promotion of specific products to specific audiences, NBC tried another tack.

Approaching a number of companies that had large sales or investments in Latin America, NBC offered to sell them 15 minutes of shortwave airtime every night for a year for $25,000. Rather than stress the ability of shortwave broadcasts to sell products, NBC argued that the most powerful impact of shortwave, at this point, would be to build "good will." As Lansford Yandell, head of International Commercial Broadcasting at NBC noted, "If you have good will, if your public relations are right, you can sell with the proper technique. If you haven't good will, you are right 'behind the eight ball' until you get it."

Based on Department of Commerce figures, Yandell estimated that there were about two million radio sets in Latin America that could receive shortwave programs, with the largest portion of them in Argentina (900,000), Brazil (360,000), and Mexico (175,000). But more important than the numbers, according to Yandell, were the types of people who listened to shortwave. Although there was very little evidence as yet to support these assertions, Yandell claimed that a good portion of the Latin American shortwave audience consisted of government and political officials and members of the upper class. He argued that the good will potential of shortwave with these groups was particularly important. "These are the people who determine the policies of the governments down there. In the hands of this important class of listeners rests the power of taxation, of import restrictions, and if worse comes to worse, of confiscation."[1]

In early November 1939, the network announced that the United Fruit Company was the first sponsor to sign with NBC shortwave. It would broadcast a daily 15-minute evening news broadcast in Spanish. The series began on December 1, 1939. With Associated Press supplying the news, the NBC International Division prepared and translated the actual program script into Spanish, subject to final editorial approval by United Fruit. The program was to have no product advertising by United Fruit, but only institutional announcements. According to the United Fruit representative, the series "is being sponsored strictly in the interest of good will. . . . All announcements will be directed solely towards creating a better understanding between the United States and the countries of Latin America where [United Fruit] does business and has extensive investments." In addition to United Fruit, RCA Manufacturing Company, a subsidiary of NBC's parent company, also signed on as an advertiser. It sponsored three shows consisting of musical selections on which commercials for RCA shortwave equipment and record players were aired.[2]

Standard Oil was NBC's third sponsor. In early February 1940, the oil company sponsored a shortwave broadcast to Latin America of the Godoy-Louis championship fight in Madison Square Gardens. Using the broadcast as a chance to do some elementary market research, NBC offered to send picture postcards of Louis and Godoy to anyone in the shortwave audience who would write the network. Over the next 2 months, more than 23,000 requests were received from all parts of Latin America. Such evidence of a large listening audience gave NBC greater confidence in the commercial viability of shortwave. In late March 1940, it issued its first rate card for international shortwave advertisers. There were high volume discounts and rebates for long term contracts. Thus, although the standard rate for 1 hour of evening prime time was $300, the actual cost of a 1-year contract for a weekly 1-hour program was $180 per prime time hour. Through such discounts and rebates, NBC hoped to attract a large number of advertisers committed to long term contracts.[3]

In May, both the Waldorf-Astoria Hotel in New York and Adams Hat Stores, Inc. signed with NBC. The Hotel sponsored a weekly program of dance music broadcast from its ballroom, with the hope of attracting future Latin American visitors to the United States as hotel customers. Adams Hat Stores, which exported hats and other male apparel to Latin America, signed a 1-year contract sponsoring prize fights from Madison Square Gardens. Also in the fall, the S.C. Johnson Company, makers of Johnson Wax, began sponsoring a weekly program in Spanish and English, with news from Hollywood.[4]

Because programs about Hollywood were popular in Latin America, an interest in shortwave advertising also was expressed by the movie industry, which saw the medium as potentially useful in promoting Hollywood films in the region. Columbia, MGM, Warner Brothers, Paramount, Universal, and RKO announced plans to jointly sponsor a series of shortwave programs aimed at Latin America. The goals of the programs were to promote United States film exports to Latin America in general, individual pictures and film stars, and overall good relations between the United States and Latin America. The film companies hoped to assist in the creation of hemispheric good will by "increasing South American acceptance of Hollywood and American ideas as expressed in American movies generally." Although both NBC and the film companies were initially enthusiastic about the projected programs, problems arose between the companies and NBC over the specific type of program content. Eventually NBC submitted detailed specifications to the movie firms of the type of program content appropriate to the shortwave service. After a brief flurry of activity and press announcements, the movie industry lost interest in the idea and the entire project was dropped.

Aside from NBC, the Crosley Broadcasting Company was also quick to take advantage of the commercial possibilities of shortwave. In October 1939, Crosley announced that it would begin selling time on shortwave broadcasts transmitted from its newly installed 50 kw transmitter. While most of Crosley's shortwave fare consisted of regular NBC material, the company, hiring Spanish and Portuguese announcers, writers, and production assistants, added 3½ hours of Spanish and 1 hour of Portuguese programming. Its basic rate was $200 an hour which, with the regular discounts, was far below that of NBC. By August 1940, Crosley had signed contracts with four advertisers. Carter Medicine Company (Carter's Little Liver Pills) bought two daily spot advertisements. A shaving company sponsored a weeknight news program. Perhaps the most ambitious of Crosley's sponsored programs was the 15-minute effort titled *Charles Amenas* (Pleasant Talks), sponsored on alternate week nights by International Cellucotton Products Company (Kleenex) and Prince Pat Ltd., a Chicago cosmetic company. The program featured a woman commentator from Puerto Rico named Concha Gandia, who discussed Hollywood fashion, trends, and gossip.[5]

Although both Westinghouse and General Electric attempted to interest advertisers in their shortwave services, neither was very successful in attracting clients. In October 1939, Westinghouse appointed F.P. Nelson as head of shortwave sales and activities. Although Nelson actively recruited advertisers, by the end of 1941 he was only able to secure Westinghouse Manufacturing Company as a sponsor. In December 1941, another sponsor almost signed on, but, with the United States entry into the war, Westinghouse's operation was put on a wartime footing and all commercial activity was dropped.[6]

General Electric continued to rely mainly on simulcasts of regular NBC network programming, and did not attempt to develop shortwave as a commercial medium. However, it did attempt to offer special programming to Latin America by giving advertisers free time on its shortwave transmissions in return for their providing programs directed at Latin American audiences. Westinghouse's first nonpaying sponsor was Tide

Water Associate Oil Company, exporter of oil products to Latin America. It provided musical programming twice a week, featuring Xavier Cugat's orchestra. Other companies that took advantage of General Electric's free air time were Condé Nast Publishing Company (*Vogue*), Gillette Razor Blade Company, Royal Baking Powder, Mohawk Carpet Company, and the American Express Company. Their programming generally consisted of musical selections.[7]

CBS made no attempt to commercialize its service. Of all the major shortwave broadcasters, its shortwave facilities were the least developed. It had two transmitters, each operating at 10 kw. Much of CBS shortwave effort during 1940 was devoted to upgrading its shortwave service, not only to meet the Federal Communications Commission power require-ment of 50 kw, but also to be able to offer an effective service that would attract advertisers in the future. In September 1940, CBS's plans for two new 50 kw transmitters were approved by the Commission. While it was building its new units, CBS continued to broadcast over its lower power transmitters and also expanded its shortwave staff and programs. One hundred thousand dollars was allocated to shortwave services in 1940 by CBS, compared to $93,000 in 1939 and $50,000 in 1938. Shortwave staff was increased from 17 in May 1939 to 25 in December 1940. In order to get visibility on the southern continent, CBS announced in the spring of 1940 that it was expanding its 11-year-old, highly successful domestic educa-tional radio program, *American School of the Air*, to include topics and subjects dealing with Latin America. Renamed *School of the Air of the Americas*, the program was to be relevant to Latin American audiences and could be used for educational purposes. CBS translated the scripts into Spanish and Portuguese, and made arrangements with various Latin American radio stations for local broadcast. When it went on the air in October 1940, the program was heard in 10 Latin American countries, in-cluding Cuba, Argentina, Chile, and Brazil. CBS also translated and made available classroom material to supplement the broadcasts.[8]

Overall, the progress made by commercial shortwave during 1940 must have been very disappointing to the broadcasters. By the beginning of 1941, out of nearly 450 hours of programs broadcast to Latin America, fewer than 20 were paid for by advertisers. To most United States adver-tisers, the potential of shortwave was largely unknown. Moreover, in of-fering commercial service, the shortwave broadcasters were competing for the advertisers' dollars with the broadcast export advertising agencies (such as Broadcast Abroad, Inc.), which already had well developed orga-nizations for putting radio advertisements on the air in Latin America. These agencies were able to tailor commercials to individual markets and were able to offer their clients more detailed information about the Latin American radio audiences, their tastes, and their listening habits. In order to overcome their lack of marketing information, shortwave broadcasters urged listeners to send letters and, as in the case of the Louis-Godoy fight, tried a number of special gimmicks to encourage listener response. Through such means, the broadcasters hoped to develop information about the size, location, nature, and tastes of their Latin American audiences.[9]

Based on the mail response to their programs, shortwave broadcasters found that news programs were by far the most popular item, given the war in Europe and the generally unsettled international situation. As a result, shortwave broadcasters expanded their newscasts. The backbone of the NBC schedule was eleven 15-minute news broadcasts made on the hour. Musical programs were the second most popular type, particularly those consisting of classical music. General network entertainment and comedy shows did not do very well. NBC, and later CBS, turned from relying on simple simulcasts of network programming to developing an entire different schedule of programs for foreign audiences.[10]

Initially there was a fear that Latin American listeners would object to commercial programs on shortwave. Both the Federal Communications Commission and the broadcasters themselves insisted that the advertising be done tastefully in order not to alienate listeners. As one commentator noted, "The advertising over the shortwaves, at least at the start, is . . . expected to be mainly institutional, so that South American audiences will be accustomed to the interjection of the commercial factor gradually."[11] However, as regular network commercials and advertisements were always part of the pre-1940 shortwave simulcasts, the commercials on shortwave represented nothing new. Overall, there was no apparent objection from Latin American listeners. A number of the advertisers on NBC, such as Adams Hats, reported increased sales in Latin America, which they attributed to their shortwave programs.[12]

In spite of the disappointing start and the numerous marketing problems they faced, shortwave broadcasters exuded hope and confidence that advertising by shortwave would play an increasingly important role in the export trade. Crosley's general manager, in a year-end review of the shortwave activities in 1940 declared: "We have numerous plans and innovations in mind to improve service of WLWO, and are confident that by the end of 1941, this station will be a vital factor in the Latin American market." Representatives from NBC and CBS made similar encouraging prognoses. Yet, as broadcasters attempted to develop shortwave as a commercial medium, the war in Europe, and its effect on inter-American relations, began to have a greater impact on the nature and direction of the broadcasters' shortwave activities and efforts.

World War II and the Western Hemisphere

Bound by neutrality legislation and a great deal of public sentiment against involvement, the Roosevelt Administration responded cautiously to the outbreak of war in Europe in September 1939. Its first goal was to insure hemispheric neutrality and security. In line with the various consultative pacts signed at the inter-American conferences, foreign ministers of the American republics met in Panama in late September 1939. The principal objective was to consider ways to keep the American nations out of the war and to deal with the economic problems resulting from the war. The conference produced a statement defining the rights and duties of the American republics as neutral nations. In addition, a neutrality zone averaging 300 miles in width around the shores of the American continents was established, and the European belligerents were told to keep their warships outside this zone. With regard to the economic problems, the conference set up an advisory committee to study and propose solutions to trade disruptions caused by the war. The administration was also considering various ways it could increase United States trade with the southern continent, hoping to replace European suppliers and markets for Latin American goods. Overall, the administration, as reflected in its participation in the Panama conference, felt that the war could be restricted to Europe. Thus, throughout the fall and winter of 1939–1940, Roosevelt attempted to play a role in negotiating a settlement of the European conflict.[13]

However, with the Nazi invasion of Denmark and Norway in April 1940 and, more spectacularly, with the invasion of Holland, Belgium, and France in May, it was evident that the hope of containing the European war was fast fading. The defeat of France in June 1940 changed the entire focus of United States policy in Latin America. With Germany in control of all of Western Europe and not much chance given for Britain's survival, the prior goal of insuring hemispheric neutrality was transformed into actively organizing against the Nazi threat to the hemisphere. Throughout the spring, as German armies swept through Belgium and France, Roosevelt received increasingly ominous reports of Nazi subversion in Latin America. By May, he concluded that continued Nazi victories in Europe would lead to attempts by Germany to overthrow existing Latin American governments. He also feared that control of the Dutch and French Caribbean possessions would be transferred to Germany. Moreover, he saw Germany's likely acquisition of the French fleet and West African bases as a prelude to an attack on Brazil and the rest of South America.

In late May, Roosevelt ordered the initiation of secret talks between the United States and Latin American military officials, and also ordered naval ships to present a show of force off the coasts of Brazil and Uruguay. Congress passed a resolution stating that the United States would not recognize the transfer of any European possession in the Western Hemisphere to a non-American power.

In the face of the new crisis, the American foreign ministers met again in July in Havana to develop more comprehensive plans for the defense of the hemisphere. Although there was opposition from countries such as Argentina, Brazil, and Chile, which did not want to take an explicit anti-

German position, the no-transfer rule embodied in the earlier Congressional resolution was adopted in principle. Another important measure declared that any aggression by a non-American power against an American nation would be considered aggression against all, that consultation would follow, and that American nations would then enter into agreements to ensure cooperation in defense. Thus, the basis was laid for a number of bilateral agreements between the United States and Latin American nations for the construction of Allied military bases in Latin America.

Aside from the strictly military aspects of hemispheric defense, there were a number of other closely related problems the Roosevelt Administration had to confront in order to secure the Western Hemisphere. Approximately half of Latin America's import and export trade was with Europe. The Latin American countries were left with huge surpluses. The inability of Latin America to market its goods could have grave political consequences for the United States. It was feared that the economic dislocation caused by the cut-off in European trade would result in the political destabilization of a number of pro-United States regimes in the region. If the United States was to gain Latin American cooperation, it would have to insure a secure economic base in the region.[14]

Coupled with the fear of economic destabilization in the region was the concern over the possible existence of a "Fifth Column" in Latin America that would exploit these economic troubles. Throughout the latter part of the 1930s, the United States was aware of the growing Nazi economic and cultural activity in the region. Yet, after the fall of France, when the notion of a "Fifth Column" was used to explain the quick Nazi victories, the Germany activity in Latin America was seen as having a very ominous meaning. Moreover, Nazi propaganda was becoming more explicitly anti-United States. Based on the monitoring done by the Princeton Listening Center, prior to the invasion of the Low Countries, the largest portion (38 percent) of Nazi shortwave program content aimed at the Americas consisted of criticism of Great Britain; the smallest portion (20 percent) consisted of criticism of the United States. Content praising the German Fatherland and United States isolation comprised 20.5 percent and 21.5 percent, respectively. After the fall of France, criticism of the United States increased to 43 percent of program content, followed by criticism of Britain (24 percent), praise of the United States isolation (18 percent), and praise of Germany (15 percent).[15]

The United States government suddenly became very concerned about what was seen as the very large Nazi presence in Latin America. Aside from Nazi shortwave propaganda and Nazi economic activity in the region, many of the reports about the Nazi threat focused on the extent to which the Germans were able to control and influence Latin American media, and thus influence Latin American public opinion against the United

States. In November 1940, for example, a Bolivian journalist charged that United States manufacturers were inadvertently supporting pro-Nazi newspapers in Bolivia. A pro-Nazi German importer in that country who distributed products for a number of United States companies was using the advertising funds supplied by the manufacturers to advertise the products in pro-German newspapers.[16]

Given the complexity of the problems, it was evident that special measures had to be taken to deal with the threat of economic dislocation and Axis penetration in Latin America. If the United States was to count upon the military, political, and economic cooperation of the Latin American governments, something more than strictly diplomatic and economic inducements and pressures would be required. As the Nazis were engaged in a major propaganda effort in Latin America, such a campaign had to be countered and, in turn, Latin American public opinion had to be mobilized behind the United States.

In this context, the government's policy on shortwave broadcasting was being reassessed. The government relied on commercial incentives to prompt expansion of United States shortwave activity to Latin America. The policy gave the government, at best, a passive role in the actual direction and development of the shortwave efforts. It was left to the broadcasters to determine the specific content and aim of the programs. The broadcasters argued that their programs, free from any government interference and control and presenting an "honest" picture of life in the United States, were the most effective means of countering Axis propaganda and promoting good hemispheric relations. However, the government was no longer certain that its foreign policy aims were being adequately served by the present arrangement. Just as it was necessary for the government to take more active measures to insure hemispheric economic stability and military defense, more direct government involvement, planning, and direction were needed in the cultural realm.

Government Shortwave Involvement 1940–1941

After the commercialization of shortwave in 1939, the Bureau of Foreign and Domestic Commerce, particularly its Electrical Division headed by John Payne, was still the most active government agency promoting shortwave broadcasting to Latin America. Seeing shortwave primarily as a tool for trade promotion, Payne continued and expanded the Bureau's previous program of assistance to the shortwave broadcasters. He continually pressed commercial attachés throughout Latin America for reports on shortwave reception, audience size, and program tastes, and relayed this information immediately to the broadcasters. An important service of the Bureau was the distribution of United States shortwave program schedules throughout Latin America. In March 1940, however, the Commerce Department, as a cost-cutting move, attempted to discontinue this service. Payne, however, was able to marshal support from the shortwave broadcasters, and the program was saved.[17]

However, during the crisis in the spring and summer of 1940, government interest in shortwave broadcasting as a means of trade promotion began to be eclipsed by more explicit political considerations. Moreover, the Roosevelt Administration began to consider ways in which it could develop closer and more cooperative ties with the communications industry in general. In July 1940, the administration revealed plans for the creation of the Defense Communications Board to coordinate policy planning between the government and the communication industries. While the companies involved in point-to-point communications and the manufacture of communication products welcomed the move, the initial response of the broadcasting industry was skepticism, seeing in it an attempt by the administration to use the war in Europe as a means of gaining greater control over domestic broadcasting. However, the administration went to great pains to reassure the broadcasters that there would be "no upsetting of broadcasting" as it then functioned. It argued that the purpose of the Board was simply to coordinate government and industry efforts in line with the nation's defense needs, and that it would not become another New Deal super agency. Eventually broadcasters were satisfied that the Board was to be geared toward "long-range planning in the interest of the national defense, rather than immediate interference with the operations of communication."[18]

The Defense Board, officially formed in the fall of 1940, was headed by James Fly, chairman of the Federal Communications Commission. Representatives from the communications industries chaired the various committees, with a government representative serving as committee secretary. The president of the National Association of Broadcasters was head of the Domestic Broadcasting Committee. Overall, the creation of the Defense Board represented the first step in the organized cooperation between the government and industry that grew to great proportions during the war.

A committee on shortwave broadcasting was included in the initial planning and final composition of the Defense Board. When formed, the committee was headed by a Westinghouse executive and was comprised of representatives of all the companies involved in shortwave broadcasting, plus representatives from the government departments and agencies that had an involvement and interest in the field. The entire issue of using shortwave broadcasting as part of an overall defense program was a sensitive one, given the furor created the previous year over the Federal Communication Commission's "culture rule." Yet, as *Broadcasting* noted, "it is not unreasonable to expect that the Government—perhaps through the State Department—will seek to have international station licenses transmit programs geared to offset insidious propaganda from abroad."[19]

Aside from the planning for and creation of the Defense Communications Board in late 1940 and early 1941, there was other evidence of growing government concern and involvement in shortwave broadcasting. The government was not yet prepared to develop any type of programming to counter Axis propaganda. However, it closely monitored the broadcasters' activities and encouraged them to boost their transmission power, develop more effective reception, and obtain more information about audience characteristics and tastes in Latin America in order to build more programming. In late July 1940, headed by the president of the National Association of Broadcasters, a delegation of representatives from all the commercial shortwave broadcasting companies met with State Department officials to discuss conditions and operations of United States shortwave broadcasting. Broadcasters told State Department officials that they were planning to invest more than $2 million in order to bring their stations up to the 50 kw transmission power requirement set by the Federal Communications Commission. Citing "hemispheric solidarity considerations," the State Department was particularly concerned about broadcasters' plans for future operations. The broadcasters responded that increased expenditures of over $1 million were planned for improved operations and new program features.[20]

In line with the increasing political emphasis put on shortwave by the government, the State Department began to take over a number of the activities of the Commerce Department and the Bureau of Foreign and Domestic Commerce. The cost of the advance program schedules sent to Latin America was assumed in part by the State Department. In the fall of 1940, it launched a world-wide survey of shortwave reception, with particular emphasis on Latin America.[21]

Roosevelt took an active interest in shortwave, and personally encouraged the broadcasters' efforts. While campaigning for his third term in Ohio in October 1940, Roosevelt took part in the dedication ceremonies for Crosley's new 50 kw shortwave transmitter. Delivering a speech from his campaign train that was then relayed to the ceremonies, Roosevelt praised the job that United States shortwave broadcasters were doing in furthering hemispheric unity and friendship. Also participating in the ceremonies were the chairman of the Federal Communications Commission and Latin American dignitaries.[22]

Later that month, the President invited William Paley to the White House to talk about the Latin American radio situation. Because Paley was planning a trip to Latin America as part of CBS's expansion in the region, Roosevelt asked him to investigate the extent of Axis influence in the Latin

American media, and to suggest possible measures to counter Axis propaganda. Paley said he would be honored to undertake the assignment and would report to the President.[23] It is not clear how much Roosevelt expected to learn from Paley's report. Nonetheless, this request was an important gesture that sought to sensitize broadcasters to the administration's foreign policy concerns and also to develop a more cooperative attitude between government and the broadcasting industry.

While still wary of government involvement, the broadcasters nevertheless willingly cooperated to help the government achieve its foreign policy aims in Latin America. No doubt such cooperation was seen as necessary to remove any excuse the government might have had to build a government station. However, as events progressed during 1940 and 1941, they did recognize that, given the critical world situation, such cooperation was necessary. Shortwave broadcasting was beginning to have a task far more important than sales promotion and entertainment, and the broadcasters were beginning to realize this. As one NBC representative noted in the fall of 1940:

> We have priced [our shortwave] service at about half what it actually costs us to operate, because we are trying to make a definite contribution to the public service of this country in the important field of foreign public relations. At first, we offered this service on two premises, sales promotion and public relations, and many companies accepted it primarily for its value in these two fields.
>
> Since the Axis' success in Europe, another very important factor has entered the picture. It is the growing conviction of Government officials and advisors, and of business leaders in this country, that the country can be served in a very important way by broadcasting to Latin America in the interest of hemispheric solidarity. Now the companies that are using our service and those that are considering it are looking at it not only for its value to their own interests, in sales promotion and public relations, but also as a means of contributing materially toward national defense.
>
> This is not being done by active propaganda, such as is used by other nations. Instead, by presenting themselves and their goods and services to Latin America, some of the leading companies of this country are giving Latin Americans a picture of the dividends that democracy pays.... In addition to this picture, they seek to convince Latin America of the fact that the purpose of U.S. business interest in Latin America is to create, not to exploit.[24]

The broadcasters were beginning to view their activity less as a pure commercial venture and more as a "public service," although the strength and intensity of this perception varied among the individual shortwave companies. In one sense, they were gradually assuming the government's definition and concerns about United States shortwave activity in Latin America. The passive, laissez-faire policy formulated in 1939, in which government aims were to be achieved by broadcasters seeking their own self-interest, was being replaced by more active cooperation between the parties.

Although mostly informal, this growing cooperation was perhaps best demonstrated in the development of Latin American shortwave networks by the United States broadcasters. One of the major problems facing broadcasters and causing considerable concern to the government was the effectiveness of reception in Latin America of United States shortwave programs. In spite of the expansion program undertaken by the shortwave broadcasters, the 22 German transmitters had a combined power of 1100 kw, over three times greater than the 320 kw output of the 12 United States transmitters. The Federal Communications Commission's 50 kw transmission power requirement was meant to boost the power of all United States shortwave stations. Due to delays, however, the Commission had to extend the July 1940 compliance deadline, first to January 1941, and then to July 1941. Yet, even with such a boost in power, it was becoming apparent that United States broadcasts would not reach a sizable Latin American audience. As more survey information about Latin American listening habits was collected, it was becoming clear that most Latin Americans, including those with all wave receivers, much preferred listening to their own local radio stations. Overall, the audience for foreign shortwave programming was very small. The Germans had recognized this fact earlier, and had started buying time on local Latin American stations for relay rebroadcasts of German programs. In contrast, while United States shortwave broadcasters occasionally relayed special shortwave programs to local stations for rebroadcast over medium or long wave, most broadcasts were made for direct shortwave reception.[25]

For both the political and commercial concerns of the government and shortwave broadcasters, a shortwave rebroadcasting network had a great advantage over direct broadcasting. Not only would a larger audience be reached, but broadcasters would have a far better idea of the size and characteristics of their audience, thus making the medium far more useful to advertisers. Moreover, relay broadcasting could be developed to the point where a North American exporter could select those cities where he would want his advertisements and sponsored programs heard. The local distributor or dealer could cut in on the sponsored program with announcements telling where the product was available locally. Overall, shortwave network broadcasting had both the advantages of local radio advertising and the advantages of a centralized network. For the government, the broadcast of United States programs on local Latin American radio stations would mean that a far wider audience would be reached, and, hopefully, influenced in favor of United States hemispheric aims.

NBC was gradually developing a system of local broadcasting, making arrangements with a number of Latin American stations for special rebroadcasts of selected sponsored shortwave programs.[26] CBS, however, planned to develop a Latin American network based on the United States model. One of the topics discussed when Paley and Roosevelt met in October 1940 was CBS's proposed network. Roosevelt welcomed the idea. In late December 1940, returning from a 7-week tour of various Latin American countries, Paley announced that he had signed affiliate contracts with 64 radio stations in 18 of the 20 Latin American republics, and had prospects for additional affiliates. Most of the contracts were for a 5-year period beginning September 1941, when CBS's two new 50 kw transmitters were to be ready for operation. In contrast to NBC's arrangement with local Latin American stations, each of CBS's affiliates was obligated to carry a daily minimum of 1 hour of CBS programming. Initially, CBS was planning to send 20 hours a week of specially prepared programs to its affiliates. Moreover, CBS was to offer technical assistance to its Latin American stations to insure they could pick up and rebroadcast all of CBS's shortwave transmissions. In signing up the various affiliates, Paley picked the most powerful and popular radio stations in each major Latin American city. In some cities such as La Paz and Rio de Janiero, this meant signing contracts with government-owned but commercially-run stations.[27]

In announcing the Latin network, Paley stressed the role that it would play in creating better inter-American relations and furthering the goals of the Good Neighbor Policy. He later met with Roosevelt and discussed both the network and the problems of Axis propaganda in Latin America, reporting to him what he saw during his trip south. Roosevelt was very happy with the success of Paley's trip, and was glad that United States programs would be heard in most Latin American countries over local radio. As Paley stated after the meeting, "The important thing is that each of these stations has agreed to carry a minimum of one hour a day of broadcasting from the United States, which will give us a dominant position in Latin America compared with any other nation. The Germans, of course, have purchased time on the radio, but we still have the dominant position based on this arrangement." The industry, however, did not ignore the commercial potential of the network. As *Broadcasting* editorialized, "Obviously, the CBS move is to promote better relations with Latin America in harmony with the policies adopted by our government. Yet the commercial possibilities are there—through the promotion of United States commodities, particularly brand name products. On the long haul, there should be a worthwhile return for American advertisers."[28]

On the heels of the CBS announcement, representatives from Crosley left for Central America to sign up affiliate stations for another network centered around Crosley's WLWO station in Ohio. Crosley was able to organize a network of 28 affiliate stations in Central America, the Caribbean, Colombia, Ecuador, Peru, and Venezuela.[29] In July, John Royal, NBC vice-president in charge of shortwave activities, left for South America to line up affiliates for the proposed NBC Latin network. Before leaving, he met with Under Secretary of State Sumner Welles to discuss NBC's plans. In Mexico, Royal signed the 21 stations of the Cadena Radio-Difusora Mexicana, a network organized by the Mexican radio entrepreneur, Don Emilio Azcarraga, and containing the most powerful (200 kw) radio station in the Western Hemisphere. Most of the contracts arranged with Latin American stations were for 1 year and did not contain minimum clearance requirements. Sponsored shows were cleared on an individual basis, with both the networks and the affiliate sharing the advertising proceeds. As did Paley, Royal stressed the larger political impact that such a network arrangement was expected to have on inter-American relations. In a few cities, NBC shared affiliates with CBS. Royal felt, however, "that in these times of unsettled world affairs when both the United States and the European powers are competing for the good will of Central and South America, it is more important to get United States news and entertainment into Latin America than to worry whether the programs are originated in the studios of NBC or CBS." By the end of 1941, NBC claimed 117 stations in its network; CBS, 76; and Crosley, 24. Of the approximately 700 radio stations in Latin America in 1941, roughly one-third were affiliated with United States shortwave networks.[30]

In line with expanding their shortwave organization into Latin America, these broadcasters also were developing special programming to the region. By summer 1941, all United States shortwave broadcasters were transmitting a total of approximately 65 hours of programming a day to Latin America, with over half of the programming especially prepared in Spanish and Portuguese. Roughly 80 percent of NBC's output, and 50 percent of Crosley's was specially programmed material. With its Latin American network operations awaiting completion of its new transmitters, CBS at this point was only preparing about one-third of its shortwave output especially for Latin American audiences. The other commercial shortwave broadcasters transmitted lesser numbers of hours and programs. As mail response showed, the most popular programming was news, followed by music and entertainment.[31]

Keenly aware of the political role shortwave broadcasts were playing in inter-American relations, broadcasters endeavored to counter Axis propaganda and promote United States goals in the region. Except for news, much of the specially prepared programming was light entertainment. But many of the unsponsored programs prepared by the networks dealt with public affairs and were aimed at creating closer ties between the United States and Latin America. One major example was CBS's *School of the Air of the Americas*, which was produced on local Latin stations live from CBS prepared scripts. *School of the Air* programs, for example, dealing with music were expanded to contain discussions of Latin American music as well as music from North America. Discussions of literature included Latin American authors.[32]

Economic aspects of inter-American relations did not escape notice. One *School of the Air* program entitled "Americans at Work" dramatized the production of important American commodities and products. The Latin American products discussed were cocoa, rubber, coffee, and bananas. In the fall of 1940, Republic Steel produced a series for Latin American audiences entitled "Your Faithful Servant—Industry." Broadcast over the General Electric shortwave station, the program was "a running dramatization of the part industry is playing in the development of the Americas." Typical of programs in the series were "Tailor-made Weather (The Story of Air Conditioning)," "The Story of the Printed Word (The Story of the Paper Pulp and Printing Industry)," and "At Home and at Work (Furniture and Shop Equipment)." According to the Latin American distributors of Republic Steel, the programs were very popular and did much to increase the understanding on the part of the Latin American audiences of United States industries. On the other hand, any mention of Latin American industrial development was ignored.[33]

Aside from such public service programs, the shortwave broadcasters endeavored to insure that the United States point of view on world matters was constantly before the Latin American public. Speeches on foreign policy by Roosevelt, Hull, and other administration officials were broadcast to Latin America both in the original English and later in Spanish and Portuguese translations.

Although the major focus of the shortwave broadcasters' activity was on Latin America, they also broadcast programs to Europe, particularly in the morning hours when shortwave transmission to Latin America was plagued with static. Initially, these programs were simulcasts of network programs. However, during the spring and summer of 1941, as the possibility of United States involvement in the European war increased, the administration began to ask the broadcasters to offer their cooperation in broadcasting special programs to Europe. In May 1941, at the request of the State Department, NBC shifted its operations to a round-the-clock "war-time" basis. German, French, and Italian announcers were hired in order to expand the network's shortwave service to Europe. Later that month, NBC broadcast a message by Roosevelt to the French people, urging them not to collaborate with Germany. The message, repeated every hour for 10 hours, also contained a talk by a French NBC announcer in which the French audience was asked rhetorically whether the Vichy government served them or the Germans. It was the first time the traditional American shortwave presentation of news was replaced with a direct and explicit political appeal to people in another country. Yet, even though broadcasts to Europe were assuming an important role in the shortwave broadcasters' activity and United States cultural warfare in general, prior to Pearl Harbor the major focus of United States foreign cultural and information activity was Latin America.[34]

Thus, throughout 1940 and into 1941, shortwave broadcasters attempted to ward off active government involvement in broadcasting to Latin America by demonstrating their willingness and readiness to cooperate with government efforts to protect the position and interests of the United States in Latin America in the face of the Axis threat to the hemisphere. Broadcasters acknowledged the important political role that their shortwave service was playing, and were willing to expand their activities to an extent not yet justified by the hope of commercial return. Through the Defense Communications Board and informal meetings with members of the State Department, the White House, and other government agencies, broadcasters kept the government informed of their efforts and, in turn, were told of government policy aims and goals. Hopefully, through such consultation, some type of coordination would emerge between the government's policy aims in Latin America and the broadcasters' shortwave activity in the region.

However, as the situation deteriorated in Europe and the prospects of a war in Asia grew, the government began to assume a larger and more active role in defining the direction and nature of the private broadcasters' activities. The process was a gradual one that given the worsening world crisis and the growing need of the government to engage in information and cultural warfare, the broadcasters were helpless to stop.

The OCIAA and Shortwave Broadcasting to Latin America

The government agency that gradually assumed the largest role in shaping government policy, action, and involvement in cultural and information activities in Latin America was the Office of the Coordinator of Inter-American Affairs (OCIAA).[35] The individual who played a major role in the creation and subsequent activities of the OCIAA was Nelson Rockefeller, the 32-year-old (in 1940) grandson of John D. Rockefeller, founder of the worldwide Standard Oil empire.

Rockefeller developed an early interest in the affairs of Latin America. During the 1930s, he made a number of trips there in connection with the affairs of Standard Oil, which had major holdings in a number of Latin American countries. He was impressed by the numerous social and economic problems of the region and, while he welcomed Roosevelt's Good Neighbor Policy as a progressive advance, he thought it was not enough. He felt a major problem was the lack of understanding between the United States and Latin America. While Latin Americans, according to Rockefeller, misunderstood the economic and political values and institutions of the United States, North American businessmen and investors knew or cared little about the culture and social and economic needs of the region. Rockefeller argued that United States investors had a responsibility to help solve the region's many problems. Speaking about Standard Oil's Latin American holdings at an annual meeting of company stockholders in the late 1930s, he argued that

> In the last analysis, the only justification for ownership is that it serves the broad interest of the people. We must recognize the social responsibilities of corporations and the corporation must use its ownership of assets to reflect the best interests of the people. If we don't they will take away our ownership.[36]

Rockefeller, a liberal Republican, viewed capitalism as a progressive force that could be directed toward socially useful ends. He felt that a program of planned private investment and government cooperation could help alleviate many of the problems of the region and assist its overall economic, social and political development. In 1937, he met with aides of Roosevelt to discuss the possibility of a joint industry–government program for inter-American economic development. While the administration expressed interest, nothing came of it.[37]

However, in Spring 1940, the Nazi victories in Europe made Latin American economic and political cooperation critically important, and Rockefeller's interest in Latin America was remembered by administration aide Harry Hopkins. At Hopkins' request, Rockefeller and his aides prepared a memorandum on the need for immediate United States action in Latin America in light of the critical war situation. In mid-June, Hopkins forwarded the document to Roosevelt.

The Rockefeller memorandum urged that, in order to counter the Axis threat, economic measures be taken to "secure economic prosperity in Central and South America, and to establish this prosperity in the frame of hemispheric economic cooperation and dependence." The measures suggested included efforts to absorb surplus Latin American agricultural and mineral products, various steps leading to the freest possible flow of trade, encouragement of both private and government investment in Latin America, and other steps to improve the economic stability of the region and foster closer inter-American economic and political ties. To implement these proposals, Rockefeller urged the creation of a special advisory committee and assistant to the president to coordinate both the activities of the various departments and broader industry-government efforts geared towards the fulfillment of the proposed measures.

In addition to economic measures, Rockefeller also felt a cultural effort was essential to the success of the economic program. "A vigorous [cultural] program," Rockefeller asserted, "should be pursued concurrently with the economic program. The main lines of a cultural program are fairly obvious, but here again, it is a question of personnel and the use, in a non-traditional way, of government funds where private agencies are unable or unwilling to act, or in matters where the activity of private agencies is less appropriate."[38]

Roosevelt was impressed with Rockefeller's ideas and gave the memorandum to various department heads for study and comment. By the end of July, the administration decided to create such a coordinating unit. Although a number of candidates were considered to head the new organization, Rockefeller emerged as the prime choice. While Roosevelt was impressed with Rockefeller, he no doubt must have appreciated the symbolic and political value of having a scion of the Rockefeller clan work for his administration. In early August, Roosevelt offered him the job. Although excited by the offer, Rockefeller was concerned about the effect such an appointment would have on his plans for a future political career. He sought the advice of Wendell Wilkie, the newly nominated Republican presidential candidate. Wilkie declared that the Axis threat to the Americas was far above partisan politics and urged him to take the job. Rockefeller accepted the post.[39]

On August 16, 1940, Roosevelt approved the official order creating the coordinating office for inter-American affairs. Rockefeller was designated its coordinator. In his new post, Rockefeller was to review existing laws, coordinate research by the several government agencies, and recommend new legislation that might be essential to the effective realization of the basic objectives of the administration's program. He also was to serve as head of the Inter-Departmental Committee on Inter-American Affairs, which was charged with considering and correlating departmental proposals concerning Latin America.

Although the Rockefeller memorandum emphasized the threat that economic problems posed to hemispheric security, Roosevelt and other administration officials were as concerned about the threat of Nazi propaganda. One of the major responsibilities of the new OCIAA unit, in addition to its coordinating function, was to undertake measures to counter such a threat. In drawing up the order establishing the OCIAA, Roosevelt personally saw to it that the coordinator, among his other duties, was charged

> with the formulation and the execution of a program in cooperation with the State Department which, by effective use of Governmental and private facilities in such fields as the arts and sciences, education and travel, the radio, press, and the cinema, will further national defense and strengthen the bonds between the nations of the Western Hemisphere.[40]

Before Rockefeller was offered the job as head of the OCIAA, the White House seriously considered appointing CBS President William Paley head. Paley, however, let the White House know that he was not interested.[41] No doubt this gesture was another move on the administration's part to create closer ties between the broadcasters and the White House. However, it does emphasize the fact that the White House perceived the development of an information campaign as one of the main activities of the OCIAA. Moreover, the initial concern that prompted the Rockefeller memorandum—the economic dislocation caused by the war—eventually assumed a minor role in the OCIAA's activities. These economic problems were dealt with by other departments and agencies. In September 1940, as a form of "lend-lease" aid to Latin American nations, Congress increased the lending authority of the Export-Import Bank from $200 to $500 million. Moreover, as war-related production increased in the United States, Latin American nations found a growing market in this country for their products. By the end of 1941, most of the severe economic difficulties had been alleviated by increased exports to the United States. After 1942, the major economic problem facing Latin America was the unavailability of imported manufactured goods and replacement parts, due to conversion to defense production in the United States.

Although the OCIAA did engage in a number of economic, commercial, and health projects, its major activity throughout the war was in cultural and information affairs. This campaign was designed to create and maintain hemispheric political and economic solidarity. As outlined in one early account of its activities, the OCIAA goals were

> to persuade the Latin Americas to take joint defensive action with us against the German menace which many of them do not admit exists. . . [to] persuade them that in the end the planes that are now only on our planning boards will conquer German bombers that have struck down eight countries in twenty-two months. . . [to] convince them that we know the answer to the economic as well as the military defense of the hemisphere. . . [to] convince them that somehow we will help them get rid of the same agricultural surplus we have not been able to get rid of ourselves, and. . . above all things [to] convince them, all of them, that the "Good Neighbor" policy is not a temporary expedient designed to get us out of a tough spot, but a sincere and permanent reversal of our nineteenth century policy of "dollar diplomacy" and "manifest destiny."[42]

To fulfill these goals, the OCIAA launched a broad and well coordinated campaign involving the press and radio and film industries.[43]

The OCIAA was the first government agency created to engage in cultural and information campaigns directed at audiences outside the United States. With its creation, the practice of cultural diplomacy initiated during the later 1930s as a small part of the Good Neighbor Policy was greatly expanded and intensified in the face of the Axis threat to the hemisphere. However, its preeminence in the information field was not uncontested. In order to centralize the government's growing informational activities both domestically and at the international level, the administration created the Office of the Coordinator of Information (COI) in July 1941. Immediately, there were jurisdictional disputes between the COI and the OCIAA. The COI and its successor, the Office of War Information (OWI), viewed Latin American informational activities as part of their domain, and tried to usurp OCIAA's activities. However, Rockefeller was able to mobilize support from both the State Department and the White House to keep Latin American information programs in the hands of the OCIAA. He argued that the goals and practices of United States cultural and information activities in Latin America were distinct and far different from the government's information campaigns in Europe and Asia. After a number of bureaucratic skirmishes, Rockefeller was able to get the COI and OWI to accept his claims. The COI, and later the OWI, were responsible for United States information activities in Europe, Asia, and Africa, while the OCIAA had control of information activities in Central and South America.[44]

As organized in the fall of 1940, the OCIAA consisted of four major sections: Cultural Relations, Communications, Commercial Development, and Trade and Financial. The head of the Communications section was James Young, former chief of the Bureau of Foreign and Domestic Commerce. Many of the Bureau's promotion and information activities in Latin America were taken over by the OCIAA. Within the Communications section were the Radio, Movies, and Press Divisions. In line with Rockefeller's policy of close business–government relations, the heads of the media divisions were drawn from private industry. In charge of the Press Division, for example, was Karle Bickel, former president of United Press and then-current chairman of Scripps-Howard's Radio Division. John Jay Whitney, a motion picture executive and chairman of the board of Freeport Sulphur Company, was head of the Motion Picture Division. Don Francisco, president and part owner of the major advertising agency Lord and Thomas, was appointed head of the Radio Division. Later, Francisco replaced Young as head of the OCIAA's Communication activities. Also working for the Radio Division were Merlin Aylesworth, former president of NBC, and Sylvester Weaver, an advertising executive who, after the war, would play a major role in the development of television programming. As with the heads of the other OCIAA divisions and sections who came from industry, these individuals took a drastic cut in pay to work with the OCIAA. Whitney, for example, left an $80,000-a-year position, and Francisco a $120,000-a-year position, to come to work for the OCIAA in $8,000-a-year posts.[45]

One of the first tasks of the OCIAA and the Radio Division was an evaluation of United States shortwave broadcasting capabilities and the development of a program to improve and expand United States shortwave service to Latin America. At first, the assessments and proposals for shortwave were wide-ranging and varied. Rockefeller, during one of the early meetings of the Executive Committee of the OCIAA, suggested that one solution to the shortwave problem was to consolidate the six shortwave companies into two major competing organizations. Hopefully, the incentive of competition would improve their shortwave programming to Latin America. Young, on the other hand, felt that the major problem facing United States broadcasting to Latin America was the lack of transmission power, and suggested that all the companies be consolidated into one, with all transmitters broadcasting the same program in different frequencies.[46] Although these discussions were remarkably prescient in view of later developments, at the time they reflected an unrealistic assessment of how much cooperation the OCIAA could expect from the broadcasters. The furor over the "culture" rule was still a very recent memory. No doubt there would be an uproar among broadcasters if the government, this time in the form of the OCIAA, stepped in and proposed the reorganization of the United States shortwave broadcasting industry. While the broadcasters were becoming more open to direct government–industry cooperation, there was a limit to what was feasible. Understandably, these proposals were never publicized or seriously considered at that time.

The OCIAA's actual program was far more modest and was aimed at working within the existing framework of industry–government relations. As reported to Roosevelt in December 1940, the OCIAA's goals were to improve the program quality and technical capabilities of existing shortwave services with the aim of increasing Latin American audiences for United States programs. Moreover, the OCIAA sought to encourage United States advertisers in Latin America to support those radio stations willing to give favorable publicity to United States policy aims, and to boycott pro-Axis and anti-United States stations.

Before any money was spent on specific projects, more information had to be gathered on the actual shortwave situation in Latin America. Early in 1941, Francisco made a 3-month tour of the region to survey the possibilities of developing and expanding radio operations to and in the Latin American Republics. His report, though, painted a very dismal picture. United States stations were outpowered by European stations. Moreover, United States programs, though popular, were inferior to standard United States fare, primarily due to the difficulties and expanse of securing suitable Spanish and Portuguese talent in the United States. Although there was very little information about shortwave audiences, they were estimated to be very small. The only practical way to reach a large audience was to have United States programs rebroadcast over local stations, something that NBC was currently doing and that CBS and Crosley were planning to do. With separate companies transmitting to Latin America, and with no attempt made to plan or coordinate their activities, the strength of the United States shortwave effort in Latin America was seriously diluted. As Francisco noted, in order to prevent direct government involvement, and for reasons of patriotism and prestige, the stations were improving their facilities and programs. Yet, he argued, there was a limit to the improvements that could be expected. The possibilities of advertising revenue were decidedly limited, and the shortwave broadcasters would not continuously sink more money into their operations with little hope of return.

The ideal solution, according to Francisco, would be the consolidation of all shortwave activities into one company and the centralization of their operations. Under such a plan, shortwave broadcasting would be noncommercial, with most of the time on the shortwave service being bought and programmed by the government. However, as Francisco noted, that plan would require "radical changes in fundamental national policy," and "would undoubtedly subject the administration to widespread and bitter criticism from the press, radio industry, Congress, general industry, and the public at large."

Given the situation, the only alternative open to the OCIAA was to work with the individual shortwave broadcasters and encourage them to improve their service by coordinating their efforts, increasing their transmission power and radio coverage in Latin America, and improving program quality. Francisco also outlined other steps the OCIAA could take to improve United States radio operations. Among these were advertising United States shortwave programs in Latin American newspapers, collecting audience and marketing information about Latin America which could be of use to the broadcasters, and sending special United States programs to local Latin American stations via point-to-point transmission and transcriptions.[47]

Throughout 1941, based on Francisco's recommendations and other internally originated suggestions and proposals, OCIAA's radio efforts were aimed at improving the transmission and programming capabilities of United States shortwave services and improving the reception of United States programs in Latin America. With regard to the latter, in January 1941, the OCIAA approved a $25,000 expenditure for advertising the United States shortwave schedule in the Sunday edition of major Latin American newspapers. However, one of the major attractions of United States programs, particularly the news, was that they were not government-controlled. Thus, the OCIAA felt that "in order to avoid even a suspicion of government influence. . . it might be advisable to have these advertisements [also] advertise radio sets," with the possibility of radio manufacturers paying for the ads.[48] Later in July, the OCIAA embarked on a more ambitious program to expand the Latin American radio audience for shortwave by encouraging United States radio sets for the Latin American market. This program was moderately successful and by the end of 1941, over 400,000 low cost sets had been sent to Latin America. After the United States' entry into the war, however, the War Production Board halted the manufacture of these sets, even though the OCIAA argued that the program was essential to the war effort.[49]

Aside from attempting to expand the radio audience for United States programs, the OCIAA tried to increase the availability of such programs in Latin America. In April 1941, the OCIAA approved a $50,000 appropriation for a 15-minute daily news broadcast to be transmitted over local stations in Argentina, Uruguay, Bolivia, and Brazil. CBS was to prepare and produce the news program, which would then be transmitted via radiotelephone by the American Telephone and Telegraph Company (ATT) to Latin America, and there distributed to the various radio stations via the facilities of the International Telephone and Telegraph Company (ITT) in the region. The cost was extremely low due to the cooperation of the private companies involved. CBS agreed to prepare and produce the news show for only a nominal fee. ATT charged only half its radiotelephone rate. And ITT offered to pick up the first $20,000 of the cost of distributing the program in Latin America.[50]

Another OCIAA project, a $450,000 survey of Latin American media, markets, and audiences, involved radio as well as the press. The study was carried out under contract by the export branch of the American Association of Advertising Agencies, with Hadley Cantril of the Princeton Public Opinion Research Project as director. The study had a number of closely related purposes. In describing the proposed study with a Congressional appropriations committee, Rockefeller declared that a major goal of the project was to analyze Latin American public opinion, media, and totalitarian propaganda techniques. It was part of a larger OCIAA effort to combat Axis propaganda and penetration in Latin America by identifying pro-Axis media. However, in explaining this project to the advertising and broadcasting industry, Rockefeller presented it as a means of developing information about Latin American markets and media that could be useful to exporters. Overall, the project was a good example of how Rockefeller and the OCIAA tried to mesh government aims with private business interests. The entire effort was one part of a larger blacklisting project by which the OCIAA identified pro-Axis firms and media to be boycotted by United States exporters. By identifying such newspapers, radio stations, and magazines, and also those which simply ran advertisements from business firms that had been designated as pro-Axis, the OCIAA hoped to deprive them of United States advertising revenue and channel such revenue toward media that had a pro-United States position. Also, the increased information on Latin American markets and consumer tastes would expand United States exports and, hopefully, increase export advertising revenue. It was expected that some of this increased revenue would be spent on shortwave advertising.[51]

In attempting to improve shortwave transmission and program quality, the OCIAA had to deal directly with the private broadcasters. Such improvements could go only so far as the broadcasters were willing to cooperate. The OCIAA's scope of action, therefore, was limited.

It encouraged the companies to upgrade their power as soon as possible to 50 kw in accordance with the Federal Communications Commission's regulation. It also urged them to employ narrow beam transmission in order to increase the effective transmission power of their broadcasts. The OCIAA welcomed CBS, Crosley, and NBC's announcement of the creation of their Latin American networks. Seeing such networks as a way of expanding Latin audiences through local rebroadcasting, the government encouraged and assisted their efforts. In mid-1941, for example, CBS was experiencing difficulties in building its new transmitters due to the growing restrictions placed on strategic materials. The OCIAA intervened, and claimed that the inauguration of the CBS Latin American network was a national priority and that CBS should receive the material necessary for the completion of the transmitters. Francisco, arguing for CBS, emphasized that "The operation of the Columbia chain will be one of the most helpful things that has yet happened in Latin America for the betterment of communications between the republics and the strengthening of our influence among the people of the southern republics." OCIAA's efforts helped CBS secure the needed materials.[52]

However, while it was possible for the OCIAA to try to improve the technical aspects of shortwave service, the organizational and programming aspects were a more sensitive area. In December 1940, for example, Francisco publicly noted that the OCIAA was considering the possibility of asking industry to organize some type of bureau to coordinate the international radio activities of all the American republics. Given that, among the American republics, the United States was the only country involved in extensive international radio broadcasting, this was a veiled hint that United States shortwave broadcasters should coordinate their Latin American activities. While John Royal, head of NBC's international division, welcomed the idea, Paley of CBS was strongly opposed. He argued that the government's interest could be best served by letting the individual broadcasters compete.[53]

In May 1941, *New York Post* columnist Dorothy Thompson criticized efforts of the shortwave broadcasting companies and argued that "it was illogical for private business to control and operate the most effective means of having America heard abroad." Shortwave radio, she said, belongs in the hands of the government. "Both the government and the networks wish, apparently, to avoid an airing of the question—the government because it fears it will be accused of trying to 'take over' the broadcasting companies; the broadcasting companies because they fear an 'entering wedge.'" She urged that all shortwave operations be taken over by the State Department, and that broadcasts be integrated with the nation's official foreign policy.[54]

Responding to Thompson, Edmund Chester, CBS shortwave director, agreed that shortwave played a crucial role in international affairs. Yet, he argued that any effect shortwave would have as a political medium would be destroyed if it became controlled directly by the government. "Once an effort is defined as propaganda, it has lost its intended value in Latin America. The quickest way to define any kind of campaign for the Latin American [as propaganda] is to make it a government effort. That simplifies matters. They know it is propaganda. . . . Shortwave listeners are just as intelligent as longwave listeners. They know good programs cost money and that the democratic way to pay for such programs is through the sale of time for commercial programs."[55]

Yet, despite such sentiments, shortwave broadcasters were gradually allowing greater government involvement and direction. Ironically, the *New York Post* column appeared the same week that NBC announced that, at the request of the State Department, it was going on a 24-hour "war-time" basis and expanding its European staff. Moreover, during the previous month, perhaps responding to the intent of Francisco's earlier suggestion, the six shortwave broadcasters announced that they had appointed a former Associated Press correspondent as an industry coordinator of international operations. His job was to develop more effective international shortwave reception through the coordination of transmission and programs. The shortwave companies stated that their decision to establish this position reflected their desire "to make more effective use of their powerful shortwave facilities in the interest of national defense."[56]

The next month, the COI announced a program to counter Axis propaganda in cooperation with private broadcasters. Both the COI and the OCIAA would provide the shortwave broadcasters with a 15-minute daily news report aimed at countering the claims and accusations of Axis radio propaganda. The news reports would be distributed to the industry coordinator, who would oversee and coordinate their transmissions by the various broadcasters. This marked the first entrance of the government into the field of international news distribution, and the first entrance of the OCIAA and the COI into direct programming activities.[57]

Further government-directed coordination of shortwave occurred in October 1941 when, under the direction of the COI, all international transmitters were linked by wire. This was primarily a move to improve United States shortwave broadcasting to Europe. It enabled stations to share and exchange the currently small number of programs aimed at

European audiences that were produced by the shortwave broadcasters. The new set-up enabled the government to monitor all shortwave broadcasts to Europe. However, officials were quick to point out that "censorship is not involved, merely the checking of material after it is aired."[58]

While the OCIAA was very careful how it treated the commercial shortwave broadcasters, its relations with the one noncommercial station, World Wide, were on a far different plane. Soon after the OCIAA was organized in the fall of 1940, OCIAA officials contacted Walter Lemmon in order to negotiate for the possible use of World Wide's facilities for occasional broadcasts that the OCIAA might want to make. However, after discussing the idea with Lemmon, OCIAA officials dropped the plan, as the OCIAA was not yet prepared to do any programming. Moreover, they felt that World Wide's transmitters were not very powerful. World Wide, however, was experiencing financial difficulties, and Lemmon argued that, since his station was the only nonprofit shortwave station, it should receive government financial assistance in any case. While the OCIAA felt that the station's power, not its nonprofit status, was the key issue, it was nonetheless concerned about the possibility of World Wide going off the air, resulting in a reduction of one-sixth of the United States transmitting power. In February 1941, the OCIAA gave the station $10,000 to keep it going. By summer, however, World Wide was again in financial straits and appealing for help. This time the OCIAA arranged a 1-year contract with World Wide. The OCIAA paid $200,000 for 700 hours of broadcasting time "to promote better relations and strengthen the bonds between the American republics." In addition, the OCIAA would oversee the financial operation of World Wide and required that the station's program personnel be approved by the OCIAA. Thus, by fall 1941, the OCIAA was subsidizing and exercising a good deal of control over the one noncommercial shortwave station.[59]

Before the end of 1941, the OCIAA had greatly expanded the scope of government involvement in shortwave broadcasting to Latin America. It was subsidizing one station, providing a series of news programs, and assisting shortwave broadcasters in improving their technical transmission and programming. In addition, the OCIAA was actively trying to increase the Latin American radio audience for United States programs through the sale of low-cost all-wave receivers. It was providing the broadcasting companies with detailed information about market and audience characteristics that would be useful to potential shortwave advertisers.

The cooperation of commercial broadcasters, of course, was voluntary. The major reason for cooperation at first, aside from prestige and patriotism, was the fear that, without it, the government would step in and take matters in its own hands. But by the end of 1941, this fear had become less compelling. As the nation turned toward war, the administration went to great length to insure that many segments of private industry alienated by New Deal reform measures developed cooperative attitudes toward the defense program. By the latter part of 1941, it was clear that "Dr. Win-the-War," to use a phrase later coined by Roosevelt, was well on his way to replacing "Dr. New Deal." Rather than institute measures that gave the government extensive control over an increasingly war-oriented economy, as was the case in Great Britain, Roosevelt relied on a broad policy of voluntary cooperation between business and government.

Broadcasters gradually came to fear a government station less as "an entering wedge" in domestic broadcasting. The new chairman of the Federal Communications Commission, James Fly, previous general counsel for the Tennessee Valley Authority (TVA), assured broadcasters that the government would never attempt anything in the field of domestic broadcasting like the TVA experiment in government ownership. Fly vigorously pursued the Commission's investigation of the networks that eventually led to the sale by NBC of one of its domestic radio networks and the formulation of regulations concerning the network–affiliate relations. Yet, such actions were balanced by his activities as head of the Defense Communications Board. There he was charged with, and successfully realized, a broad program of government-industry cooperation in all aspects of electrical communication. Overall, while the Commission under Fly was to insist that broadcasters be regulated and held accountable under antitrust statues, the limits of the changes the administration was trying to accomplish in broadcasting were becoming clear. The basic private, profit-oriented structure of the industry was not to be threatened.[60]

With such assurances, the commercial shortwave broadcasters were able to reevaluate their activities more realistically. It was becoming increasingly evident that, despite the wide promotion by Crosley and NBC, the commercial potential of shortwave as an advertising medium was negligible. According to one estimate, commercial shortwave broadcasters spent over $1,500,000 in 1941 on direct operating costs alone. This was expected to increase to $2,000,000 in 1942. However, total revenues for commercial service in 1941 were only $150,000. Such initial losses, of course, could be justified if there was reason to believe that the service, at some point in the future, would move into the black. However, there was little reason to expect such a development. There was no evidence of any increased interest on the part of advertisers in shortwave. At the end of 1941, Crosley had only eight shortwave sponsors; NBC, six (including RCA); Westinghouse, one (Westinghouse itself); and General Electric, four nonpaying sponsors who were given free air time for the programs they produced. CBS, with its Latin American network not yet in operation, did not offer commercial time. The programs presented by sponsors were mostly 15-minute, low budget productions consisting of either news or music. As one observer at the end of 1941 noted, "Shortwave still needs some giant advertiser to put its commercials on the map."[61]

It was becoming less likely, however, that such a "giant advertiser" would be found in the near future. Under various administration military preparedness measures, exports of products containing strategic materials were curtailed and more and more industrial production was being shifted from the export market to war-related needs. Aid to the Allies required that ships formerly used in United States–Latin American trade be diverted to transporting goods to Britain. The export business to Latin America experienced a crisis. Between 1941 and 1942, United States exports to the region declined 18 percent, from $1,035 million to $848 million.[62] Under such conditions, it would be years before the commercial broadcasters could expect to make a profit on their shortwave activities.

In the face of these considerations, the strong unified opposition against a government station on the part of the commercial broadcasters, a unified front demonstrated at the 1938 Congressional hearing and again during the uproar over the "culture" rule, began to break up. NBC and Crosley, the two companies most actively involved in selling commercial time and, most likely, the companies that had lost the most money in shortwave, were the most in favor of greater government involvement and activity. In conferences with the OCIAA in the fall of 1941, representatives from these two companies broached the possibility of government takeover and operation of all shortwave facilities.[63] Although Crosley had adequate technical facilities for its Latin American network, it had vastly underestimated the difficulties of setting up a shortwave commercial operation aimed at Latin American audiences. Although a powerful regional station, the Crosley broadcasting operation lacked the resources to follow through on its plans. Located in Ohio, it was in no position to develop a full programming schedule to Latin America. Crosley wanted out.

NBC was also losing money. In the first 10 months of 1941, NBC reported a loss of $245,000 on its shortwave service.[64] Yet, an equally important factor behind the company's openness to greater government involvement was that NBC was a subsidiary of RCA, a company that was no stranger to close government–industry collaboration. RCA President David Sarnoff was far more mindful of the international political dimension of shortwave broadcasting. Moreover, RCA was heavily involved in Latin America through the export of electrical equipment and the operation of radio communication facilities. Sarnoff and the company were willing to cooperate with the government in any way necessary to protect United States interests and investments in the region. Such cooperation would be easier if it meant relinquishing the unprofitable commercial shortwave service to the government.

The positions of Westinghouse and General Electric were similar to that of RCA. Their shortwave broadcasting activities were subsidiary to their manufacturing activities. Moreover, their shortwave stations were part of the NBC network. In general, they tended to follow the lead of NBC/RCA in shortwave broadcasting matters.

CBS was the only commercial shortwave broadcaster that, by the end of 1941, openly opposed any direct government involvement in shortwave broadcasting. Its Latin American network was not yet in operation, and it was transmitting with only 10 kw of power. Of the major shortwave companies, CBS was, at this point, the least involved in actual shortwave operations. Its opposition was due to the hope that its Latin American network would succeed commercially where the other broadcasters had failed. Moreover, as a company whose primary business was broadcasting, in contrast to RCA, Westinghouse, and General Electric, it was more wedded to the principle of opposition to active government involvement in broadcasting. CBS, of course, recognized the political aspect of shortwave broadcasting, but argued that privately operated broadcasting, without the onus of government control, censorship, and propaganda, would be far more effective in achieving the broad foreign policy aims of creating a positive opinion of the United States in the minds of the Latin Americans. CBS wanted to cooperate with the government, but on a voluntary basis, and on terms agreeable to the company.

War-Time Shortwave

With the United States entry into the war in December 1941, there was an expectation that the government would take over all communication facilities deemed necessary to the war effort, as it had in World War I. Some of the OCIAA officials anticipated that the government would immediately assume control of all shortwave facilities and operations. At last, it would seem, the OCIAA had a clear and unarguable mandate for direct intervention in international broadcasting.

In a brash and urgent memorandum entitled "A Proposal to Utilize International Radio for Victory," written shortly after the attack on Pearl Harbor, OCIAA radio officials proposed a program for war-time radio operations. While radio operations directed to the war zones in Europe and Asia were to be overtly propagandistic and geared to the specific needs of the Armed Forces, radio programming to Latin America still was to maintain its information/entertainment nature. The major and only goal of United States shortwave activity to Latin America was to provide "sound radio showmanship, [and] to create a flow of outstanding program attractions which would reveal the American nation as a powerful, personable, friendly, idealistic neighbor who is at war, and who will win its war."[65] The memorandum called for the immediate creation of a government radio corporation that would take over and operate all shortwave facilities. Previous objections, such as that a government station would endanger the status of private domestic broadcasting or that government originated programs would be discounted as propaganda, were dismissed as no longer valid in a war situation.

Despite such urgent words, prompt, direct government action in broadcasting and in communications generally was not forthcoming. The government–industry cooperation that the administration strove to cultivate was now bearing fruit. Upon hearing of the attack at Pearl Harbor, Sarnoff, a reserve colonel in the Army Signal Corps, immediately wired Roosevelt, informing him that all RCA facilities and personnel were at his disposal. The communications industry as a whole expressed a similar commitment to close industry–government cooperation in the crisis. Drastic government takeover was not necessary.

In the field of broadcasting, despite years of antagonistic relations between the administration and domestic broadcasters, the government had little problem in getting both the networks and the local stations to follow the directions and guidance of the COI and, later, the OWI. Although voluntary, broadcasters strictly adhered to the government's censorship guidelines. Following the OWI's directions, domestic radio programming began to play an important role in the war effort by promoting—generally free of charge—war bond sales, scrap drives, and other war-related campaigns.

In return for such cooperation, the administration made no move to touch the commercial, private, profit-oriented structure of United States broadcasting. Indeed, the government took steps, through indirect subsidization, to strengthen it. With many consumer goods all but disappearing from the market due to the shift to war production, radio, along with the print media, faced a drastic decline in advertising revenue. To correct this, the Treasury Department, in the summer of 1942, declared that a company could deduct advertising expenses even if it had no goods to sell to the public. This Treasury decision encouraged companies to continue to advertise and, during the war years, most radio stations experienced excellent financial health.

Shortwave broadcasters demonstrated a similar cooperative attitude. Immediately after the news of Pearl Harbor, all stations switched to 24-hour operations and greatly expanded their transmission of news to Europe and Latin America. The amount of news programming broadcast over CBS's 10 kw transmitter, for example, increased more than 400 percent during the first days of the war. The shortwave stations quickly added to their staffs, particularly trying to build up their European news broadcasts. Both the COI and the OCIAA provided background reports and general guidelines for the broadcasters. Also, the COI set up a post to monitor all United States programs in order to insure that no information of potential use to the enemy would be broadcast. Although compliance with government directives was voluntary, during the first few months of the war, there was little question of broadcasters acquiescing to government wishes in the area of content. At the request of the Army, both NBC and CBS began to transmit their more popular network programs overseas for the entertainment of United States troops. Crosley, in early spring 1942, voluntarily turned over all its shortwave program time to the COI.[66]

Such cooperation during the first months of the war was effective in achieving immediate government aims in the area of shortwave broadcasting. However, these informal voluntary arrangements could not last indefinitely. Broadcasters were being called upon to expand their shortwave operations to Europe and Asia as well as maintain their current level of broadcasting to Latin America. As the war progressed, no doubt the demands on shortwave would grow. Yet broadcasters were bearing most, if not all, of the cost of providing these services. While the broadcasters continually emphasized their patriotic motives in doing this, there was, no doubt, a limit.

Likewise, both the CIO and the OCIAA felt that the pre-war arrangement of indirect guidance and encouragement and voluntary cooperation was no longer adequate in a war-time situation. The broadcasters performed admirably in the weeks after Pearl Harbor. However, as the war progressed, the COI and OCIAA radio needs became more specialized. They could not rely on the voluntary cooperation of the broadcasters to accomplish their expanded propaganda tasks. If the United States was to wage an effective shortwave campaign, the government needed to exercise direct control over operations.

During the late winter and early spring months of 1942, representatives from the COI, OCIAA, and the broadcasters proposed and discussed various plans under which the government would take over and operate the nation's shortwave service. Rockefeller and the OCIAA, arguing that shortwave was a commercial failure and never could be expected to provide adequate facilities or programs, called for the creation of a government or combined government-industry-owned corporation to take over and operate the shortwave facilities. Rockefeller's plan would mean government ownership of shortwave stations. Most likely, it would have a very significant impact on the post-war development of shortwave.

The COI, on the other hand, offered what it called a "voluntary plan of cooperation" by which the government would lease all the time on all the stations. All programming would be centralized under the direction of the government. This plan would replace government ownership with government subsidization and leave open the post-war development of shortwave. Both the OCIAA and the COI agreed that, in any plan, shortwave transmission would be divided between the OCIAA and the COI, with the COI controlling and programming the time between 1:00 A.M. and 4:00 P.M. for transmission to Europe and Asia, and the OCIAA controlling the time between 4:00 P.M. and midnight for programs to Latin America. In presenting their different plans, the COI and the OCIAA strongly insisted, in what by now were ritualized statements, that they had no intention of stepping into the domestic broadcasting field.[67]

Publicly reversing a position maintained for almost a decade, the commercial shortwave broadcasters, with one exception, expressed no preference for either plan, nor did they suggest an alternative plan. They were willing to go along with anything, including government ownership. All they requested was that all government agencies involved make a definite decision on a unified policy and then tell the broadcasters.

The one exception was CBS and William Paley. Paley's reluctance to give blind approval to anything the government proposed was understandable. After more than 2 years of planning and spending over $500,000 on the construction of two new 50 kw transmitters, the CBS Latin American network was scheduled to go into operation, finally, in May 1942. While NBC, Crosley, Westinghouse, and General Electric were more than willing to write off their shortwave operations as unprofitable, CBS's shortwave system had not yet had a chance to prove itself. It was evident that there would not be any immediate profit in the system, given war conditions. However, Paley felt that commercial shortwave could play a big part in post-war United States–Latin American trade. Moreover, as broadcasting was CBS's major activity, he was reluctant to simply write off the entire Latin American operation.

To government proposals, he presented his own alternative. He proposed that all United States private shortwave broadcasters be organized into two privately owned organizations which would be run in close cooperation with the government, but would not be controlled by it. This would maintain and encourage a competitive system of international broadcasting. Such a system would, in the words of Paley, "maintain the competitive situation which has played an essential part in the development of domestic broadcasting, whose service is unparalleled anywhere else in the world."[68] As all the other commercial shortwave companies were currently programmed by NBC, it was evident that Paley hoped to expand the domestic NBC and CBS domination of broadcasting onto an international level. In any event, his Latin American network would remain intact.

The other private broadcasters offered Paley no support. Both the COI and the OCIAA rejected his proposal. Their major objection was that, as the nation's shortwave facilities were limited, it was wiser to aim for complete coordination than to divide the stations into two completely separate and competing groups. A more important but unstated objection was that the government would not have the kind of control it desired over the programming and organizational aspects of the shortwave system.

Although rejecting Paley's proposal, the OCIAA was careful not to alienate him. At this point, his cooperation and the use of CBS's Latin American network organization were deemed essential to the OCIAA radio campaign in Latin America. That the OCIAA and the government were courting Paley was evident at the ceremonies dedicating the CBS Latin network in late May. Among the speakers were Vice-President Henry Wallace, Sumner Welles, and Nelson Rockefeller. Also, speeches and remarks arranged with the assistance of the Department of State were received via shortwave from President Somoza of Nicaragua, President Rios of Chile, and President Medina of Venezuela. While all speakers used the opportunity for profuse praise of inter-American solidarity and good neighborliness, Welles, Rockefeller, and Wallace made certain that Paley and CBS received an equal amount of commendation and expressions of gratitude.[69]

Throughout the spring and early summer, officials from the OCIAA and the COI discussed the various plans. Eventually, the Federal Communications Commission, the Bureau of the Budget, and the White House were brought into the discussions. For a time, the discussion of the shortwave issue was held up due to a larger policy debate concerning the overall organization of all the government information activities. At one point, it was suggested that all OCIAA information activities be consolidated in the proposed Office of War Information. Rockefeller was able to mobilize State Department support, however, and was able to keep the Latin American information program separate from the OWI when it was formed in late June.

Generally, the administration's preference was for no radical alterations in the existing relations between the broadcasting industry and government. Thus, the Rockefeller plan for a government broadcasting corporation was dropped in favor of a leasing arrangement. During July, officials from the FCC, OWI, and OCIAA began meeting with the various shortwave companies regarding the leasing of all the time on their shortwave service. Overall, NBC was agreeable to any type of leasing arrangement as long as program quality was maintained. Since NBC and CBS would be doing most of the programming themselves under contract to the government, such concerns were not significant.[70]

Paley, on the other hand, was opposed to any leasing arrangement, as he felt it destroyed "the principle of free radio which...is the primary virtue of American shortwave as distinguished from that of other countries." He did not want to send out programs paid for by the government, even if such programs were prepared by CBS. He argued on behalf of his two competitive network plans, which, according to Paley, would be backed by government financing where necessary. Paley admitted that he was alone in his opposition to the government plan. Nonetheless, he declared "he was not willing to yield as it was a principle with him and not a question of dollars and cents."[71] His opposition was based on the fear that a government leasing arrangement would destroy any hope for CBS's Latin American network. It would lose its identity as a separate, distinct organization in the minds of its audience and would come to be regarded by Latin Americans as primarily a United States government propaganda medium. Yet, in spite of Paley's strong show of opposition, it was felt by the OCIAA's representatives who met with Paley that something could be worked out to meet Paley's objections.

Through late summer into early fall, the OWI and the OCIAA negotiated the specifics of a leasing arrangement. The resulting contract between the government and the broadcasters, signed in late October and going into effect November 1, reflected a compromise. Time on all shortwave stations would be leased by the government at cost, plus depreciation. The government would program all stations and determine the time of operation and direction of transmission. The OWI would occupy two-thirds of the transmision time (1:00 A.M. to 4:00 P.M.), and the OCIAA one-third (4:00 P.M. to midnight). Actual shortwave programming would be done on a contract basis, with the government having the right to approve all scripts before broadcast.[72]

The shortwave service to Europe, Asia, and Africa was consolidated into one operation. As a concession to Paley, however, the OCIAA allowed both NBC and CBS to maintain, in large part, their individual Latin American networks. Program contracts were signed by the OCIAA with NBC and CBS to provide programming to Latin America. In preparing and overseeing the Latin American programming, the OCIAA worked with each network individually. While the small Portuguese and English program services of NBC and CBS were merged, their Spanish language service was kept separate. Moreover, the OCIAA assigned the transmitters of the other shortwave broadcasters for use by the networks in their Latin American operations. CBS transmitted over its own transmitters, plus those of Crosley and one of World Wide's two transmitters. NBC used General Electric and Westinghouse's transmitters, in addition to RCA's, plus the other one of World Wide. Although the government was leasing all the time on the service, the "Voice of America" call was not used, and each network was allowed to introduce individual programs such as "CBS Presents" or "NBC Presents."[73]

Thus, Paley's proposal of two competitive networks was put into effect, in part, in Latin America. The major changes were that the government was subsidizing the entire affair and also had control over programming. The overall effect of the leasing contract was to bolster NBC's and CBS's presence in the region. With the addition of the transmitters of the other companies, NBC's and CBS's overall transmission of power was increased, and they would be able to continue to operate like private commercial networks by maintaining their own identity.

To sweeten the deal, the government announced in August that it planned to build 22 new shortwave transmitters of 50 to 100 kw power to augment the existing 14 transmitters. These new transmitters, owned by the government, would be licensed to the private broadcasting companies and would be operated in accordance with the overall leasing arrangement. Moreover, these new transmitters, estimated to cost around $7 million, would be controlled by the government only for the duration of the war. After the war, private broadcasters would have the option to buy them.[74]

The response to this overall arrangement between the broadcasters and the government was favorable. Westinghouse, Crosley, and General Electric were happy to have the government bear the cost of their transmitters. They made no objections to the fact that their shortwave broadcasting was subsumed under the NBC and CBS services and that their shortwave stations would become mere technical appendages. *Broadcasting* praised the leasing contracts and the plans for the new shortwave transmitters as an abandonment of the principle of government shortwave ownership and operation and the institution of government-industry "partnership" in the field of international broadcasting.[75]

The only dissenting voice was that of Walter Lemmon of World Wide. Although his station was the first to be subsidized by the government, he was the only shortwave broadcaster to balk at the leasing arrangement. Under this arrangement, World Wide would not be engaged in any programming activities, and, instead, would turn its transmitters over to NBC and CBS programs. Lemmon argued that the unique educational character of his station would be destroyed. He felt that his station should maintain its distinct identity, and he would not sign any leasing arrangement until he was assured that the educational programs of his station would be maintained. The OCIAA and OWI, however, had a different explanation for his reluctance. On November 2, 1942, they released a terse joint statement saying that, although Lemmon's station was currently being subsidized by the government, he had refused to sign the leasing contract because he was unsatisfied with the price the government was willing to pay for use of his facilities. The price he was demanding was higher than any of the other broadcasters had asked and would, in the opinion of the OWI and the OCIAA, yield World Wide, a nonprofit company, a very sizeable profit on its operations. Three days later, the government seized the station and began operating it as part of the overall OCIAA/OWI system. This was the only forcible government seizure of a private broadcasting station to occur during the war.[76]

While the industry welcomed the OCIAA/OWI leasing arrangement, among radio officials at the OCIAA, there were second thoughts about the whole deal. Although NBC generally proved to be very cooperative, relations with CBS were troublesome. A little over a month after the leasing arrangement went into effect, the Radio Division reported to Rockefeller that it was experiencing serious difficulties with CBS. One main trouble point was control of program content. Under the programming contract, the OCIAA indicated general guidelines and goals for specific shows. CBS then wrote the script, and produced and broadcast the show. However, CBS was very reluctant to allow OCIAA review of the script before actual broadcast. Since OCIAA was ultimately responsible for all broadcast content, OCIAA radio officials were understandably chagrined by CBS's behavior. They attributed all the problems to "a lack of understanding and an obstructionist attitude" on the part of CBS, which "stands stubbornly on what it believes to be its principles and contends every inch." Overall, the network did not seem to appreciate the fact that the government was paying for all the programming and, as any regular commercial sponsor, had the right of general supervision over program content.[77]

Also, OCIAA officials were very much aware of the fact that, by allowing NBC and CBS to maintain their network identities and by assigning them the use of the transmitters of the other shortwave companies, they were, in effect, subsidizing a monopoly over Latin American radio by the two networks. Since OCIAA officials found the implications of this distasteful, particularly since CBS tried to take advantage of the situation. Even though the transmitting stations of Crosley and World Wide broadcast only CBS programming, they still identified themselves over the air by their original call letters and station name. CBS wanted their station identification changed to "This is the Columbia Broadcasting System transmitting on the 25 meter band." According to the CBS representative who proposed this, "I believe this. . . would avoid giving the impression that we are just another government-run radio set-up." Feeling this would assist CBS in obtaining a monopoly in international shortwave broadcasting at the expense of the other licensees, the OCIAA rejected the suggestion.[78]

Other problems became apparent. The highly vaunted CBS network of Latin American affiliate stations was not living up to expectations. Numerous reports were received by the OCIAA that CBS affiliates in Latin America were not broadcasting OCIAA feature programs. OCIAA programs, for example, were not being cleared by CBS affiliates in Brazil, Bolivia, Chile, El Salvador, Honduras, Peru, Venezuela, and Argentina. Many of the affiliates were unable to pick up the shortwave transmission with consistently good quality for local rebroadcasting. Similar, although far less numerous, complaints were received about NBC affiliates. Moreover, where both NBC and CBS affiliates did broadcast the network and OCIAA programs, the competition between the local affiliates tended to split the audience.[79]

As OCIAA officials assessed the situation in early 1943, the major problem with the radio operation in Latin America was an over-reliance on direct shortwave broadcasts and local rebroadcasts of shortwave programs. Shortwave operations were being carried out by NBC and CBS operating as two competing networks. This system diluted available transmission power and split local Latin audiences. Also, with two network organizations to coordinate, the OCIAA had numerous problems exercising effective control over program production and activities. One OCIAA radio staff member, in a memorandum recounting the numerous problems he had encountered, expressed his frustration with the present set-up:

> Why should the two shortwave networks, which unquestionably owe their very existence to the Government complicate our operations instead of doing everything they can to help us? I say that they owe their very existence to the government, because, after thoroughly testing shortwave broadcasting from every possible angle commencing over two years ago, I became absolutely convinced that commercially they would never be able to meet their expenses.[80]

To deal with the inadequacies of shortwave, the OCIAA began to develop alternative methods of reaching Latin American radio audiences. One very successful alternative was the use of transcriptions. Spanish and Portuguese programs were developed and produced by the OCIAA in the United States, transcribed onto records, and then sent to local Latin American radio stations. Another alternative was local live production of OCIAA-prepared scripts. While these two alternatives proved to be very useful, due to the time lag between production and actual broadcast, they could not replace shortwave broadcasts and rebroadcasts in the extremely important areas of news, topical, and current events programming.

In early spring 1943, OCIAA officials began to consider reorganizing the entire Latin American shortwave operation. They saw that the major problem was NBC and CBS operating as two competing networks in Latin America. This created problems in the supervision, transmission, and reception of the programs to Latin America. The obvious solution was for the OCIAA to exercise its power under the contract and merge the two networks into one operation in Latin America.

In May 1943, John Ogilvie, associate director of the Radio Division, wrote all shortwave broadcasters informing them that, effective July 1, the current two-network Spanish program service would be merged into one; NBC and CBS would program alternate hours. Under this plan, "the best and most important programs of CBS and NBC. . .would be broadcast simultaneously on the maximum number of transmitters in an effort to secure better reception and coverage.[81] Overall, the amount of individual NBC and CBS programming would be cut in half, saving the OCIAA a considerable amount of money and also increasing its ability to control and direct programming.

As expected, none of the shortwave broadcasters voiced opposition to the plan with the exception of Paley and CBS. A merger of the two networks would lead CBS's Latin network to lose its identity and become "another government-run radio set-up." Whereas, before, Paley could define how much government involvement he would allow by cooperating voluntarily in CBS's shortwave activities, at this point he was bound by the program and leasing contract he had signed with the government. Being no longer in control of the situation, he tried to negotiate a less drastic alternative. He suggested that, rather than merge the two shortwave networks, all shortwave transmitters be used simultaneously for OCIAA feature programs, returning to the two-network operation at all other times. OCIAA's desire for more effective coverage would be satisfied without having to sacrifice the dual network operation and CBS's distinct network identity in Latin America.

OCIAA officers, after studying Paley's suggestion, rejected it as technically unfeasible. The switching of transmitters from dual to single network transmissions would require a 15-minute period in which the transmitters would have to go off the air for technical adjustments for each changeover. Moreover, Paley was unable to gather any support from the other shortwave broadcasters. NBC officials were strongly in favor of the OCIAA proposal as they felt it would greatly improve coverage and reception in Latin America of United States programs.[82]

Paley had to admit defeat. He accepted the fact that, for the duration of the war, the CBS Latin network was to give way to OCIAA control. In a letter to Francisco, he noted that the OCIAA decision was a disappointment. Nonetheless, he stated, CBS would cooperate fully. Perhaps as a consolation prize, the first two new government shortwave transmitters to be built were licensed and delivered to CBS in late summer 1943.[83]

On July 1, 1943, the merger of the programming service of the two networks was instituted. Afterwards, reception of United States shortwave was greatly improved and affiliate stations in Latin America were able to pick up shortwave programs for rebroadcasting to local audiences much better than before. Moreover, the OCIAA was able to exercise far more control and guidance in specific program content, thus enabling it to reach Latin American audiences with programs which corresponded more closely to its specific political aims.

For the duration of the war, relations between the OCIAA, the OWI, and the broadcasters were generally trouble-free, and no further objection or opposition was voiced to government control of shortwave. CBS cooperated fully. This, no doubt, was due in part to the fact that Paley left for Europe in fall 1943 to serve as a civilian consultant to the Office of War Information, with the rank of honorary colonel. The next year, he became chief of Radio Broadcasting within the Psychological Warfare Division of the Supreme Headquarters of the Allied Expeditionary Forces. Working under Eisenhower, he was responsible for the allied forces' radio propaganda efforts in connection with the D-Day invasion. No doubt, from this experience, he learned to appreciate the government's concern about the control of international broadcasting. In any event, for the rest of the war, Paley paid little attention to CBS's Latin American network.

OCIAA Activities in Latin America

With the problems with the shortwave broadcasters settled, the OCIAA could concentrate all of its energies on developing and implementing an information campaign in Latin America. In contrast to the OWI, which broadcast toward war areas, OCIAA's efforts were aimed at audiences in nations not actively engaged in the war. Before Pearl Harbor, the major aim was to evoke "passive collaboration," or a unity which emphasized the defense and solidarity of the hemisphere. This campaign was considered a success, for, in the words of Rockefeller, "when the critical moment—declaration of war against this country—arrived, all the other American republics, without exception, volunteered some expression of allegiance to the U.S. cause."[84]

After the United States entry into the war, the aims became more specific. The information activities sought to evoke full, active hemispheric collaboration by making a case for the breaking of diplomatic relations with the Axis powers, followed hopefully by a declaration of war; full military cooperation; the suppression of subversive Axis activities—including propaganda—throughout the hemisphere; and a coordinated economic program for the production and control of critical materials. The emphasis on these various aims changed with the course of the war. In the first year and a half of the war, emphasis was placed on convincing Latin America that the United States would win. News and programs dealing with the progress of the war and the power of the Allies were highlighted. This was meant to counteract any defeatist Axis propaganda and encourage Latin Americans to get on the winning side. In addition, the OCIAA highlighted the part Latin America was playing in the war by portraying efforts aimed at the acquisition of strategic materials and the development of various United States-supported economic projects in Latin America. In the latter part of 1943 and on into 1944, with victory in sight, the OCIAA, looking to the post-war world, began to deemphasize the war and increase attention given to hemispheric economic interdependence, solidarity, and post-war planning.[85]

OCIAA's efforts, however, were complicated by a number of problems. The Latin American media were heavily dependent on United States export advertising, particularly since European export advertising totally dried up after 1939. Although there were no precise figures, it was generally estimated that in the early 1940s, approximately 40 percent of all print and radio advertising revenue in Latin America came from United States companies doing business in the region.[86] Initially, the OCIAA tried to take advantage of the Latin media's dependency on United States advertising dollars by urging United States exporters to boycott pro-Axis media outlets and support those radio stations and publications friendly to United States policy aims. However, with the United States entry into the war, there was a decline in United States exports to the region. Exporters, in turn, began to cut back on their advertising expenditures, creating serious financial difficulties for the pro-United States media. For newspapers and magazines, there was the additional problem of a heavy dependency on North American newsprint, shipments of which were curtailed due to shipping shortages.

To the OCIAA, this was a grand opportunity to further insure the cooperation of the Latin American media in its information activities. In August 1942, Rockefeller was able to persuade the Treasury Department, in line with its ruling on domestic advertising, to allow companies to deduct as a business expenses all export advertising, even though they actually had no products to sell. He then contracted over 1,300 United States companies doing business in Latin America and urged them to maintain or even increase their pre-war level of advertising in the Latin American media. He argued that this would be a significant, and tax-deductible, contribution to the war effort. Also looking forward to the post-war market, he noted that it would be important for them to keep their names before the Latin American public.[87]

The overall response by United States exporters was very positive. A survey conducted by the OCIAA in early 1943 revealed that 65 percent of 376 exporters intended to maintain or increase their Latin American advertising. Despite the fact that United States exporters had little or no goods to sell, expenditures by United States advertisers in the region grew from $8 million in 1942 to $16 million in 1944 and $20 million in 1945. In order to assist exporters, the OCIAA issued thematic guidelines and directions to be followed by advertisers in writing their advertising copy. Thus, much of the advertising, in addition to keeping the exporter's name before the Latin public, stressed the various propaganda points (e.g., inter-American solidarity, and the Allied war effort) that the OCIAA was trying to get across. By mid-1943, the OCIAA had been in contact with over 1,500 firms, assisting them in their advertising in Latin America. This included both Latin American print and local radio advertising.[88]

The primary task of OCIAA's activities in this area was to direct United States advertising toward pro-Allied media, and use such advertising to win Latin American support for United States policy. However, in some instances, United States advertising was utilized to pressure some newspapers and radio stations to drop advertising from black-listed firms. In

Mexico City, for example, a number of newspapers were informed that, unless they discontinued advertising from suspected pro-Axis firms, United States motion picture advertisers, who carried several full pages of advertising daily, would withdraw their advertising. The Mexican newspapers gave in.[89]

In conjunction with its black-listing and advertising projects, the OCIAA's press section began to supply news releases, feature stories, photographs, and other editorial material to Latin American publications and radio stations. By mid-1944, the OCIAA estimated that it was distributing a daily average of four items of information material to each of over 1,000 leading newspapers in Latin America. It also estimated that approximately 75 percent of the material was being used. Also, the OCIAA expedited shipment of newsprint to those publications it found to be friendly to the Allied war cause.

An important element in the OCIAA's media activities, particularly in radio, was the OCIAA coordinating committee that existed in each of the American republics. These committees oversaw OCIAA activities on a local level. They had official government status, worked in conjunction with the local United States embassy, and were funded by the OCIAA. However, their connections to the OCIAA or the State Department were not publicized. The local committees were comprised of prominent local United States citizens, most of whom were employees of Latin American subsidiaries of United States companies. The coordinating committee in Argentina, for example, was headed by an official from the local branch of the Standard Oil Company. Committtee members included employees of Ford, National City Bank, Armco, and General Motors. The press-radio division of the Argentine committee was run by representatives of the local branches of RCA, McCann Erickson, N.W. Ayers, and J. Walter Thompson. In time, the coordinating committee became an effective field organization for the OCIAA.[91]

OCIAA radio operations were divided between direct shortwave and shortwave rebroadcasting, and local radio broadcasts based on transcriptions and local live productions. Time on local radio stations was bought by the OCIAA. In the case of the shortwave rebroadcasts on the local affiliates of NBC and CBS, the local stations received their fee through the networks. For transcription broadcasts and local live productions, the local coodinating committee made all the arrangements, bought the time on the local station, and checked the actual broadcast. The majority of programs transmitted over shortwave were news and commentary, all focusing on the war. Both shortwave and transcribed programs also included musical and variety shows (including a Spanish version of the "Hit Parade") and dramatic productions. The dramatic productions tended to emphasize war themes and topics. The following example of radio shows, taken from an OCIAA program handbook, gives an idea of the programs produced by the OCIAA and broadcast by shortwave, transcription, or live local production:

> "Cavalcade of America"—The struggle for freedom in the United States. . . . Places special emphasis on the part played by American citizens in the fight.
>
> "Hero's Tribute"—Re-enacted dramatization of the American fighting men on the far-flung battle fronts of Europe.
>
> "The Mysterious One"—Based on authentic information of pro-Axis activities. . . . Takes the form of fictionalized drama depicting a typical Latin American, his sincere admiration of the United States and the United Nations . . . . An extremely powerful means of making clear to the masses what pro-Axis activities really mean in terms of their own independence, their own economic welfare, and the existence of their nations' soverign states [sic].
>
> "Believe it or Not for South America"—These programs present interesting facts with particular reference to the war and the hemispheric defense effort.
>
> "Fighting Youth"—Patterned after "Major Bowes' Amateur Hour." Programs center around a master of ceremonies who interviews men in the Army camps. Performers discuss their training to defeat the enemy, describe Army life, and talent is demonstrated in singing and playing of musical instruments.[92]

As is evident, OCIAA shows attempted to achieve the overall goal of creating Latin American support for the war effort and establishing closer ties between the United States and Latin America. How successful the individual shows were was never really precisely determined. A number of programs, however, were popular enough that, after the war, regular commercial sponsors in Latin America took them over and continued producing them.[93]

The OCIAA involvement in producing and broadcasting these programs over Latin American radio was not a secret. However, the OCIAA generally tried to keep as low a profile as possible. Initially, the OCIAA prohibited local coordinating committees from seeking local commercial sponsors for the transcribed and locally produced OCIAA radio programs. However, by 1943, it had changed that policy, both to save money and to take "the sting from our propaganda message because the show is not automatically suspected of being government inspired."[94]

Although the immediate major goal of OCIAA's information activities was to counter Axis propaganda and mobilize Latin American public opinion in support of United States policy, a concomitant, but not as well articulated, objective of OCIAA officials involved the "modernization" of Latin American media. With few exceptions, the OCIAA radio staff came from backgrounds in advertising or commercial radio broadcasting.[95] In trying to reach Latin American radio audiences, they applied their knowledge, assumptions, and biases acquired from working in United States broadcasting to the Latin American radio situation. Many of them felt that, compared to the United States, much of Latin American radio was vastly underdeveloped, and that few Latin Americans understood or appreciated the potential of radio. OCIAA radio officials tied the success of their Latin American activities to their ability to upgrade and modernize the medium. This attitude is well expressed in a memorandum written in 1941 proposing (prematurely) major subsidization of NBC and CBS program and network activities in Latin America in order to consolidate the networks' presence in the region and build major radio audiences. The memorandum argued,

> We will find ourselves, at the cost of a million dollars or so, revolutionizing the radio picture in Latin American, bringing to those countries the same benefits that accrued to our nation from the development of chain radio. We will build the habit of listening on one side, and we will create the star show philosophy on the other. We will make radio not only more desirable from the quality of offerings, but more exciting in the sale of more sets, the greater use of sets, and as our audience builds, we will have the means of educating, influencing, and informing the peoples of the other republics.[96]

After 1943, the OCIAA emphasized the role that advertising would play in extending and developing markets in Latin America for United States goods, and saw much of its information activity as preparing for this. Much of the information gathered by the OCIAA on Latin American media and markets was made available to United States advertisers and exporters. In 1943, the OCIAA put together a "media cost plan" for United States exporters "which enable[d] a manufacturer to form a quick rough estimate of the cost of an advertising program in Latin America to fit almost any budget." In 1944, the OCIAA compiled all its information on radio, press, and magazine advertising rates and market size in Latin America into a book made available to United States exporters. This publication represented the first comprehensive guide to Latin American advertising media and was heartily welcomed by exporters.[97]

Overall, the impact and success of the OCIAA's information activities in Latin America are difficult to gauge. Rockefeller estimated, for example, that Motion Picture Division's material at its peak was viewed by over 40 million Latin Americans weekly, the Radio Division output was heard by 15 to 20 million daily, and the Press Division's material reached 40 to 60 million Latin Americans monthly.[98] However, no efforts were made to study or measure the effect of such output on Latin American public opinion. No substantial surveys were conducted and, other than from anecdotal accounts, there is no clear evidence that OCIAA's efforts were successful in countering Axis propaganda or mobilizing public opinion in favor of the United States.

The greatest observable impact of OCIAA's activity was not on public opinion, but on the structure and operation of the Latin American media. Exploiting the media's dependence on United States advertising revenue, the OCIAA acted to strangle those publications and radio stations not supporting United States interests or war aims, and to bolster those media that did. In the press, it accomplished this largely through the willingness of United States advertisers to follow OCIAA's guidelines and directives. In radio, this practice was complemented by direct United States government payments to radio stations. It was estimated that, by the end of the war, the United States government, through the OCIAA, was the largest radio time user and revenue producer for Latin American broadcasters.[99] While the OCIAA may not have won the support of the Latin American masses, it nevertheless must have gained the allegiance of the Latin American media owners.

Aside from its political impact on the Latin American media, the OCIAA information activities had a more basic effect of assisting the development of the Latin media, particularly the newer medium of radio, along the lines of the United States model. One goal of the OCIAA was to further develop Latin American media as advertising outlets for United States exporters to the region. Moreover, the OCIAA, through its radio programming activities and support of NBC and CBS efforts, played a great role in determining the character of Latin American radio. Program formats and styles began to resemble those of the United States. As the Latin American correspondent for *Variety* noted happily after the war,

Ten years ago Latin American radio was attuned to the Old World. The tastes of its directors and listeners were altogether European. Today Latin American radio, celebrating its twenty-fifth anniversary, is distinctly of the New World. . . .

Advertising agencies, some local, many branches of North American firms, find radio one of their best media. In the smaller places, the stations do the whole job themselves, getting their own business, developing programs and doing their own collecting. . . . Bigger stations. . . are following the trend from the United States and are producing more and more live programming, especially during evening hours. These stations and others like them time their productions and program them as in the United States. Broadcasters who once imported their top talent, ideas, equipment and way of operation from Europe now look to the United States. They bring down *yanqui* artists and even struggle through the hot-pix-stix language of *Variety*, the U.S. radio and theatrical weekly, to catch up with what's new. They have their own programs cut and fitted to the tastes of local listeners. But they've borrowed many ideas, from quiz shows to commentators and man-in-the-street interviews.[100]

Notes

1 Lansford P. Yandell, "How to Build Good Will and Sales by Short Wave Broadcasts," *Export Trade and Shipper*, 13 May 1940, p. 4; "Radio Programs and Listeners in Latin America," ibid., 21 October 1940, p. 7.

2 "AP News Selected for Latin American Series," *Broadcasting*, 15 November 1939, p. 48; "Foreign Time Sold by NBC," ibid., 15 November 1939, p. 30; *New York Times*, 9 November 1939, 34:4; "NBC Sponsored International Broadcasts," *Variety 1940/1941 Radio Directory*, pp. 347–348.

3 Yandell, "How to Build Good Will;" "Foreign Rate Card is Issued by NBC," *Broadcasting*, 1 April 1940, p. 37. *New York Times*, 23 March 1940, 20:4.

4 "American Radio Dominates Latin Waves," *Broadcasting*, 1 October 1940, p. 30. In testimony on the Chavez-McAdoo bill in 1938, Frederic Willis of CBS noted that they received numerous requests from Latin American shortwave listeners for more news about Hollywood fashions and personalities. To this, Senator Bone remarked, "Maybe we are ruining South America with Hollywood. U.S., Congress, Senate, *Hearings Before a Subcommittee of the Committee on Interstate Commerce on S. 3342...*, 75th Congress, 3rd Session, 1939, p. 106.

5 "Movie Shortwave Series on NBC's Latin Service Starts by End of Month," *Broadcasting*, 15 September 1940, p. 44; "Movie Firms and NBC Consider Proposals for Latin Shortwave Service," *Broadcasting*, 1 November 1940, p. 100; *New York Times*, 14 August 1940, 5:8; "Sale of South American Time Planned by New Crosley International Station," *Broadcasting*, 1 November 1939, p. 40; "WLWO Starts Service to Latin America with Four Sponsors Already Secured," ibid., 1 September 1940, p. 36.

6 *Broadcasting—1941 Yearbook*, p. 311; Westinghouse Electric Company, "History of Shortwave Broadcasting," (no date), mimeo, Broadcast Pioneers Library, Washington, D.C., p. 36.

7 "Tydol's GE Shortwave," *Broadcasting*, 1 June 1940, p. 30; "Sponsors Supply Programming to GE," ibid., 15 December 1940, p. 95; "Latin Serenade," *Business Week*, 19 July 1941, p. 34.

8 "CBS Given Authority for International Outlet; Plans Shortwave Center," *Broadcasting*, 1 September 1940, p. 36; "Education Project CBS Extended to Latin America," ibid., 15 March 1940, p. 78; "CBS School Program Entering Its 12th Year, Reaches Latin Nations," ibid., 1 October 1940, p. 64.

9 Beth Alene Roberts, "United States Propaganda Warfare in Latin America, 1938-1942" (Ph.D. dissertation, University of Southern California, 1943), p. 406; "Reaching via Ether for Latin Trade," *Business Week*, 13 January 1940, p. 46.

10 Charles J. Rolo, *Radio Goes to War* (New York: G.P. Putnam's Sons, 1942), p. 241; "American Radio Dominates Latin Waves."

11 "Shortwave Radio Opens to Commerce;" *Commerce*, January 1940, pp. 16–17; "Commercial Series for Latin Nations Viewed as Aid to Hemispheric Relations," *Broadcasting*, 15 October 1940, p. 26.

12 "The Story of Advertising by Radio in 1940 and the Outlook," *Export Trade and Shipper*, 20 January 1941, pp. 18–19.

13 Robert Dallek, *Franklin D. Roosevelt and American Foreign Policy, 1932–1945* (New York: Oxford University Press, 1979), pp. 216–218.

[14] Samuel L. Bailey, *The United States and the Development of South America, 1945-1975* (New York: New Viewpoints, 1976), pp. 38-39.

[15] Harold N. Graves, *War on the Short Wave* (New York: Foreign Policy Association, 1941), pp. 37-38.

[16] *New York Times*, 19 November 1940, 42:3; 20 November 1940, 40:3.

[17] Payne to Wilson, 13 March 1940, Radio General 1940 file, Box 544, BFDC.

[18] "Communications Defense Board Projected," *Broadcasting*, 1 July 1940, p. 9; "Defense Board Given Limited Authority," ibid., 1 October 1940, p. 11; "Long Range Defense Program Under Way," ibid., 13 January 1941, p. 14.

[19] "Communications Defense Board Projected."

[20] "Heavy Expenditures for New Equipment to Bolster Service to Latin America," *Broadcasting*, 1 August 1940, p. 126.

[21] "Shortwave Survey," ibid., 1 November 1940, p. 91.

[22] "Roosevelt Praises Role of Radio in American Unity," ibid., 1 November 1940, p. 80.

[23] William S. Paley, *As It Happened—A Memoir* (Garden City: Doubleday, 1979), pp. 141-142.

[24] "Commercial Series as Aid to Hemispheric Relations."

[25] Allen Brewster Maxwell, "Evoking Latin American Collaboration in the Second World War—A Study of the Office of the Coordinator of Inter-American Affairs (1940-1946)" (Ph.D. dissertation, Fletcher School of Law and Diplomacy, 1971), p. 75; "Shortwave Power Boost is Extended to July 1," *Broadcasting*, 27 January 1941, p. 15; Hohberg to Payne, 9 February 1940, Latin American Radio 1940 file, Box 2731, BFDC.

[26] "NBC to Start Regular Pickups by Stations in Latin America," *Broadcasting*, 1 December 1940, p. 28.

[27] "CBS Latin Hookup Covers 18 Nations," ibid., 1 January 1941, p. 18; William Paley, "Radio Turns South," *Fortune*, April 1941, p. 77.

[28] *New York Times*, 27 February 1941, 10:6; "Radio Pan-america," *Broadcasting*, 1 January 1941, p. 38.

[29] "Shouse to Tour Latin Countries," *Broadcasting*, 27 January 1941, p. 15; "Merchandising Set-Up in Latin Nations Included in Crosley Rebroadcast Net," ibid., 8 August 1941, p. 51.

[30] "Royal to Leave on Latin American Tour to Promote NBC Activities to the South," *Broadcasting*, 21 July 1941, p. 3; "Network in Mexico Ties up with NBC," ibid., 25 August 1941, p. 11; "NBC's Latin American Hook-up Completed with 92 Stations," ibid., 8 September 1941, p. 26; "Latin American Networks of U.S. Broadcasting Companies," *Broadcasting—1942 Yearbook*, p. 400; Rolo, *Radio Goes to War*, p. 247.

[31] Charles J. Rolo and R. Strausz-Hupe, "U.S. International Broadcasting," *Harper's*, August 1941, pp. 306-307.

[32] "CBS Makes Plans for School Series," *Broadcasting*, 1 August, 1940, p. 137.

[33] "Republic Steel Extends GE Shortwave Service," *Broadcasting*, 1 January 1941, p. 54-b; Advertising-Radio-Latin America file, Box 2506, BFDC.

[34] "NBC's Shortwave on Wartime Basis," *Broadcasting*, 5 May 1941, p. 18; "NBC Includes Direct Appeal to French in Shortwave Message of President," ibid., 19 May 1940, p. 12.

[35] When the OCIAA was originally created in August 1940, it was named the Office for the Coordination of Commercial and Cultural Relations between the Ameri-

can Republics. The next year it was reorganized and renamed the Office of the Coordinator of Inter-American Affairs. For the sake of convenience, the OCIAA designation will be used throughout.

36 Quoted in Joe Alex Morris, *Nelson Rockefeller— A Biography* (New York: Harper & Brothers, 1960), p. 115.

37 U.S., Office of Inter-American Affairs, *History of the Office of the Coordinator of Inter-American Affairs* (hereafter cited as *OCIAA History*), by Donald W. Rowland, Historical Reports on War Administration (Washington, D.C.: Government Printing Office, 1947), p. 6.

38 *OCIAA History*, Appendix, pp. 279–280.

39 Morris, *Rockefeller*, p. 132.

40 *OCIAA History*, p. 280; p. 7, footnote 8.

41 Paley, *As It Happened*, pp. 140–141.

42 James B. Reston, "Our Second Line of Defense," *New York Times Magazine*, 29 June 1941, p. 7.

43 As this study is focusing primarily on the radio activities of the OCIAA, its involvement with the other media will be mentioned only when relevant. For accounts of the OCIAA's other media activities, see *OCIAA History*, Chapters 4–8, and Maxwell, "Evoking Latin American Collaboration," Chapters 1–5, 13. Other studies which are devoted, in part, to an examination of the OCIAA's activities are Roberts, "Propaganda Warfare in Latin America," and Gaizka de Usabel, "American Films in Latin America: The Case History of United Artists Corporation, 1919–1951" (Ph.D. dissertation, University of Wisconsin, 1975), pp. 389–477.

44 For a discussion of the relations between the OCIAA and the COI and OWI, see *OCIAA History*, pp. 195–205, Morris, *Rockefeller*, pp. 154–169, and James P. Warburg, *Unwritten Treaty* (New York: Harcourt, Brace and Company, 1946), pp. 79–96. For a comprehensive study of the OWI and its activities, see Allan M. Winkler, *The Politics of Propaganda—The Office of War Information* (New Haven: Yale University Press, 1978).

45 "Francisco, Bickel on Defense Body," *Broadcasting*, 1 November 1940, p. 17; U.S., Congress, House, Committee on Appropriations, *Hearings on the Second Deficiency Appropriations Bill for 1941*, 77th Congress, 1st Session, 1941, pp. 694, 718.

46 Executive Committee Minutes, 12 September 1940, Box 5433, OCIAA.

47 Francisco to Rockefeller, 16 April 1941, Shortwave Misc. I file, pp. 1–2, 6–9, Box 243, OCIAA.

48 Executive Committee Minutes, 15 January 1941, ibid.

49 *OCIAA History*, p. 59; Maxwell, "Evoking Latin American Collaboration," p. 82.

50 Executive Committee Minutes, 23 April 1941, Box 5433, OCIAA.

51 "Latin Board Plans Advertising Study," *Broadcasting*, 17 February 1941, p. 10; "Cantril Discusses New Latin Board," ibid., 3 March 1941, p. 28; *Hearings on the Second Deficiency Appropriations Bill for 1941*, pp. 696–714.

52 Francisco to Peck, 15 October 1941, Box 243, OCIAA; Robert William Pirsein, "The Voice of America—A History of the International Broadcasting Activities of the United States Government, 1940–1962" (Ph.D. dissertation, Northwestern University, 1970), pp. 15–16.

[53] "Francisco Favors Creation of Bureau to Coordinate Hemisphere Broadcasting," *Broadcasting*, 1 December 1940, p. 28.

[54] Quoted in "Foreign Broadcast Office in State Department Urged in Column by Dorothy Thompson," ibid., 12 May 1941, pp. 118.

[55] "Federal Control of Broadcast is Conceived as Threat to Effectiveness," ibid., 19 May 1941, p. 30.

[56] "Firms Operating International Stations Name Stanley Richardson Coordinator," ibid., 12 April 1941, p. 12.

[57] *New York Times*, 4 May 1941, IV:6:1.

[58] "Program Line ties Shortwave Stations, Permitting Combined Use of Facilities," *Broadcasting*, 27 October 1941, p. 51.

[59] Executive Committee Minutes, 18 September, 1940, 13 November 1940, 18 December 1940, 12 February 1941, Box 5433, OCIAA: *OCIAA History*, p. 59.

[60] "Federal Operation of Stations is Called Objectionable by Fly," *Broadcasting*, 1 January 1941, p. 54-A.

[61] "Shortwave Stations Rally to the Call," *Broadcasting*, 29 December 1941, p. 20. Charles J. Rolo and Robert Strausz-Hupe, "Reaching for Trade Through Ether," *Barron's*, 22 December 1941, p. 9.

[62] U.S., Department of Commerce, *Statistical Abstract of the United States*, 1946, p. 910.

[63] "A Proposal to Utilize International Radio for Victory," December 1941, Shortwave Misc. I file, Box 243, OCIAA.

[64] NBC International Shortwave: Statement, 27 November 1942, File 38, Box 101, National Broadcasting Company Archives, State Historical Society of Wisconsin, Madison, Wisconsin.

[65] Memorandum, December 1941, Misc. Shortwave I file, Box 243, OCIAA.

[66] "Shortwaves on 24 Hour Basis," *Broadcasting*, 15 December 1941, p. 18; "NBC's Top Series Go by Shortwave to Forces Abroad," ibid., 9 March 1942, p. 54; "Wartime Shortwave operations Up to FDR and Budget Bureau," ibid.

[67] "President May Settle Shortwave Dispute," *Broadcasting*, 23 February 1942, p. 10.

[68] "Shortwavers Put Plan of Operation up to Government," ibid., 2 March 1942, p. 16.

[69] "CBS Opens New Latin Hookup, Radio Praised by High Officials," ibid., 25 May 1942, p. 22.

[70] "Wartime Shortwave Operation Up to FDR;" *OCIAA History*, p. 61; Memorandum: NBC First Conference Re: Leasing Time, 4 August 1942, Leasing of Time file, Box 243, OCIAA.

[71] Memorandum, 8 August 1942, ibid.

[72] "US Poised to Lease All Shortwave Stations," *Broadcasting*, 2 November 1942, p. 7; Summary of Facilities Contract between Government and International Broadcasters, 15 December 1942, Shortwave Programming File, Box 241, OCIAA.

[73] Radio Division Report, 1 June 1943, Misc. Reports file, Box 966, OCIAA; Pirsein, "The Voice of America," p. 30.

[74] "Radio Steps into Leading Wartime Role"; "22 New Shortwave Outlets Projected," *Broadcasting*, 24 August 1942, p. 62.

[75] "Govt. Ownership, Operation Out, 'Partnership' Concept Goes Forward,"

ibid., 31 August 1942, p. 13.

[76] "Shortwave Outlets Geared for African Push," ibid., 16 November 1942.

[77] Memorandum, 7 December 1942, Shortwave Programming file, Box 241, OCIAA.

[78] Memorandum, 7 December 1942; Larson to Ogilvie, 11 December 1942; Shortwave Misc. II file, Box 243, OCIAA.

[79] Haydon to Ogilvie, 24 December 1942; Kranz to Haydon, 19 November 1942; NBC-CBS file, Box 242, OCIAA.

[80] Haydon to Francisco, 28 November 1942, Shortwave Misc. II file, Box 243, OCIAA.

[81] Ogilvie to Paley, 4 May 1943, Shortwave Misc. III file, Box 243, OCIAA.

[82] Francisco to Rockefeller, 4 May 1943, ibid.

[83] Paley to Francisco, 13 May 1943, ibid.; "CBS Gets First Plant in Shortwave Program," Broadcasting, 12 July 1943, p. 43.

[84] U.S., Congress, House, Committee on Appropriations, Subcommittee on Deficiency Appropriations, Hearings on the First Supplemental National Defense Appropriations Bill for 1943, 77th Congress, 2nd Session, p. 560.

[85] Maxwell, "Evoking Latin American Collaboration," pp. 32, 35.

[86] "Defense May Restrict Latin American Radio," Broadcasting, 10 October 1941, p. 59. U.S., Congress, House, Hearings on the National War Agencies Appropriations Bill for 1944, 78th Congress, 1st Session, p. 304.

[87] "Export Advertising Permitted in Spite of Market Loss," Broadcasting, 12 October 1942, p. 56.

[88] New York Times, 12 January 1943, 34:2, 2 February 1945, 23:5; OCIAA History, pp. 20-21; "U.S. Sponsors Pushing Latin Market," Broadcasting, 9 July 1942, p. 40.

[89] Maxwell, "Evoking Latin American Collaboration," p. 134.

[90] U.S., Congress, Senate, Committee on Appropriations, Hearings on the National War Agencies Appropriation Bill for 1945, 78th Congress, 2nd Session, p. 86.

[91] Report: Radio Division, 1 June 1943, Misc. Reports file, Box 966, pp. 145–162, OCIAA.

[92] Ibid., pp. 40–41.

[93] U.S., Congress, House, Committee on Appropriations, Hearings on National War Agencies Appropriations Bill for 1946, 79th Congress, 1st Session, p. 523.

[94] Report: Radio Division, 1 June 1943, Misc. Reports file, Box 966, p. 31, OCIAA.

[95] "Here is Radio Division's Staff of Experts," in Don Francisco, "Short Wave Miracle," Printer's Ink, 15 October 1943, p. 97.

[96] Memorandum, 4 October 1941, Procedures Misc. file, Box 241, OCIAA.

[97] William A. Anderson, "The Rising Tide of U.S. Advertising in Latin America." Export Trade and Shipper, 1 January 1944, p. 11; New York Times, 27 July 1944, 26:3. After the war, the OCIAA's activities in Latin American market research were carried on by advertising agencies. In November 1946, the New York Times reported the first contingent of Latin Americans arriving in this country to be trained in United States marketing research techniques and advertising practices. 10 November 1946, III:6:4.

[98] Maxwell, "Evoking Latin American Collaboration," pp. 146–147.

[99] Ray Josephs, "Latinos Tune In," The Inter-American, September 1945, p. 39. Josephs was the Latin American correspondent for Variety.

[100] Ibid., pp. 17, 18–19.

CHAPTER 6

CONCLUSION AND POSTSCRIPT

By the fall of 1943, the merger between the two networks completed the change from the former policy of voluntary government–industry cooperation to one of explicit government control and direction. This change came about gradually over a period of 4 years and, with the exception of CBS and World Wide, very little opposition was voiced either from the shortwave broadcasters or the broadcasting industry as a whole. Indeed, most of the commercial broadcasters welcomed the change.

The change in government policy in shortwave was based on the need to insure Latin American solidarity and military, economic, and political cooperation after the Axis victories in the spring of 1940. The Good Neighbor Policy formulated and implemented by Roosevelt prepared the ground for many of the policies and practices pursued by the United States in its wartime relations with the other American republics. Military and economic ties between the United States and Latin American nations were tightened. In addition, the United States acted to expand its presence in Latin American cultural life. As Rockefeller argued in his June 1940 memorandum to Roosevelt, any United States program in Latin America must be done in conjunction with an effort to persuade the Latin American public to accept the leadership of the United States in hemispheric economic, political, and military matters. The creation of the OCIAA, and its information and propaganda activities, reflect the fact that cultural diplomacy in Latin America during World War II became an important component of United States economic, military, and political efforts in the region.

Shortwave broadcasting played an essential role in the cultural campaign by the United States in Latin America. While shortwave had both a commercial and political value in inter-American relations, prior to 1940 administration policy emphasized its role in promoting trade. After 1940, the administration began to view it more explicitly as a political instrument aimed at cultivating Latin American support for United States foreign policy aims and war goals.

However, in defining new goals for shortwave broadcasting, the administration had to contend with the shortwave broadcasters. Whereas, before, it had been assumed that, by providing for the commercialization of shortwave service the broadcasters would assist in achieving larger United States political goals in hemispheric affairs by their own individual efforts, in a crisis situation the arrangement was no longer satisfactory. The United States government began to exercise more explicit political direction over the activities of the shortwave broadcasters. The broadcasters, in turn, accepted such direction. At first, their cooperation was more a reflection of the fear that, if they did not cooperate, the government would have to enter the field, a prospect with ominous implications for domestic broadcasting. In cooperating, the broadcasters, however, began to assume more and more of the government's definition of their own activities. In a short time, the broadcasters saw shortwave less as a commercial endeavor and more as an explicit political effort aimed at achieving the government's goals in Latin America. Broadcasters undertook on behalf of the government the task of countering Axis propaganda and convincing Latin Americans to accept United States leadership in the world crisis. Once they defined their activity largely as an appendage of United States foreign policy, it was only logical that the government became more involved. By 1943, the government had assumed complete control of their activities. The expected outcry from domestic broadcasters against explicit government control of broadcasting, of course, did not occur. On one level, one could explain this lack of protest by arguing that the broadcasters saw this as an extraordinary war-time measure setting no precedent for peace-time relations between the government and broadcasters. Once the war was over, shortwave would become depoliticized and placed again in the hands of commercial broadcasters.

Yet this obscures a larger dynamic. As the world situation deteriorated and the possibility of United States entrance into the war increased, the administration actively sought the cooperation of the broadcasting industry. As planning for the mobilization of United States war resources and energies proceeded, the administration acted to give the leading representatives from the various sectors of the communication industry a major role in shaping government policies and practices in their respective fields. At first, broadcasters were suspicious. However, by the time war actually came, the administration had successfully assured them of its good faith and very limited goals in the field of domestic broadcasting. Much of the suspicion and hostility between the broadcasting industry and the government was dissipated in the warmth of close war-time collaboration.

Thus, the major reason behind the private broadcasters' activity in shortwave—the fear of a government shortwave station as an "entering wedge" into a control of domestic broadcasting—was no longer valid. The commercial shortwave broadcasters, losing enormous amounts of money in order to achieve the primarily political goals of the administration in hemispheric affairs, were ready to turn their services over to the government. The one commercial broadcaster who objected, William Paley, argued on behalf of the earlier arrangement of voluntary cooperation between the government and industry. He did not base his position on the spectre of the "entering wedge," which had dominated all earlier discussion of government shortwave involvement. Rather, he argued on behalf of the principle of "free radio." Yet, as he was willing to use his shortwave service to accomplish the explicit political tasks in Latin America which the administration outlined, his argument of "free radio" was not very compelling. To many within the OCIAA, it was simply a cover to protect CBS's interests in Latin America. In his fight for voluntary cooperation, he was neither able to win the support of his fellow shortwave broadcasters nor the domestic broadcasting industry in general.

In a sense, by 1943 a settlement had been reached between the government and the broadcasters on the issue of international broadcasting. Recognizing the important role such broadcasting played in world affairs, broadcasters accepted government control of shortwave as necessary to the United States' political position in hemispheric and world politics. They were willing to accept the fact that the rules, assumptions, and relations applied to domestic broadcasting were not relevant to international broadcasting. In turn, the administration assured the broadcasters that its control of international broadcasting would have no effect on the government's role in domestic broadcasting. It would not be used as an "entering wedge." A strict separation between international and domestic broadcasting was thus defined.

This definition of international broadcasting as primarily a tool for foreign policy was further affirmed in 1944 by a report issued by the Department of State on postwar international United States broadcasting. Written by Columbia University professor Arthur MacMahon, the report recommended the continuation of United States government broadcasting activities after the war. The question of direct government ownership, finance, and control of broadcasting facilities and operations was left open, thus allowing for the possibility of some degree of participation by private broadcasters. Nonetheless, the political nature and purpose of such broadcasting was emphasized.[1]

It was evident that the pre-war system of United States international broadcasting was neither desirable nor feasible. After the war, the private commercial broadcasters did not rush to reclaim their stations. With one exception, private broadcasters continued to lease their transmitters to the government. Both NBC and CBS continued to provide programming to the government until 1948, when the government took over all shortwave programming activities. For a while after the war, CBS tried to revive its private Latin American shortwave service. CBS transmitted the program features prepared under contract to the government, along with simulcasts of its regular network fare, to its affiliated stations in Latin America. In the years immediately after the war, CBS also added a number of new affiliated stations in Mexico, Columbia, and Panama. No attempt, however, was made to sell commercial time. As a good portion of CBS's post-war energies and resources were bound up with the development of television broadcasting, it did not vigorously pursue the development of a Latin American network. In 1948, the network liquidated its Latin American system and activities as part of a general withdrawal from all shortwave broadcasting and programming.[2]

Walter Lemmon's World Wide station, seized during the war, was returned to him in spring 1946. He attempted to renew his educational broadcasting activities, but again faced financial difficulties. Although he sought both government subsidies and program contracts to keep his station going, he was unsuccessful and his station limped along on meager resources. In the late 1940s and early 1950s, his broadcasts began to assume a more directly political character as he broadcast programs attacking communism and promoting global free enterprise. In the late 1950s, he tried to sell commercial time on his station. However, feeling that the field of international commercial broadcasting was beyond the development of one individual, he sold his World Wide station to Metro-Media for $800,000 in 1959. That company tried to develop the station as a medium for shortwave commercials, and had a fair amount of success. Advertising revenue in 1962 equaled about $400,000. However, the station was still losing money, and Metro-Media finally sold it to the Mormon Church, which used it for international religious broadcasts.[3]

The post-war withdrawal of private broadcasters from international broadcasting was matched by greater government involvement. Yet implementation of a post-war shortwave policy and programming activities was not without problems. While everyone accepted the inadequacies of private, commercial shortwave activities and the need for government direction in that field, the precise nature and extent of postwar government shortwave activity was open to a great deal of debate. The State Department argued for a government monopoly of shortwave activity. Yet Congress was not prepared to grant one. After the war, the shortwave activities of the OCIAA and OWI were transferred to the State Department. The Department created the International Broadcasting Division (IBD) at the end of 1945 to carry out shortwave activities which were collectively called the Voice of America (VOA). Over the next 3 years, the VOA has a precarious existence as it sought to justify to Congress and the public the need for government shortwave activities. Following the trend of postwar demobilization in late 1945 and 1946, personnel and programming were cut drastically. Over 60 percent of OWI and OCIAA employees working in the IBD were discharged by April 1946, and programming dropped from a wartime high of 1,176 hours weekly to 446 by December 1945. The number of languages broadcast dropped from 41 to 24. Requested appropriations for 1947 and 1948 were reduced drastically by Congress, necessitating further cutbacks in personnel and service. Also, the Associated Press and United Press withdrew their news service from the VOA in early 1946. They felt their credibility was compromised by supplying news to a government sponsored service. In addition to these problems, the VOA was continuously attacked by members of Congress for employing individuals whose loyalties were suspect.[4]

In spite of these problems and reduced resources, the VOA continued its activities. As the nature of the post war world became more clear, and the conflict between the United States and the Soviet Union began to emerge as the central element in United States foreign policy, the need for continued shortwave activities became more pronounced. In March 1947 President Harry Truman, in an appeal to Congress for aid for the pro-Western governments of Turkey and Greece beleaguered by Communist guerilla movements, declared that the United States should be willing and able to engage in ideological, if not military, confrontation with the Soviet Union in order to protect United States interests throughout the world. The Cold War was on.

Just as the fear of Nazi subversion in Latin America in the late 1930s galvanized government action in shortwave broadcasting, the fear of Soviet penetration in countries heretofore considered friendly to the United States interests galvanized the Truman administration and Congress to upgrade the VOA. In January 1948 Congress passed the Smith-Mundt bill, which gave government shortwave activities permanent legal status. Also, appropriations to the VOA were increased, allowing it to hire more personnel and expand programming and hours. With the outbreak of the Korean War, the importance of its activities increased, as did its budget. In 1953 the VOA was transferred from the State Department to the newly formed United States Information Agency, which consolidated all government informational and cultural activities.

In the expansion of such shortwave and other information activities, Latin America was generally ignored or relegated to a very low priority. This neglect was only part of the larger framework of postwar foreign policy in which little active attention was given to Latin America and its problems. During the war, when the United States needed Latin American support and raw materials, United States policy makers spoke warmly of close United States–Latin American solidarity and partnership. Such rhetoric led many Latin Americans to believe that, after the war, such cooperation would continue, and that the United States government would focus its attention on Latin America. Many hoped that United States assistance through government loans and aid to Latin American nations would help these countries in their own economic and social development. Such hopes were not realized. Now, more than before, because of the war, Latin America was tightly integrated into the United States dominated hemispheric system. For the United States, Latin America was "safe" and did not need any further special attention. The major focus of United States foreign policy now was in Europe and in the Far East, both areas recipients of United States government aid and military assistance. Latin Americans were urged to depend upon private United States investment for their own developmental needs. With its dominance in hemispheric economic and political affairs unchallenged, the United States in post-war world affairs could safely ignore the economic and social problems of Latin America while turning its major attention and efforts towards the problem of creating a new world order.

This relegation of Latin America to the backwaters of United States foreign policy was reflected in the decline of United States shortwave service to the region. In 1947 the 9 hours of daily broadcasts to Latin America comprised roughly 28 percent of all government originated or sponsored shortwave broadcasts. By 1951, although total VOA programming had increased 60 percent to 48 hours of daily programming, service to Latin America had decreased to roughly 5 hours daily, or 10 percent of all broadcasts. In 1953, specially prepared Spanish and Portuguese programs were cut totally. By 1956 VOA programming totaled around 145 hours daily. The bulk of the broadcasts consisted of specially prepared programs in 43 languages. Aside from broadcasting in the major European and Asian languages, the VOA aired regular programs in Hindi, Urdu, Arabic, Persian, Vietnamese, Slovene, Georgian, Armenian, and Telegu. Broadcasts to Latin America consisted only of 1 hour of daily programming, less than 1 percent of total VOA output. Moreover, that 1 hour was in English.[5] It was evident that, to the policymakers in the State Department and the officials at the VOA, Latin American merited little special attention.

With the success of the Cuban revolution in 1959, this lack of concern turned quickly to near panic. Latin America could no longer be considered securely strapped into the United States sphere of influence and interest. After first trying to oust Castro in the unsuccessful Bay of Pigs invasion, the United States developed a strategy of trying to isolate and contain the revolutionary energies of Cuba, and to prevent their spread to other Latin American countries. The Alliance for Progress, promoted by the Kennedy administration as an ambitious program for beneficial social change and material betterment, was aimed at providing an alternative to the revolutionary change that so threatened United States interests in the hemisphere.

The Alliance consisted of two major strategies. The first was the provision of developmental and economic aid to Latin American countries that would enable them to confront and solve many of their serious social and economic problems. This aid would be conditional on the implementation of various social and political reforms. The overall goal was to weaken both the oligarchical right and the revolutionary left. Hopefully, the democratic moderate middle, those new emerging "modernizing" middle class elements that the United States so much pinned its hopes on would be strengthened and provide the stable, popular, pro-United States regimes that Washington so much wanted in the region. The second element in the Alliance strategy was a vast increase in military aid and assistance to the Latin American military to enable them to deal with the rise in guerilla activity. During the 1960s it became evident that the first part of this grand strategy vastly underestimated the depth of the social and political problems facing Latin America. It also wrongly assumed that many of these problems could be solved without upsetting United States private and government interests in the region. Moreover, this strategy vastly overestimated the size, strength, and potential of the moderate middle elements. Finally, as the military organizaions in the various Latin American countries were modernized and strengthened by United States military aid, they began to play a more active role as a coherent institution in the political life of their countries. Military coups became a common phenomenon as the various social democratic or Christian Democratic governments failed to cope with the political or social problems. Although social and political reforms were halted by military takeovers, the United States generally was not greatly concerned, as the resulting military governments provided a far stronger bulwark against any threatening revolutionary change.

The reemergence of Latin America as a problem area for the United States was reflected in the quick upgrading of VOA broadcast service to the region. In March 1960 VOA Spanish broadcasts to Latin America were resumed, and in August 1961 Portuguese broadcasts were begun again. By 1962, 82 hours of weekly programming in both languages, comprising roughly 17 percent of total VOA foreign programming, was beamed to the region.[6] In addition to the increase in VOA services, the Central Intelligence Agency in 1960 built and operated a radio station on the Grand Swan Island off the coast of Honduras. "Radio Swan" was technically owned by the Gibralter Steamship Corporation, whose president was a former head of United Fruit and former State Department intelligence official. Supposedly a private commercial medium wave station aimed at Spanish-speaking audiences throughout the Caribbean and Central America, Radio Swan was a CIA operation aimed at destabilizing the Castro government. During the Bay of Pigs it broadcast appeals to the Cuban population to rise and overthrow Castro. It continued to broadcast anti-Castro appeals until 1967, when it seemingly went off the air. It reappeared again in 1975, this time located in the Honduran city of San Pedro Sola. It is run by Cuban exiles and continues to broadcast vehement anti-Castro programming.[7]

During the 1960s and into the 1970s, the installation of military and authoritarian governments in such countries as Brazil, Uruguay, Chile, and Argentina acted for a time to hold back the threat of revolutionary change in the region, thus allowing the United States to focus its energies on Vietnam, Europe, China, and the Soviet Union. Together with already existing military regimes in countries such as Nicaragua and Paraguay, these governments, friendly to United States interests and beholden to United States aid, acted as guarantors of the United States position in the hemisphere. Relying primarily on repression and violence, these regimes contained the Cuban threat and made the region safe again for United States interests.

In the late 1970s and early 1980s, new threats to United States dominance emerged as the social and economic problems intensified and the forces of progressive change could no longer be held back. The Carter administration, as had the Kennedy administration 16 years earlier, tried to cope with the pressures for change by developing a policy that hoped to manage the energies of these forces into channels not threatening to United States interests in the region. The human rights policy of the Carter administration hoped to lessen the repressive nature of many of the Latin American regimes and allow moderate political elements to play a larger role in dealing with the increasingly urgent social and economic problems. While, in some instances, the Carter policy did help moderate the repressive and violent nature of some of the military regimes and allow for political openings for more moderate and progressive elements, on the whole, human rights was never the underlying principle upon which United States Latin America policy was organized. The most important element was still fighting off the threat of revolution. And it was this second goal that dominated United States actions in the region.

In the late 1970s the problems were most acute in Central America, a region based on an agricultural export economy with societies almost feudal in nature, consisting of a large peasant class, a small ruling oligarchy that generally controlled a major portion of a nation's land and resources, and an almost nonexistent middle class. Given the vastly unequal distribution of income and land, this region was a prime site for revolutionary change. In 1979 the Somoza regime in Nicaragua, installed in the 1930s and heavily supported by the United States, fell to the Sandinistas. While the new government was committed to a revolutionary social transformation of Nicaraguan society, it was pragmatic enough not to try and alienate the United States. In El Salvador a similar process of revolutionary change was unfolding. Here, however, the United States was committed to insuring that the experience of Nicaragua would not be repeated. It worked to insure that the major social ills, such as the problem of land distribution, were confronted in order to forestall a victory by the revolutionary guerilla movement operating in the country. The United States sought to solve the problem of threatening revolutionary change by creating a moderate government that would eschew the repressive violence of the previous oligarchs, confront the social problems of the country, and defeat the guerilla movement, yet at the same time support United States interests in the region.

While the Carter administration sought to achieve this goal with as little direct United States intervention as possible, the Reagan administration, once in office, defined the situation in Central America primarily in the context of the conflict between the United States and the Soviet Union. To the administration, guerrilla activity in El Salvador was not as much a reflection of the grave social and economic problems of the country as it was a result of a direct Soviet and Cuban challenge to United States interests in the region. The United States responded with increasing military aid to the El Salvadorean government and greatly expanding its own military presence in the region.

As had other administrations in the past, the Reagan administration turned to radio broadcasting as a potential weapon. The VOA was already maintaining a full service of 84 hours a week in Spanish aimed at Latin America. However, the VOA charter mandated objective news presentation, and many of the VOA staff with backgrounds in regular news organization were committed to professional journalistic values of objectivity and nonsensationalism. Such a style of broadcasting did not match the Reagan administration's aggressive foreign policy approach in the region. Drawing upon an idea first put forward by the Council on Inter-American Security, a conservative think tank, the administration proposed to Congress in 1982 the creation of a medium wave station aimed at Cuba. This station, named Radio Martí after the hero of Cuban independence, was to be similar to Radio Free Europe and exist independently from the VOA. It would be staffed by Cuban exiles and be overtly propagandistic in its programming. Its overall purpose would be to destabilize the Cuban government and thus, according to the administration, lessen the Cuban and Soviet threat to Central America.

Opposition to Radio Martí quickly appeared. A number of Democratic congressmen objected to the station on the grounds that it would worsen the already bad United States–Cuban relations and increase tensions in the region. One congressman proposed calling the legislation authorizing the station the "John Foster Dulles War Mentality Memorial Radio Broadcasting to Cuba Act." Another objection more serious to pro-administration congressmen was the threat of Cuba jamming the station once it was built. Radio Martí would operate on the same medium wave frequency as station WHO in Des Moines, Iowa. WHO was a powerful clear-signal station that served the farming communities of the midwestern and plain states. While Radio Martí broadcasts would normally not interfere with WHO, it was estimated that a powerful jamming signal from Cuba on the same frequency would reduce the effective coverage of WHO from 800 to 45 miles. Moreover, there was a concern that such a station would encourage Cuba to jam other medium wave commercial stations in retaliation. For these reasons, the National Association of Broadcasters opposed the legislation. The bill passed the House in August 1982, but was killed by a filibuster in the Senate in December. The next year the legislation was reintroduced, and, after a series of negotiations between opponents and supporters of the bill, it was approved by Congress in September 1983. In its final compromise form, Radio Martí would be under the direction of the VOA and subject to VOA programming standards; thus the programs would be "objective, accurate, balanced and. . . present a variety of views." It would operate on a noncommercial medium wave frequency already used by the VOA. To protect commercial broadcasters from possible Cuban jamming, the bill authorized government compensation to commercial broadcasters for any technical expenses incurred as a result of Cuban interference.[8]

While the final legislation lessened the belligerent nature of initial proposal to some degree, Radio Martí does represent a serious provocation that is in line with the entire character and tone of the Reagan administration's Latin American policy. In a sense the administration's aggressive actions in Central America, from increasing military aid and activity in Central America, to the invasion of Granada, to the construction of Radio Martí, bespeaks a return to the "Big Stick" policy of Theodore Roosevelt. But such a policy is less a return to the exciting days of United States power and empire building, and more a reflection of failure. Since the turn of the century, the overriding goal of United States policy in Latin America has been the construction of a hemispheric system of economic, political, and military relations based primarily on United States interests and needs in the region. But given the nature of United States military, economic, and political of such needs, the resulting system has been unable to accommodate meaningful social change and progress in the region, or any degree of national autonomy and self-determination by any of the Latin American nations. While the United States has tried different approaches, such as the Good Neighbor Policy, the Alliance for Progress, and Carter's Human Rights Policy, all have been failures and the basic contradiction between United States interests and Latin American realities remain. The militaristic policies of the Reagan administration are a frank admission of that contradiction. If the Reagan administration is successful, albeit such a success would only be momentary, no doubt it would apply these policies to other parts of the globe where United States interests are similarly contested.

Latin America was and is a laboratory and testing ground, not only for the practices and methods of United States economic and political imperialism, but also for the control and use of communications and media to achieve its goal of domination. Yet the hegemony of the United States has not remained uncontested. With varying degress of success there have been challenges, the most notable occurring today in Central America. One should remain hopeful. Just as Latin America served as a testing ground for imperialism, it can equally become a testing ground for liberation.

Notes

[1] Arthur McMahon, *Memorandum on the Post-War International Information Program of the United States* (Washington, D.C.: Department of State, Publication 2438, 1945).

[2] Press Release, 9 August 1946, 18 October 1946, CBS Library, New York, New York: *Variety*, 7 July 1948, 28:1; "Voice Withdrawal," *Broadcasting*, 5 July 1948, p. 26.

[3] "Regains Station," *Business Week*, 11 May 1946, p. 51; Paula Burton, "Factors in the Attempt to Establish a Permanent Instrumentality for the Administration of the International Broadcasting Services of the United States" (Ph.D. dissertation, New York University, 1949), pp. 184–200; *Wall Street Journal*, 27 March 1962, I:3; *New York Tribune*, 16 October 1962, 14:2.

[4] Robert William Pirsein, "The Voice of America: A History of the International Broadcasting Activities of the United States Government, 1940–1962" (Ph.D. dissertation, Northwestern University, 1970), pp. 110–135.

[5] Ibid., pp. 133, 210, 358.

[6] Ibid., p. 424.

[7] Howard H. Frederick, "Ideology in International Telecommunication: Radio Wars Between Cuba and the United States" (Ph.D. dissertation, The American University, 1984), pp. 7–11; Donald R. Browne, *International Radio Broadcasting: The Limits of the Limitless Medium* (New York: Praeger, 1982), pp. 149–151.

[8] *Congressional Quarterly Weekly*, 7 August 1982, p. 1900; 10 July 1982, p. 1656.

BIBLIOGRAPHY

Archival Sources

Broadcast Pioneers Library, Washington, D.C.
David Sarnoff papers, David Sarnoff Library, Princeton, New Jersey.
CBS News Division Library, New York, New York.
National Broadcasting Company Archives, State Historical Society of Wisconsin, Madison, Wisconsin.
United States National Archives:
General Records of the Department of Commerce, Record Group 40, National Archives Building, Washington, D.C. (abbreviated in notes as COM).
Records of the Bureau of Foreign and Domestic Commerce, Record Group 151, National Archives Building, Washington, D.C. (BFDC).
Records of the Office of Inter-American Affairs (Office of the Coordinator of Inter-American Affairs), Record Group 229, Washington National Record Center, Suitland, Maryland (OCIAA).
Records of the Board of War Communication, Record Group 259, National Archives Building, Washington, D.C. (WARCOM).
Records of the Office of War Information, Record Group 208, Washington National Records Center, Suitland, Maryland (OWI).

Unpublished Material

Burton, Paulu. "Factors in the Attempt to Establish a Permanent Instrumentality for the Administration of the International Broadcasting Services of the United States." Ph.D. dissertation, New York University, 1949.
Campbell, Archer Stuart. "American Export Trade and Exporting Methods." Ph.D. dissertation, University of Virginia, 1932.
Frederick, Howard, H. "Ideology in International Telecommunications: Radio Wars Between Cuba and the United States." Ph.D. dissertation, The American University, 1984.
Harris, William G. "Radio Propaganda in Latin America." Senior thesis. Princeton University, 1939.

Lichty, Lawrence Wilson. "'The Nation's Station,' A History of Radio Station WLW." 2 vols. Ph.D. dissertation, Ohio State University, 1964.

Maxwell, Allen Brewster. "Evoking Latin American Collaboration in the Second World War—A Study of the Office of the Coordinator of Inter-American Affairs (1940–1946). Ph.D. dissertation, Fletcher School of Law and Diplomacy, 1971.

Pirsein, Robert William. "The Voice of America—A History of the International Broadcasting Activities of the United States Government, 1940–1962." Ph.D. dissertation, Northwestern University, 1970.

Roberts, Beth Alene. "United States Propaganda Welfare in Latin America." Ph.D. dissertation, University of Southern California, 1943.

Sarnoff, David, "Relationship of Radio to the Problem of National Defense." Lecture delivered before the Army War College, 31 January 1927. Mimeo, David Sarnoff Library, Princeton, New Jersey.

Sidel, Michael Kent. "A Historical Analysis of American Short Wave Broadcasting 1916–1942." Ph.D. dissertation, Northwestern University, 1976.

de Usabel, Gaizka. "American Films in Latin America: The Case History of the United Artists Corporation, 1919–1951." Ph.D. dissertation, University of Wisconsin, 1975.

Westinghouse Electric Company. "History of Shortwave Broadcasting." Broadcast Pioneers Library, Washington, D.C., n.d. (Mimeographed)

Periodicals and Yearbooks

Advertising Age
Broadcast Advertising
Broadcasting
Broadcasting—1935 Yearbook
Broadcasting—1942 Yearbook
Bulletin of the Pan American Union
Business Week
Commerce
Commercial and Financial Chronicle
Congressional Quarterly Weekly
Export Trade and Shipper
Moving Picture World
Newsweek
New York Times
Scientific American
United States Daily
Variety 1940/1941 Radio Directory

Official Documents

McMahon, Arthur. *Memorandum on the Post-War International Information Program of the United States.* Department of State Publication 2438. Washington, D.C.: Government Printing Office, 1945.

United Nations. Department of Economic and Social Affairs. *Foreign Capital in Latin America.* New York: United Nations, 1955.

United Nations. Economic Commission for Latin America. *External Financing in Latin America.* New York: United Nations, 1965.

U.S. Department of Commerce. *Statistical Abstract of the United States 1946.* Washington, D.C.: Government Printing Office, 1946.

U.S. Department of Commerce. Bureau of Foreign and Domestic Culture. *Advertising in Brazil.* Trade Information Bulletin No. 838. Washington, D.C.: Government Printing Office, 1937.

U.S. Department of Commerce. Bureau of Foreign and Domestic Culture. *Advertising Methods in Argentina, Uruguay, and Brazil,* by J.W. Sanger. Special Agent Series No. 190. Washington, D.C.: Government Printing Office, 1920.

U.S. Department of Commerce. Bureau of Foreign and Domestic Culture. *Advertising Methods in Cuba,* by J.W. Sanger. Special Agent Series No. 178. Washington, D.C.: Government Printing Office, 1919.

U.S. Department of Commerce. Bureau of Foreign and Domestic Culture. *Advertising Methods in Chile, Peru, and Bolivia,* by J.W. Sanger. Special Agent Series No. 185. Washington, D.C.: Government Printing Office, 1919.

U.S. Department of Commerce. Bureau of Foreign and Domestic Culture. *Broadcasting Advertising in Asia, Africa, Australia, and Oceania.* Trade Information Bulletin No. 799. Washington, D.C.: Government Printing Office, 1932.

U.S. Department of Commerce. Bureau of Foreign and Domestic Culture. *Broadcasting Advertising in Europe.* Trade Information Bulletin No. 787. Washington, D.C.: Government Printing Office, 1932.

U.S. Department of Commerce. Bureau of Foreign and Domestic Culture. *Broadcasting Advertising in Latin America.* Trade Information Bulletin No. 771. Washington, D.C.: Government Printing Office, 1931.

U.S. Department of Commerce. Bureau of Foreign and Domestic Culture. *Statistical Abstract of the United States, 1936.* Washington, D.C.: Government Printing Office, 1936.

U.S. Department of Commerce. Radio Division. *Radio Service Bulletin.*

U.S. Congress. *Congressional Record.*

U.S. Congress. House. *Report on Communication Companies.* House Report No. 1273, 73rd Congress, 2nd Session, 1934.

U.S. Congress. House. Committee on Appropriations. *Hearings on the National War Agencies Appropriation Bill for 1944.* 78th Congress, 1st Session, 1943.

U.S. Congress. House. Committee on Appropriations. *Hearings on the National War Agencies Appropriation Bill for 1946.* 79th Congress, 1st Session, 1944.

U.S. Congress. House. Committee on Appropriations. *Hearings on the Second Deficiency Appropriations Bill for 1941.* 77th Congress, 1st Session, 1941.

U.S. Congress. House. Committee on Appropriations. Subcommittee of Deficiency Appropriations. *Hearings on the First Supplemental National Defense Appropriations Bill for 1943,* 77th Congress, 2nd Session, 1942.

U.S. Congress. House. Committee on Naval Affairs. *Hearings Authorizing the Secretary of the Navy to Construct and Maintain a Government Radio Broadcasting Station . . . and for Other Purposes (H.R. 4281).* 75th Congress, 3rd Session, 1938.

U.S. Congress. Senate. *Commercial Radio Advertising.* Senate Document No. 137, 72nd Congress, 1st Session, 1932.

U.S. Congress. Senate. Committee of Appropriations. *Hearings on the National War Agencies Appropriation Bill for 1945.* 78th Congress, 2nd Session, 1944.

U.S. Congress. Senate. Committee on Interstate Commerce. *Hearings before a Subcommittee of the Committee on Interstate Commerce on S. 3342, A Bill to Authorize the Construction and Operation of a Radio-Broadcasting Station Designed to Promote Friendly Relations among the Nations of the Western Hemisphere.* 75th Congress, 3rd Session, 1938.

U.S. Congress. Senate. Interstate Commerce Committee. *Study of International Communications, Hearings before a Subcommittee of the Committee on Interstate Commerce.* 78th Congress, 1st Session, 1945.

U.S. Federal Communications Commission. *Third Annual Report* (1937).

U.S. Federal Communications Commission. *Sixth Annual Report* (1940).

U.S. Federal Radio Commission. *Second Annual Report* (1928).

U.S. Federal Radio Commission. *Third Annual Report* (1929).

U.S. Federal Radio Commission. *Sixth Annual Report* (1932).

U.S. Federal Trade Commission. *Report of the Federal Trade Commission on the Radio Industry.* Washington, D.C.: Government Printing Office, 1924.

U.S. Office of Inter-American Affairs. *History of the Office of the Coordinator of Inter-American Affairs,* by Donald W. Rowland. Historical Reports on War Administration. Washington, D.C.: Government Printing Office, 1947.

U.S. Interdepartmental Committee to Study International Broadcasting. *Report of the Interdepartment Committee to Study International Broadcasting: Report of the Subcommittee on Programs.* Washington, D.C.: Government Printing Office, 1939.

U.S. Office of the President. Executive Order #6472, 2 December 1933.

U.S. Department of State. *Papers Relating to the Foreign Relations of the United States, 1915.* Washington, D.C.: Government Printing Office, 1924.

U.S. Department of State. *Papers Relating to the Foreign Relations of the United States, 1916.* Washington, D.C.: Government Printing Office, 1929.

U.S. Department of State. *Papers Relating to the Foreign Relations of the United States, 1933.* Washington, D.C.: Government Printing Office, 1933.

U.S. Department of State. *Report of the Delegation of the United States of America to the Seventh International Conference of American States, Montevideo, Uruguay, December 3–26, 1933.* Conference Series No. 19. Washington, D.C.: Government Printing Office, 1934.

U.S. Department of State. *Report of the Delegation of the United States of America to the Inter-American Conference for the Maintenance of Peace, Buenos Aires, Argentina, December 1–23, 1936.* Conference Series No. 33. Washington, D.C.: Government Printing Office, 1937.

U.S. Department of State. *Report of the Delegation of the United States of America to the Inter-American Conference on Problems of War and Peace, Mexico City, February 21–March 8, 1945.* Conference Series No. 85. Washington, D.C.: Government Printing Office, 1946.

Welles, Sumner. *Pan American Cooperation,* radio address, March 14, 1935. Department of State Latin American Series No. 10. Washington, D.C.: Government Printing Office, 1935.

Welles, Sumner. *The Roosevelt Administration and Its Dealings with the Republics of the Western Hemisphere*, address read at the Annual Convention of the Association of American Colleges, Atlanta, January 17, 1935. Department of State Latin American Series No. 9. Washington, D.C.: Government Printing Office, 1935.

Welles, Sumner. *The Way to Peace on the American Continent*, address before the Maryland Federation of Women's Clubs, Baltimore, April 15, 1936. Department of State Latin American Series No. 13. Washington, D.C.: Government Printing Office, 1936.

Articles

Anderson, William A. "The Rising Tide of U.S. Advertising in Latin America." *Export Trade and Shipper*, 1 January 1944, p. 11.

Bent, Silas. "International Broadcasting." *Public Opinion Quarterly* I (July) 1937, pp. 117–121.

Bernstein, Barton J. "America in War and Peace: The Test of Liberalism." In *Towards a New Past: Dissenting Essays in American History*, pp. 289–321. Edited by Barton J. Bernstein. New York: Vintage Books, 1969.

Bernstein, Barton J. "The New Deal: The Conservative Achievements of Liberal Reform." In *Towards a New Past: Dissenting Essays in American History*, pp. 263–288. Edited by Barton J. Bernstein. New York: Vintage Books, 1969.

Boyd, Douglas A. "The Pre-History of the Voice of America." *Public Telecommunications Review* 2:6 (December) 1974, pp. 38–45.

Browne, Donald R. "The Voice of America: Policies and Problems." *Journalism Monographs*, 43 (February) 1976.

Cruise O'Brien, Rita. "Mass Communications: Social Mechanisms of Incorporation and Dependence." In *Transnational Capitalism and National Development*, pp. 129–143. Edited by J.J. Villamil. Atlantic Highlands, New Jersey: Humanities Press, 1979.

Davis, H.P. "The Early History of Broadcasting in the United States." In *The Radio Industry: The Story of Its Development*, pp. 189–226. Chicago: A.W. Shaw & Company, 1928.

Dowsett, H.M. "Commercial Short Wave Wireless Communication. Part I: The Empiradio Beam Services." *The Marconi Review* 13 (October) 1929, pp. 14–30.

Dowsett, H.M. "Commercial Short Wave Wireless Communication. Part II: The 'Via Marconi' Services." *The Marconi Review* 14 (November) 1929, pp. 1–15.

Dunlap, Orrin E. "Super-Radio Spans the Atlantic." *Scientific American* 133 (October) 1925, pp. 244–245.

Fejes, Fred, "Media Imperialism: An Assessment." *Media, Culture, and Society* 3:3 (July) 1981, pp. 281–289.

Fejes, Fred. Review of *"Media Imperialism" Reconsidered: The Homogenizing of Television Culture*, by Chin-Chaun Lee. *Media, Culture, and Society* 4:1 (January) 1982, pp. 71–73.

Francisco, Don. "Short Wave Miracle." *Printer's Ink*, 15 October 1943, p. 20.

Haden, Allen. "In Defense of Rockefeller." *The Inter-American*, November 1945, p. 48.

Hallbord, H.E.; Briggs, L.A.; and Hansell, C.W. "Short-wave Commercial Long Distance Communication." *Proceedings of the Institute of Radio Engineers* 15:6 (June) 1927, pp. 467–499.

Jewett, Frank B. "The Development and Use of Radio Telephony as a Means of Communication." In *The Radio Industry: The Story of Its Development*, pp. 114–139. Chicago: A.W. Shaw & Company, 1928.

Josephs, Ray. "Latinos Tune In." *The Inter-American*, September 1945, p. 17.

Lemmon, Walter S. "International Broadcasting—A Force in World Trade." In *Report of the Thirty-Sixth Foreign Trade Convention, October 31–November 2, 1949*, pp. 197–204. New York: National Foreign Trade Council, 1950.

Leroy, Howard S. "Treaty Regulation of International and Short Wave Broadcasting." *The American Journal of International Law* 32 (October) 1938, pp. 719–737.

Mosco, Vincent and Herman, Andrew. "Radical Social Theory and the Communications Revolution." In *Communications and Social Structure—Critical Studies in Mass Media Research*, pp. 58–84. Edited by Emile G. McAnany, Jorge Schnitman, and Noreene Janus. New York: Praeger, 1981.

Nordenstreng, Kaarle and Schiller, Herbert. "Communication and National Development: Changing Perspectives—Introduction." In *National Sovereighty and International Communications*, pp. 3–8. Edited by Kaarle Nordenstreng and Herbert Schiller. Norwood, New Jersey: Ablex, 1979.

Paley, William. "Radio Turns South." *Fortune*, April 1941, p. 77 + .

Radosh, Ronald. "The Myth of the New Deal." In *A New History of Leviathan—Essays on the Rise of the American Corporate State*, pp. 146–187. Edited by Ronald Radosh and Murray N. Rothbard. New York: E.P. Dutton, 1972.

Reston, James B. "Our Second Line of Defense." *New York Times Magazine*, 29 June 1941, pp. 7–9.

Rippy J. Fred. "Notes on the Early Telephone Companies of Latin America." *Hispanic American Historical Review* 26:1, 1946, pp. 116–118.

Rodgers, W.W. "Broadcasting Complete American Programs to England." *Radio Broadcast* 4 (March) 1924, pp. 359–364.

Rodgers, W.W. "Is Short-wave Relay Broadcasting a Step toward a National Broadcasting System." *Radio Broadcast* 3 (June) 1923, pp. 119–122.

Rolo, Charles J. and Strausz-Hupe, Robert. "Reaching for Trade through Ether." *Barron's*, 22 December 1941, p. 9.

Rolo, Charles J. and Strausz-Hupe, Robert. "U.S. International Broadcasting." *Harper's*, August 1941, pp. 301–312.

Smith, Robert Freeman. "The Good Neighbor Policy: The Liberal Paradox in United States Relations with Latin America." In *Watershed of Empire—Essays on New Deal Foreign Policy*, pp. 65–94. Edited by Leonard P. Liggio and James J. Martin. Colorado Springs: Ralph Myles, Publisher, 1976.

Waldron, Webb. "Democracy on Shortwave." *Reader's Digest*, September 1941, pp. 40–44.

Whitton, John B. and Herz, John H. "Radio in International Politics." In *Propaganda by Short Wave*, pp. 1–48. Edited by Harwood L. Childs and John B. Whitton. Princeton: Princeton University Press, 1942.

Winterbottom, William A. "The World Comes to America Via Radio." *Broadcasting* 15 (June) 1934, p. 31.

Yandell, Lansford P. "How to Build Good Will and Sales by Short Wave Broadcasting." *Export Trade and Shipper*, 13 May 1940, p. 4.

Yandell, Lansford, P. "Radio Programs and Listeners in Latin America." *Export Trade and Shipper*, 21 October 1940, p. 7.

Books

Archer, Gleason L. *Big Business and Radio*. New York: The American Historical Society, 1939.

Archer, Gleason L. *History of Radio to 1926*. New York: The American Historical Society, 1938; reprint edition with addendum, New York: Arno Press, 1971.

Baerresen, Donald W.; Carnoy, Martin; and Grunwald, Joseph. *Latin American Trade Patterns:* Washington: D.C.: The Brookings Institution, 1965.

Bailey, Samuel, L. *The United States and the Development of South America, 1945–1975*. New York: New Viewpoints, 1976.

Baker, W.J. *A History of the Marconi Company*. London: Meuthen & Co., Ltd., 1970.

Barnouw, Erik. *A Tower of Babel: A History of Broadcasting in the United States to 1933*. New York: Oxford University Press, 1966.

Barnouw, Erik. The Golden Web—A History of Broadcasting in the United States, Vol. II—1933–1953. New York: Oxford, 1968.

Bemis, Samuel Flagg. *The Latin American Policy of the United States*. New York: Harcourt, Brace and Company, 1943.

Bernstein, Marvin D. editor. *Foreign Investment in Latin America*. New York: Alfred A. Knopf, 1966.

Brewer, Anthony. *Marxist Theories of Imperialism: A Critical Survey*. London: Routledge and Kegan Paul, 1980.

Brown, F.J. *The Cable and Wireless Communications of the World*. London: Sir Isaac Pitman and Sons, 1927.

Browne, Donald R. *International Broadcasting: The Limits of a Limitless Medium*. New York: Praeger, 1982.

Connell, Smith, Gordon. *The United States and Latin America*. London: Heinemann Educational Books, 1974.

Cooper, Kent. *Barriers Down*. New York: Farrar and Rinehart, 1942.

Dallek, Robert. *Franklin D. Roosevelt and American Foreign Policy*. New York: Oxford University Press, 1979.

Dalton, W.M. *The Story of Radio*. 3 vols. London: Adam Hilger, 1975.

Danielian, N.R. *A.T.T.—The Story of Industrial Conquest*. New York: The Vanguard Press, 1939.

Divine, Robert A. *The Illusion of Neutrality*. Chicago: The University of Chicago Press, 1962.

Dozer, Donald Marquand. *Are We Good Neighbors?* Gainesville: University of Florida Press, 1959.

Duggan, Laurence. *The Americas: The Search for Hemisphere Security*. New York: Henry Holt and Company, 1949.

Dunlap, Orrin E. *Radio and Television Almanac*. New York: Harper, 1951.

Eldridge, F.R. *Advertising and Selling Abroad*. New York: Harper & Brothers, 1930.

Espinosa, J. Manuel. *Inter-American Beginnings of U.S. Cultural Diplomacy, 1936-1948*, Cultural Relations Programs of the U.S. Department of State—Historical Studies No. 2. Washington, D.C.: Government Printing Office, 1976.

Frye, Alton. *Nazi Germany and the American Hemisphere, 1933-1941*. New Haven: Yale University Press, 1967.

Gantenbein, James W., editor. *The Evolution of Our Latin American Policy: A Documentary Record*. New York: Octagon Books, 1971.

Gardner, Lloyd C. *Economic Aspects of New Deal Diplomacy*. Madison: The University of Wisconsin Press, 1964.

Gardner, Mary A. *The Inter-American Press Association: Its Fight for Freedom of the Press, 1926-1960*. Austin: The University of Texas Press, 1967.

Gellman, Irwin F. *Good Neighbor Diplomacy: United States Policies in Latin America, 1933-1945*. Baltimore: The Johns Hopkins University Press, 1979.

Gil, Federico G. *Latin American–United States Relations*. New York: Harcourt Brace Jovanovich, 1971.

Glade, William P. *The Latin American Economies*. New York: Van Nostrand, 1969.

Graves, Harold N. *War on the Short Wave*. New York: Foreign Policy Association, 1941.

Green, David. *The Containment of Latin America*. Chicago: Quadrangle Books, 1971.

Guerrant, Edward O. *Roosevelt's Good Neighbor Policy*. Albuquerque: The University of New Mexico Press, 1950.

Haslett, A.W. *Radio Round the World*. Cambridge: Cambridge University Press, 1934.

Herring, Hubert. *A History of Latin America*. New York: Alfred A. Knopf, 1967.

Herring, James M. and Grosse, Gerald, C. *Telecommunication—Economics and Regulation*. New York: McGraw-Hill, 1936.

Horn, Paul V. and Bice, Hubert E. *Latin American Trade and Economics*. New York: Prentice-Hall, 1949.

Hull, Cordell. *The Memoirs of Cordell Hull*. 2 vols. New York: The Macmillan Company, 1948.

Ickes, Harold L. *The Secret Diary of Harold L. Ickes*. Vol. 2. *The Inside Struggle, 1936-1939*. New York: Simon and Schuster, 1954.

Inman, Samuel Guy. *Democracy versus the Totalitarian State in Latin America*. Pamphlet Series No. 7. Philadelphia: The American Academy of Political and Social Science, 1938.

International Telephone and Telegraph Corporation. *Annual Report*, 1930.

Ladner, A.W. and Stone, C.R. *Short Wave Wireless Communication.* 3rd ed. New York: John Wiley and Sons, 1936.

Lee, Chin Chau. *"Media Imperialism" Reconsidered: The Homogenizing of Television Culture.* Beverly Hills: Sage, 1980.

Leinwoll, Stanley. *From Spark to Satellite—A History of Radio Communication.* New York: Charles Scribner's Sons, 1979.

Leuchtenberg, William E. *Franklin D. Roosevelt and the New Deal, 1932–1940.* New York: Harper and Row, 1963.

Lieuwen, Edwin. *U.S. Policy in Latin America: A Short History.* New York: Praeger, 1965.

Lyons, Eugene. *David Sarnoff.* New York: Harper & Row, 1966.

Maclaurin, W. Rupert. *Invention and Innovation in the Radio Industry.* New York: Macmillan, 1949.

Mattleart, Armand. *Multinational Corporations and the Control of Culture.* Atlantic Highlands, New Jersey: Humanities Press, 1979.

Mecham, J. Lloyd. *A Survey of United States–Latin American Relations.* Boston: Houghton Mifflin Company, 1965.

Morris, Joe Alex. *Deadline Every Minute.* Garden City, New York: Doubleday, 1957.

Nearing, Scott and Freeman, Joseph. *Dollar Diplomacy.* New York: Monthly Review Press, 1966.

Normano, J.F. *The Struggle for South America.* Boston: Houghton Mifflin Company, 1931.

Paley, William S. *As It Happened—A Memoir.* Garden City: Doubleday, 1979.

Polenberg, Richard. *War and Society: The United States 1941–1945.* Philadelphia: J.B. Lippincott, 1972.

Radio Corporation of America. *Annual Report,* 1920.

Raushenbus, Joan. *Look at Latin America.* New York: The Foreign Policy Association, 1940.

Rippy, J. Fred. *Globe and Hemisphere: Latin America's Place in the Postwar Foreign Relations of the United States.* Chicago: Henry Regnery Company, 1958.

Rippy, J. Fred. *Latin America and the Industrial Age.* New York: G.P. Putnam's Sons, 1947.

The Rockefeller Foundation. *Annual Report 1935.*

The Rockefeller Foundation. *Annual Report 1936.*

The Rockefeller Foundation. *Annual Report 1937.*

The Rockefeller Foundation. *Annual Report 1938.*

Rolo, Charles J. *Radio Goes to War.* New York: G.P. Putnam's Sons, 1942.

Ronning, C. Neale, editor. *Intervention in Latin America.* New York: Alfred A. Knopf, 1970.

Rosenberg, Emily S. *Spreading the American Dream: American Economic and Cultural Expansion 1890–1945.* New York: Hill and Wang, 1982.

Saerchinger, Cesar. *Hello America!—Radio Adventures in Europe.* Boston: Houghton Mifflin, 1938.

Sarnoff, David. *Looking Ahead: The Papers of David Sarnoff.* New York: McGraw-Hill, 1968.

Schewe, Donald B. editor. *Franklin D. Roosevelt and Foreign Affairs.* Second

Series. 14 vols. New York: Clearwater Publishing Company, 1979.

Schiller, Herbert. *Mass Communications and American Empire*. Boston: Beacon, 1971.

Schreiner, George Abel. *Cable and Wireless and Their Role in the Foreign Relations of the United States*. Boston: Stratford, 1924.

Shepardson, Whitney H. *The United States in World Affairs—An Account of American Foreign Relations, 1938*. New York: Council on Foreign Relations/ Harper and Brothers, 1939.

Steward, Dick. *Trade and Hemisphere: The Good Neighbor Policy and Reciprocal Trade*. Columbia: University of Missouri Press, 1975.

Taussig, F.W. *The Tariff History of the United States*. New York: G.P. Putnam's Sons, 1931.

Thomas, Alfred Barnaby. *Latin America—A History*. New York: Macmillan Company, 1956.

Tribolet, Leslie Bennett. *The International Aspects of Electrical Communication in the Pacific Area*. Baltimore: Johns Hopkins Press, 1929.

Tulchin, Joseph S. *The Aftermath of War: World War I and U.S. Policy Toward Latin America*. New York: New York University Press, 1971.

Tunstall, Jeremy. *The Media Are American*. New York: Columbia University Press, 1977.

Varis, Tapio. *International Inventory of Television Programme Structure and the Flow of Programmes between Nations*. Tampere, Finland: University of Tampere, 1973.

Vyvyan, R.N. *Wireless Over Thirty Years*. London: George Routledge & Sons, 1933.

Warburg, James P. *Unwritten Treaty*. New York: Harcourt, Brace and Company, 1946.

Williams, William Appelman. *The Tragedy of American Diplomacy*, revised and enlarged. New York: Dell, 1962.

Winkler, Allan, M. *The Politics of Propaganda—The Office of War Information*. New Haven: Yale University Press, 1978.

Wood, Bryce. *The Making of the Good Neighbor Policy*. New York: Columbia University Press, 1961.

AUTHOR INDEX

SUBJECT INDEX